2nd Edition

The Complete Photo Guide to

KNITTING

**Creative Publishing
international**

First published in the United States of America by Creative Publishing international, a division of Quarto Publishing Group USA Inc.
400 First Avenue North
Suite 400
Minneapolis, MN 55401
1-800-328-3895
www.creativepub.com
Visit www.Craftside.Typepad.com for a behind-the-scenes peek at our crafty world!

ISBN: 978-1-58923-820-6

Digital edition published in 2015
eISBN: 978-1-62788-384-9

10 9 8 7 6 5 4 3 2

Library of Congress Cataloging-in-Publication Data available

Technical Editor: Rita Greenfeder
Copy Editor: Kari Cornell and Ann Wilson
Cover and Book Design: Kim Winscher
Page Layout: Danielle Smith and Laurie Young
Photographs: CPi, Chris Hubert, Rau + Barber

Printed in China

Dedication

For my ever-growing family, who constantly fill my life with joy.

Acknowledgments

I have a long list of people to thank for their help in putting this book together. Many thanks to the following yarn companies for the generous donation of their yarns for the projects and swatches in the book and for their continued support of designers everywhere: Blue Heron Yarns, Cascade Yarns, Coats and Clark, DJ International, Hampden Hills Alpacas, Knitting Fever, Lion Brand Yarn Company, Lucci Yarns, Patons Yarn Company, Plymouth Yarn Company Inc, Red Heart Yarns, Tahki Stacy Charles, Universal Yarns, and South West Trading Company.

Thanks to Sasha Kagan and Judy Pascale for sharing their expertise in special knitting techniques.

Thanks to Jeannine Buehler, Paula Alexander, Nancy Smith, Theresa DeLaBarrera, Marie Stewart, Frances Feery, and Mary O'Hara for helping me make many of the samples for the book, and to Frances Feery for helping me proofread the patterns.

Thank you to my lovely granddaughter, Nicole Valencia, and to Ava and Zoe DiGrandi for modeling the children's garments.

Thanks so much to my son, Chris Hubert, for some of the photography. I love how he photographs the children.

Last, but by no means least, a very big "thank you" to my editor, Linda Neubauer. Thank you so much for your continued support.

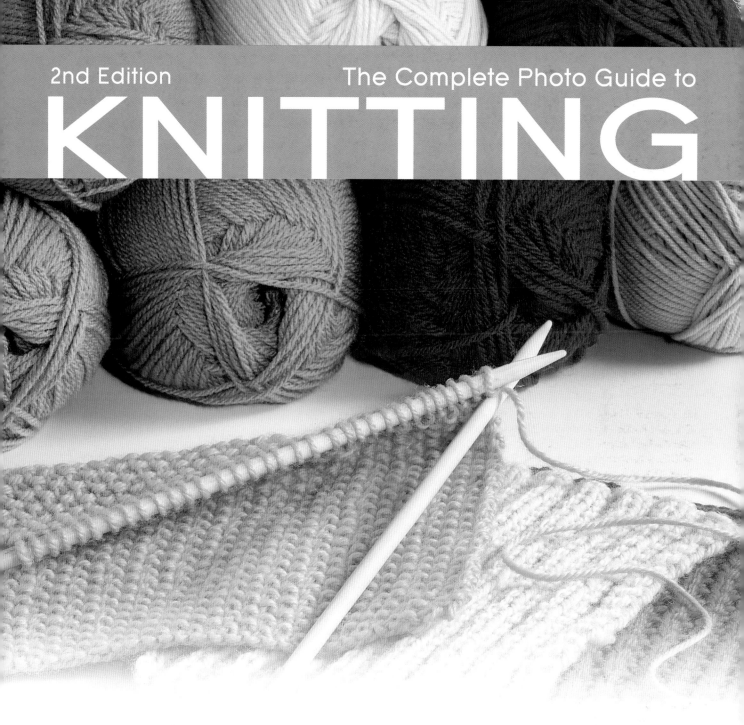

2nd Edition

The Complete Photo Guide to

KNITTING

Creative Publishing
international

CONTENTS

Introduction

It always amazes my students when I tell them that if they can knit and purl, they can learn to create all the beautiful patterns in any book.

The realization that it is almost impossible to write down all the stitch patterns that have been handed down through the ages in one volume led me to create a second edition of *The Complete Photo Guide to Knitting*. In this book, I have included twenty new stitch patterns in addition to the ones that already appeared in the first volume. And, to help you hone your skills, I have added fifteen new projects. The projects range in difficulty from very easy beginner items to more intricate garments, which may utilize several stitches in one piece.

The Knitting Basics section is packed with details about how to knit. It is intended to help beginning knitters learn the craft, but also to refresh seasoned knitters' memories about certain techniques. After all, who among us memorized the steps for grafting after our first attempt? In knitting there are many different techniques for casting on stitches, increasing and decreasing, binding off, and seaming, and each has its ideal use. Adding these techniques to your knitting repertoire will make you a more confident knitter.

The Stitch Patterns section is a collection of 220 stitch patterns, showcasing the vast range of knitted fabrics you can create. I learned some of the stitch patterns many years ago. My mom taught me several others, and I picked up a few from an old family friend who could knit as if she had a knitting encyclopedia in her brain. I learned other stitch patterns from books and knitting patterns that I studied over the years. Some stitch names have been handed down through generations of knitters; I made up some of the others to fit what I thought the stitches look like.

I have sorted the stitches into categories, including laces, textures, and ribs, but many of the stitches fit more than one category. You can dramatically change the look and drape of a stitch by changing yarn and needle size, experimenting as you go to get the look and feel that you want. Projects arranged throughout the book showcase at least one stitch from each group.

In the Specialty Knitting Methods section, I include methods for one-piece knitting, entrelac knitting, free-form knitting, knitting with beads, and intarsia.

I hope that knitters will use the patterns and techniques presented in this book to create their own wonderful designs. With the vast variety of yarn and tools available and the incredible array of stitch pattern options, the sky's the limit!

Enjoy.

Margaret

History of Knitting

Knitting, a simple technique for producing fabric from a strand of yarn or thread using two needles, is a fascinating hobby embraced by millions the world over. Unlike weaving, knitting does not require a loom or other large equipment. Knitting projects are small and portable, which made knitting especially appealing to nomadic people and continues to make knitting appealing to today's textile hobbyists.

The word *knitting* comes from the Anglo-Saxon word *cynntan*, which means to tie or knot. The ancient knotting craft was passed down from generation to generation.

Knitting histories are varied, and most histories place knitting's origin in the Middle East. Knitting spread to Europe via Mediterranean trade routes, and then to the Americas along with European colonization.

The oldest known knitting needle is on display in the Corinium Museum in Gloucestershire, England, and the oldest artifact with a knitted appearance is a type of sock. It is believed that socks and stockings were the first pieces produced using techniques similar to knitting. These socks and other clothing relics were worked in Nålebinding, a technique for making fabric by creating multiple knots or loops with a single needle and thread. Some of the pieces look similar to knitted pieces. Several pieces done in the now-obscure techniques, such as Romano-Egyptian toe-socks created in the third through fifth centuries CE (Common Era or A D), have been mistaken for knitting or crocheting.

The oldest known real-knitting examples, which were formed on two sticks by pulling loops through loops, are cotton Coptic socks found in an Egyptian tomb dating to around 1000 CE. It is fascinating to note that socks continue to be a very popular project for today's knitters and crocheters.

While members of both sexes knit today, knitting was formerly an occupation held only by men. During the Middle Ages, men trained for six years to become master knitters. After completing their apprenticeships, they had to pass an extremely difficult examination before going into business for themselves.

The earliest known knitted items found in Europe were made by Muslim knitters employed by Spanish Christian royal families. Their high level of knitting skill can be seen in several items found in tombs in Abbey of Santa María la Real de Las Huelgas, a royal monastery near Burgos, Spain. Among them are the knitted cushion covers and gloves found in the tomb of Prince Fernando de la Cerda, who died in 1275. The silk cushion cover was knit at approximately twenty stitches per inch. Numerous other knit garments and accessories dating from the mid-thirteenth century have been found in Spanish cathedral treasuries.

At this time, the purl stitch (the opposite action to the knit stitch) was unknown, and stockinette fabric, as we know it, was produced by knitting in the round on multiple knitting pins. Sometimes the knitting was cut open, a process now known as steeking.

Several European paintings dating from the fourteenth and fifteenth centuries portray the Virgin Mary knitting, including *Our Lady Knitting* by Tommaso da Modena (circa 1325 to 1375) and *Visit of the Angel* by Master Bertram of Minden (1400 to 1410).

The first known purl stitches appear from the mid-sixteenth century in the red silk stockings in which Eleanora de Toledo, wife of Cosimo de' Medici, was buried. The stockings also sport the first known lacy patterns made by yarn-over stitches; however, the technique may have been developed slightly earlier. Queen Elizabeth I of England also favored silk stockings, which were finer, softer, more decorative, and much more expensive than those made of wool. Stockings reputed to have belonged to Queen Elizabeth I still exist and demonstrate the quality of items that were specifically knitted for her. During this era the manufacture of stockings was of vast importance to many Britons, who knitted with fine wool and exported their wares. Knitting schools were established as a way of providing income to the poor.

In 1566, King Eric of Sweden had a garment inventory done; he owned twenty-seven pairs of silk stockings imported from Spain. The gauge on these stockings was about twenty-five stitches per inch. Imagine! We groan at the thought of knitting seven or eight stitches per inch using the large array of sock yarns available today.

The knowledge of knitting followed trade routes and spread around the world. Sailors were also big fans of knitting because the craft occupied their time on long voyages. Back in Europe, peasants gradually added knitting to their folk costumes, producing lovely ethnic sweaters.

Colonial-era women were avid and constant knitters. Many of the women kept daily journals of small-town life that often made references to knitting. Typically, the women would include notes such as "I knit several inches on my stocking today" and "read a little, knit a little by candlelight."

Women went on to design their own garments and then passed their techniques on to others, who then improved or changed them to suit their needs. This method of learning continued up to the nineteenth century, when magazines geared toward women came into fashion. As women began to depend on patterns supplied by magazines, the tradition of passing on patterns slowly diminished and soon became obsolete.

Over the years, the role of knitting has regularly shifted from producing high-demand luxury items to creating low-demand folk crafts and back again. In the Victorian era, knitting became a parlor art used to make all sorts of exquisitely fine laces, bags, and baby clothes. The Victorians most likely introduced fine beadwork to knitting, stringing tiny beads onto sewing thread and knitting it into fabric.

The next knitting revolution was the idea of knitwear as sportswear, which came simultaneously from British royalty and Paris designers. The Prince of Wales began wearing Fair Isle sweaters for golfing. Italian designer Elsa Schiaparelli mass-produced her "bow knot" sweater, and it became an instant hit.

In the 1930s the Depression hit, and around the world several co-ops were set up to help women earn money by knitting. When cash-pressed customers desired European-designed sweaters, knitters copied the designs for far less money. During this time, knitting flourished. Women knitted fashionable suits and jackets. Movie stars, such as Bette Davis and Joan Blondell, were shown in knitting books featuring styles of the time.

Child knitting, circa 1915. (© imagebroker/Alamy)

AMERICAN RED CROSS

OUR BOYS NEED SOX KNIT YOUR BIT

(Library of Congress)

There are many groups making chemo caps, preemie caps, blankets, comfort afghans, and comfort toys for those in need. These items are given to local hospitals or distributed through such groups as the Salvation Army and local police and fire departments. Evie Rosen, the creator of Warm Up America!, saw the program as a way for knitters to get involved in helping the homeless.

During the 1960s and 1970s knitting waned in popularity and needlepoint took over as the popular textile art. In the 1980s, with twice as many women working, the market altered in other ways. Women juggling husbands, children, households, and careers now wanted quick-completion projects. Books featuring weekend projects using bulky yarn and large needles became the vogue. Women who had only a few hours to devote to knitting wanted to see fast results.

Though knitting was at an all-time low in the 1980s, it is now experiencing a wonderful resurgence. Knitting conferences, guilds, chapters, clubs, and groups of all kinds are flourishing throughout the country. Women are busily knitting fashionable items for themselves, charity, and their family and friends.The vast array of yarn available today, ranging from moderately priced yarns to high-end designer yarns threaded with crystal, make knitting fun for everyone.

Knitters the world over continue to experiment with new stitches and techniques, new yarns, and new tools to make the knitting process easier, faster, and smoother. New methods are constantly being introduced. We are adding to knitting history every day.

During the 1940s, charity knitting blossomed. Women knitted for war efforts, sending knitted items to our armed forces and to those suffering the effects of war in foreign countries. This movement spelled a knitting comeback to yarn companies, which foresaw millions of people learning to knit.

Though experiencing a resurgence, charitable knitting was not new. Knitters have been charitable throughout history. During the Civil War, knitters provided items for their fighting forces. In 1917, during the First World War, members of the American Red Cross surveyed war-zone conditions and wrote home describing our soldiers' need for knitted mufflers, sweaters, and socks. Knitters rallied round, and The Red Cross coordinated the effort, providing yarn and instructions for shipping the finished items overseas. Such groups as Warm Up America! and Save the Children bring knitters and crocheters together to provide comfort to people in need.

References:

No Idle Hand: The Social History of American Knitting by Anne L. Macdonald

Wikipedia *History of Knitting*

A Treasury of Knitting Patterns by Barbara Walker

KNITTING BASICS

In this section, you will find all the information you need to start knitting. If you are new to knitting, use these pages to learn basic techniques and terminology. If you are an experienced knitter, refer to this section for guidance on abbreviations, needle sizes, method variations, and more.

Knitting Needles and Other Tools

Knitting needles are made of aluminum, plastic, bamboo, or wood and come in a range of sizes and styles.

The diameter of the needle determines the size of the stitch. Sizes are stated in metric measurements as well as a U.S. numbering system, as given in the chart at right. In general, smaller needles are used for knitting finer yarns, larger needles for heavier yarns.

There are also different types of needles. Straight needles come in different lengths and have a stop on one end to keep stitches from sliding off. This style is used for knitting back and forth in rows, as for a scarf or pieces of a sweater. Double-pointed needles are short with points on both ends, useful for knitting in the round on projects like socks and mittens. Circular needles are two needle points connected by a flexible cable. The points come in the usual range of needle sizes, and they also come in various cable lengths; the longer the cable, the more stitches it will hold. Besides knitting in the round, as for a one-piece sweater, circular needles are useful for knitting in rows on large projects like blankets.

Other useful items include stitch markers, stitch counters, stitch holders, and yarn bobbins for color work.

KNITTING NEEDLE SIZES

Metric Size	U.S. Size
2.25 mm	1
2.75 mm	2
3.25 mm	3
3.5 mm	4
3.75 mm	5
4 mm	6
4.5 mm	7
5 mm	8
5.5 mm	9
6 mm	10
6.5 mm	10½
8 mm	11
9 mm	13
10 mm	15
12.75 mm	17
15 mm	19
19 mm	35
25 mm	50

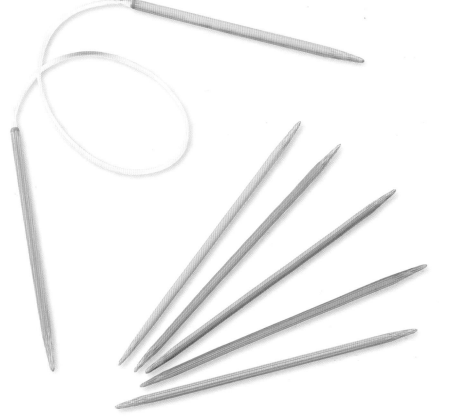

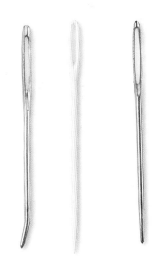

Small sharp scissors for cutting yarn and a flexible tape measure are essential for knitting. For finishing your projects, you will need a yarn or tapestry needle with a blunt end for weaving in yarn ends and hand-sewing seams.

Knitting Instructions

Knitting instructions are written in a shortened form, using standard abbreviations. This greatly reduces the space and overwhelming confusion that would result if the instructions were written out completely, word for word. Sometimes, stitch charts with symbols are included to help you understand the pattern. This happens especially when you are knitting something with cables (page 205) or intarsia (page 265).

Reading Written Instructions

Knitting patterns are often groups of stitches that are repeated a certain number of times in a row or round. Rather than repeat the instructions for the stitch group over and over, the group is enclosed between parentheses or brackets immediately followed by the number of times to work the stitches.

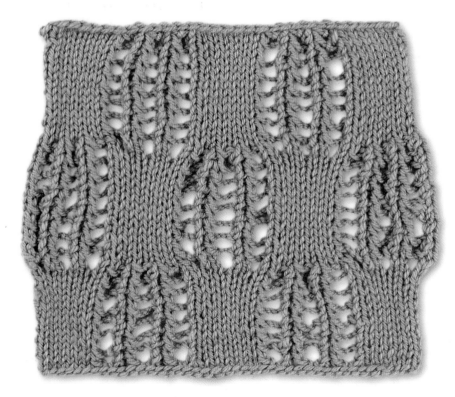

For example: (k2tog, sl 1, k1, psso) 3 times or [k2tog, sl 1, k1, psso] 3 times.

This is a much shorter way to say "knit 2 together, slip 1, knit 1, pass slipped stitch over; knit 2 together, slip 1, knit 1, pass slipped stitch over; knit 2 together, slip 1, knit 1, pass slipped stitch over."

Another way to indicate repeated stitch patterns is with asterisks. This same instruction could be written: *k2tog, sl 1, k1, psso, repeat from * two times more.

Parentheses are also used to clarify or reinforce information. They may be used at the end of a row to tell you how many total stitches you should have in that row, such as (25 sts). Sometimes this information is set off with an em dash at the row end—25 sts. Parentheses are also used to tell you which side of the work you should be on: (WS) or (RS). For multi-size patterns, parentheses enclose the variations you must apply to the different sizes. For example, a pattern may include directions for size 2 (4, 6, 8). Throughout the instructions, wherever you must choose for the correct size, the choices will be written like this: K34 (36, 38, 40).

Abbreviations

Here is the list of standard abbreviations used for knitting. Until you can readily identify them, keep the list handy whenever you knit.

beg........begin

bet........between

BO........bind off

CC........contrasting color

cm.........centimeter

cn.........cable needle

CO........cast on

Col.........color

cont........continue

dec........decrease

dpn........double-pointed needle(s)

g..........grams

inc.........increase

k..........knit

k1f&b......knit into front and back loop of same stitch

k2tog.......knit two stitches together

kwise.......knitwise

m(s)........markers(s)

MC........main color

mm........millimeters

M1.........make one stitch (increase)

oz.........ounce

p..........purl

patt........pattern

p1f&b......purl into front and back loop of same stitch

p2tog......purl two stitches together

pm........place marker

psso.......pass slipped stitch over

pwise......purlwise

rem ....remaining or remain

rep........repeat

rev St st......reverse stockinette stitch

rib.........ribbing

rnd(s)........rounds

RS........right side

sk.........skip

skp........slip 1, knit 1, pass slipped stitch over (decrease)

sl..........slip

sl1k........slip one knitwise

sl1p........slip one purlwise

sl st........slip stitch

sm.........slip marker

ssk.........slip 1, slip 1, knit these 2 stitches together (decrease)

st(s)........stitch(es)

St st........stockinette stitch

tbl.........through back loop

tog.........together

WS........wrong side

wyb........with yarn in back

wyf.........with yarn in front

yb.........yarn back

yf.........yarn forward

yo.........yarn over needle

*.........repeat from *

[ ].........repeat instructions in brackets as directed

( ).........repeat instructions in parentheses as directed

( ).........number of stitches that should be on the needle or across a row

Techniques

These are the basic techniques for knitting. If you are a beginning knitter, use these pages to help you learn to knit and improve your skills. If you are an occasional knitter, refer to this section to refresh your memory about the different stitches and stitch combinations used for shaping your knitting. Even experienced knitters will return to this section for clarification on stitch directions from time to time.

Casting On Stitches

Every knitting project begins by putting a foundation row of stitches on your needle; this is called casting on. There are several different ways to cast on stitches. The standard method—the one used if your pattern doesn't specify another method—is called long-tail cast-on.

Long-Tail Cast-On

Make a slipknot on the needle and hold the needle in your right hand. Put the thumb and index finger of your left hand between the tail and working yarn, the tail around your thumb and the working yarn around your index finger. Use the other fingers of your left hand to hold both strands snugly against your left palm **(1)**. Insert the needle upward through the loop on your thumb **(2)**. Pivot the needle to the right and go over and under the yarn on your index finger, picking up a loop **(3)**. Pull the loop back down through the thumb loop **(4)**. Let your thumb drop out of the loop and immediately wrap the tail yarn back around your thumb. Spread your fingers to snug up the new stitch on the needle **(5)**. Repeat the steps for each stitch.

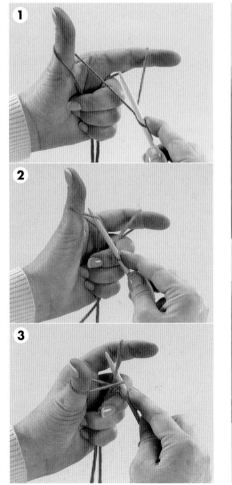

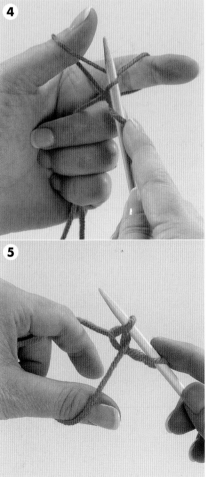

Cable Cast-On

Other cast-on methods are used in specific situations. The cable cast-on is useful if you need to add stitches to your knitting after you've already worked several rows or rounds.

Insert the right needle into the space between the last two stitches on your left needle. Wrap the yarn around your needle **(1)** and pull a loop through **(2)**. Put this loop back on your left needle. You've just cast on one stitch. Continue in this manner, adding as many stitches as the pattern calls for **(3)**.

Knit Cast-On

Notice that the knit cast-on is very similar to the cable cast-on. The difference lies in where you insert your needle. This method creates a tight, inelastic edge. Create a slipknot, and place it on your needle to create your first loop. Insert your needle into the loop knitwise. Wrap your yarn around your needle **(1)** and pull a loop through. Place this loop on your left needle **(2)**. You have just cast on one stitch. Continue in this manner until you have cast on the required number of stitches **(3)**.

Elastic Cast-On

This method is similar to the long-tail cast-on, but with an extra twist that makes the cast-on row more elastic. Use this method when the cast-on edge needs to stretch, such as for socks, mittens, and hats. Allow extra length (about 30% more) for the yarn tail when casting on with this method.

Make a slipknot on the needle and hold the needle in your right hand. Put the thumb and index finger of your left hand between the tail and working yarn, with the tail around your thumb and the working yarn around your index finger. Use the other fingers of your left hand to hold both strands snugly against your left palm **(1)**. Wrap the needle from the front under both strands of the tail yarn **(2)** and insert the tip over the back strand and into the loop between the strands **(3)**. With the back strand still on the needle, bring the needle tip toward you under and over the front strand **(4)**. Catch the working yarn, wrapping it counter-clockwise around the needle **(5)**, then bring the needle tip forward and manueuver it back through the thumb loop. Drop the loop from your thumb. Catch the tail yarn with your thumb again, forming a new loop as you snug up the new stitch on the needle **(6)**. Repeat the steps to add stitches **(7)**. Notice the extra bead of yarn under each stitch.

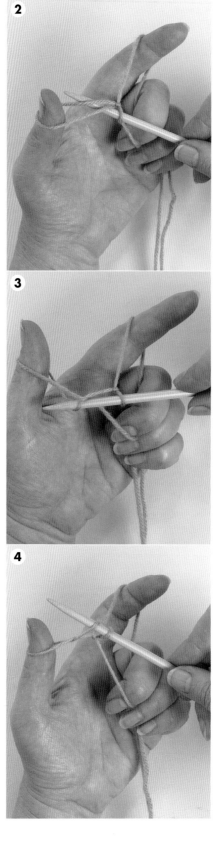

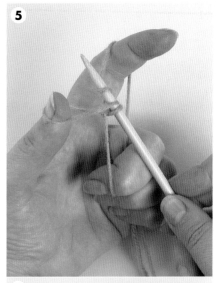

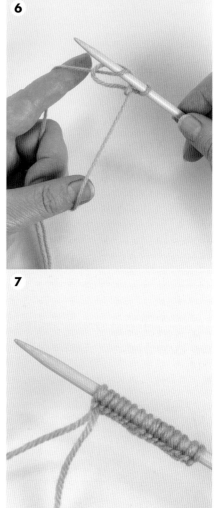

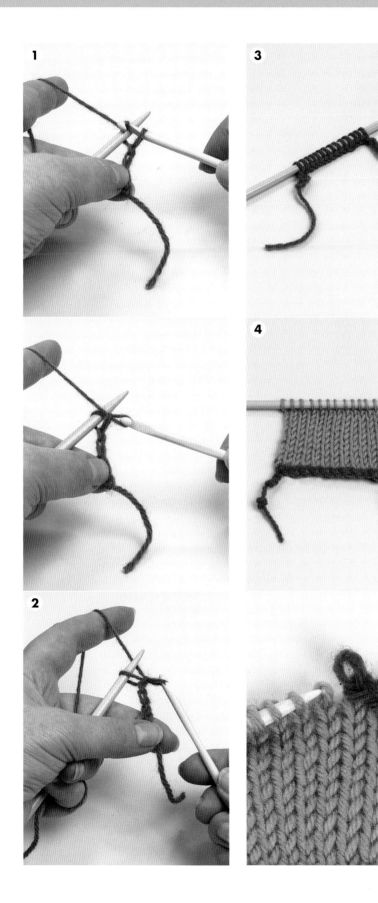

Provisional Cast-On

A provisional cast-on is a way of casting on stitches so that the cast-on row can later be removed, leaving a row of "live" stitches that can be placed on a needle and knitted in the opposite direction. There are many uses for this cast-on and many patterns call for it. There are also several ways to achieve a provisional cast-on. My favorite is to use a crochet hook to put the stitches on the needle. It is quite easy to do, and easy to remove the provisional yarn when done.

With a contrasting yarn, make a slip-knot, then chain two or three stitches with a crochet hook. Hold a knitting needle in your left hand over the working yarn that is coming from the crochet hook in your right hand. Take the hook over the needle, wrap the yarn over the hook, and pull it through the loop on the hook, making a chain (**1**). Reposition the working yarn under the needle (**2**), and make another stitch over the needle. Continue until you have made the required number of stitches. Chain two or three stitches with just the crochet hook, cut the yarn, and pull the end through (**3**). Make a knot in the beginning tail, so that you know to pull the end without the knot when it comes time to unravel the provisional cast-on. Drop the contrast yarn and, starting with the first row, knit the stitches with your project yarn. When you are ready to knit from the cast-on edge, release the stitches of the contrast yarn and pick up the live stitches with your knitting needle (**4**).

Knitting and Purling

Knit the Standard Way

To knit the standard way (abbreviated k), insert your right needle through the last loop on your left needle from left to right wrap the yarn around your right needle counterclockwise **(1)**, and pull a loop through, simultaneously dropping the stitch off of your left needle **(2)**.

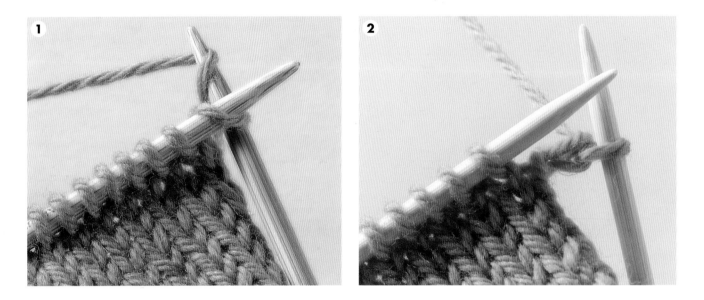

Knit Through Back Loop

To knit through the back loop (ktbl) insert your right needle through the last loop on your left needle from right to left **(3)**. The resulting stitch looks like a knit stitch but is tight and twisted **(4)**.

Purl the Standard Way

Bring your yarn to the front of the work, insert your needle right-to-left through the last loop on your left needle, wrap the yarn around the needle counter-clockwise **(1)**, and pull a loop through onto your right needle while dropping the old loop off your left needle **(2)**.

Purl Through Back Loop

To create a stitch that is twisted from the purl side, purl the stitch through the back loop (abbreviated ptbl). Insert your needle left to right through the last loop of your left needle **(3)** and continue to make a purl stitch in the same way **(4)**.

Slipping Stitches

To slip a stitch, move your stitch from the left needle to the right needle without doing anything to it. When you slip a stitch by inserting your right needle right to left into the other stitch (the same way you would if you were going to purl that stitch), you are slipping a stitch purlwise (sl 1 pwise) **(5)**. If you slip a stitch by inserting your needle through it from left-to-right (the way you would if you were going to knit that stitch), you are slipping the stitch knitwise (sl 1 kwise) **(6)**.

Binding Off

Finishing the last row or round of a knitted project so that it will not ravel is called binding off. In the conventional method of binding off, usually done from the right side, you knit the first two stitches, then, using your left needle, lift the second stitch on the right needle up and over the stitch that you've just knit. One stitch is bound off. Repeat this, one stitch at a time, until all stitches are bound off. When a pattern just tells you to bind off all stitches, this is the method to use. If the pattern tells you to bind off in pattern, you knit or purl each stitch following the stitch pattern that has been established before binding it off.

Purl Two Together Bind-Off

You can also bind off from the wrong side, or purl side of stockinette stitching. For this common method of binding off, purl two stitches together **(1)**, transfer this stitch back to your left needle **(2)**, and purl two stitches again **(3)**. Repeat this operation until you've bound off the required number of stitches.

Three-Needle Bind-Off

The three-needle bind-off method finishes two edges and joins them together at once. This is especially useful for shoulder seams of sweaters. Both needles must hold the same number of stitches. A third needle is used to bind them off and together.

Hold the two pieces that you're joining with their right sides facing each other. Then, insert a third needle knitwise through the first stitch on the front needle and through the first stitch on the back needle (**1**). Wrap the yarn around the tip of your needle, and pull a loop through both stitches as you simultaneously drop the stitches from the front and back needles (**2**). Repeat these steps to get a second stitch onto your right needle. Once you have two stitches on your right needle, use the tip of the left needle to lift the second stitch on your right needle up and over the first stitch (**3**), thus binding off one stitch. Continue in this way to the end of the row.

Stretchy Bind-Off Stitches

Two of my favorite stretchy bind-off stitches have different looks and each produces different effects.

The first one works really well with stockinette stitch, especially if you have a tendency to bind off too tightly. The second one works great when binding off in ribbing, especially at necklines.

Stretchy Bind-Off #1

Work the first two stitches, *take the first stitch over the second stitch, but leave this stitch on the left-hand needle **(1)**, knit the next stitch on the left-hand needle **(2)**, then slip both stitches off **(3)**. Two stitches remain on the right-hand needle (one stitch has been bound off); repeat from * until all stitches have been bound off **(4)**.

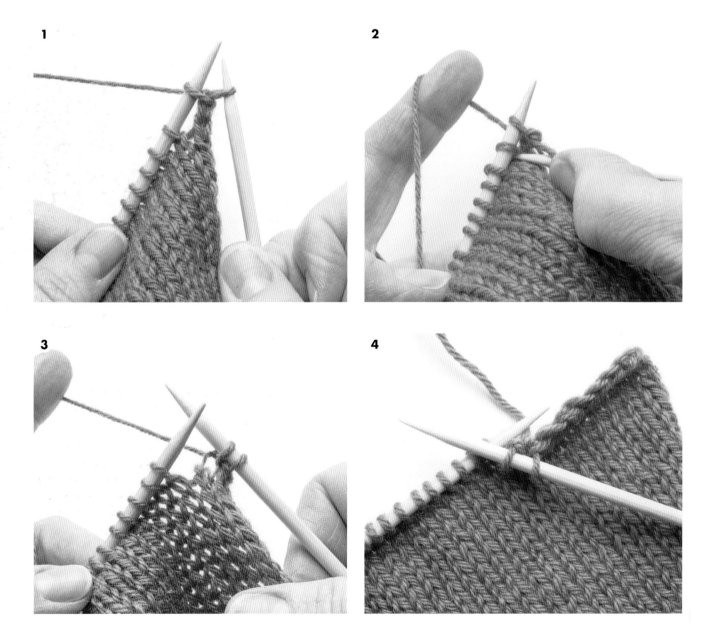

Stretchy Bind-Off #2

Work the first stitch; when the next stitch is a purl stitch, purl the stitch, insert the left-hand needle into the back of both stitches (**1**) and purl both stitches together. When the next stitch is a knit stitch, knit the stitch, insert the left-hand needle into the front of both stitches (**2**) and knit both stitches together (**3**).

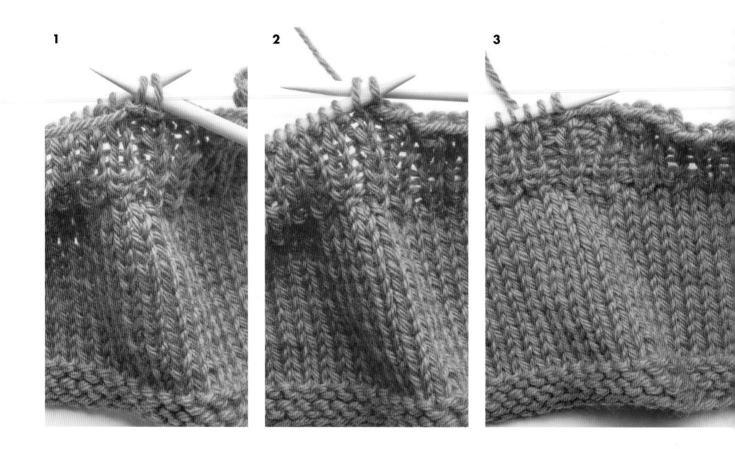

1   **2**   **3**

Picot Bind-Off

The picot bind-off creates a decorative edge and can be used on edges that will not be seamed, such as neck or front borders, baby clothes, and blankets.

Using the basic knit method, bind off the first two stitches, *turn, using knit cast-on method, cast on three additional stitches, turn, bind off all but one of the stitches by passing the second over the first until one stitch remains on right needle, bind off two more stitches; repeat from * to end of row (**4**).

Shaping

When you sew, you shape fabric with darts or tucks or simply in the way you cut the garment pieces. There are various ways to shape fabric as you knit: decreasing or increasing the number of stitches on the needle, and adding short rows into the work. Basically, adding another row or round increases the length of a shape. Increasing or decreasing the number of stitches in a row alters the width of the shape. Adding short rows causes portions of the shape to curve forward or backward.

Decreasing

Here are various ways to decrease the number of stitches. Each method has a distinct appearance.

Knit Two Together (k2tog)

Knitting two stitches together has a definite orientation: it is right-leaning. The stitch on the left always leans to the right and sits on top of the stitch on the right. Insert the needle knitwise into two stitches together, wrap the yarn around the needle (1), and pull the loop through (2).

Slip-Slip-Knit (ssk)

To create a left-leaning decrease that mirrors knitting two stitches together, use a slip-slip-knit. Slip the two stitches knitwise, one at a time (1), (2), and insert your left needle into them to knit them together. You have decreased one stitch and the right stitch leans on top of the left stitch.

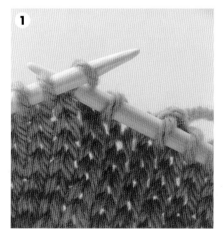

Purl Two Together (p2tog)

To create a right-leaning decrease from the wrong side of the work, purl two stitches together: insert the right needle into two stitches purlwise, wrap the yarn around the tip of the right needle (**1**), and pull a loop through (**2**).

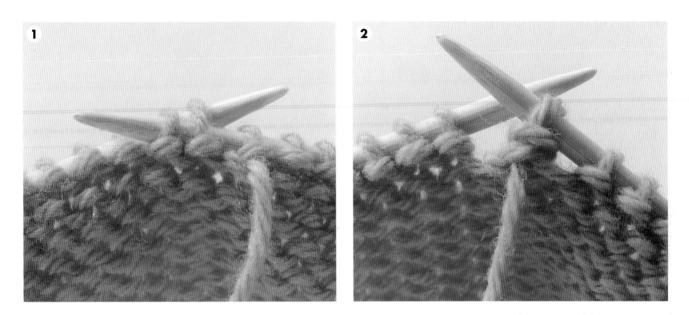

Purl Two Together Through Back Loops (p2tog-tbl)

To create a left-leaning decrease from the wrong side of the work, purl two stitches together through their back loops. Take your right needle, and, turning the work slightly to see the back, insert it left to right through your two stitches. Then, wrap your yarn around the tip of your right needle (**1**) and pull a loop through onto your right needle (**2**).

Increasing

Each of these different increase methods looks different, and is suitable for a different situation.

Bar Increase (kfb)

This is one of the simplest increases. Instructions may tell you to knit into the front and back loop of the same stitch. The new stitch that you create with this method will have a little bar at its base, which will be highly visible. Often, the bar increase is used in situations where the bar blends in with the rest of the stitches (as in garter stitch) or when the bar serves a decorative function to highlight the line at which you are increasing stitches.

Knit a stitch, but don't drop it off your left needle **(1)**. Now, insert your right needle into the back loop of the stitch **(2)**, and knit it again, now allowing the stitch to slide off your left needle **(3)**. Your single stitch will now have become two, with the second stitch branching from a little horizontal bar.

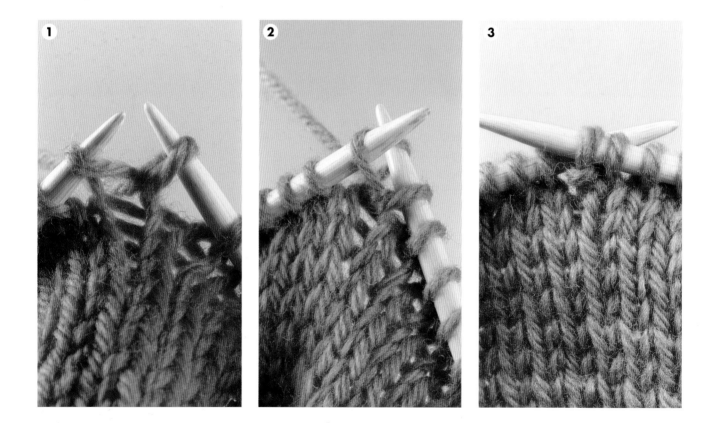

Make One Increases (M1R and M1L)

Make one increases are nearly invisible. To perform both the right and the left versions of the make one increase, you pick up the running yarn between your needles, place it on your left needle, and knit into it. How you place the running yarn on your left needle and how you knit into the resulting loop varies, based on whether you are working the right or the left version of the increase.

Make One Right (M1R)

Unlike decreases, which clearly have a direction in which they slant, increases have a slant that's much more subtle. The right-leaning version of the make one increase, abbreviated M1R, tends to be the default make one increase to use. If the instructions simply say M1, use this method. Insert your right needle under the running yarn from front to back **(1)**. Then, transfer the resulting loop onto your left needle **(2)**. Now, knit into this loop in the normal way, thereby adding an extra stitch to your row **(3)**.

Make One Left (M1L)

To work the left version of the make one increase, insert your left needle under the running yarn from front to back and transfer the loop to your left needle **(1)**. Now, knit into the back loop of this stitch, once again adding an extra stitch to your row.

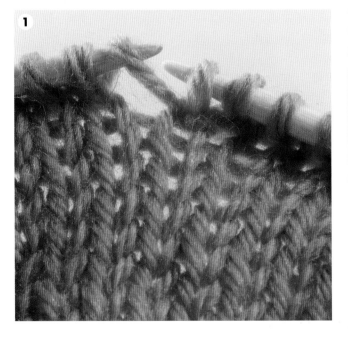

Note the subtle difference in the way these increases slant.

Lifting Up the Loop Increases (krl and kll)

To work loop increases, add an extra stitch by knitting into the head of the stitch in the row below the one you are working.

Right Loop Increase (krl)

To work the right version, use your right needle to lift up the head of the stitch that's directly below the stitch on your left needle (1). Place this loop on your left needle (2) and knit into it (3), thereby adding an extra stitch to your row.

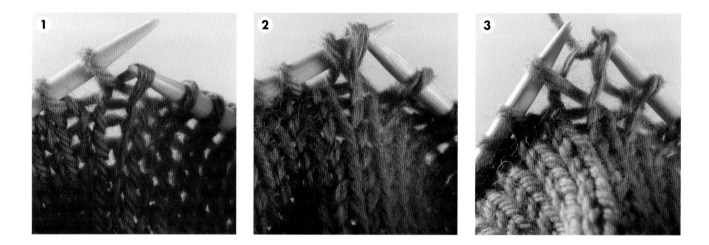

Left Loop Increase (kll)

To work the left version of the loop increase, use your left needle to lift up the head of the stitch that's two stitches below the stitch on your right needle (1). Keep this loop on your left needle. Then knit into this loop (2), adding an extra stitch to your row.

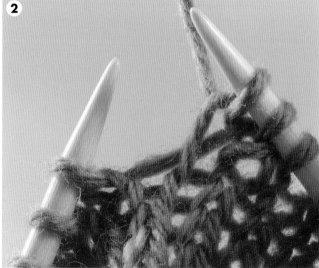

Yarn-Over Increase (yo)

The yarn-over increase, used often in knitting lace, creates a hole in the fabric. Bring your yarn forward, wrap it counterclockwise around the right needle, and return it to the back of the work **(1)**. In the next row, knit or purl this wrap like any other stitch. The yarn-over increase leaves a hole **(2)**.

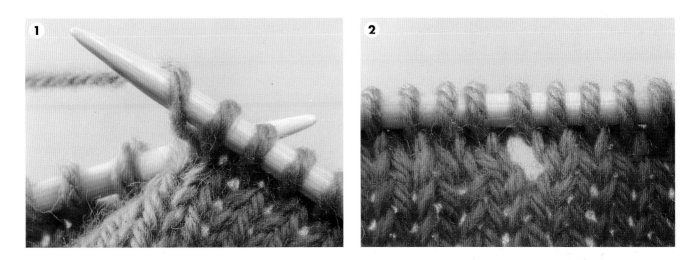

Short Rows

A short row is exactly what it sounds like: a row that you add into your knitting that has fewer stitches than the number of stitches on your needle. Instead of knitting all the stitches on the needle, you knit only some of them, turn your knitting, and purl back to the beginning of your row, thus adding a short row into your knitting.

If you add short rows to one side of your knitting, you are making one selvage of the work longer than the other selvage **(1)**.

If you add short rows to the center of your knitting, you are making the central length of your work longer than the selvage length. This will result in a central bulge **(2)**.

Short rows on one side

Short rows in the center

Wrapping and Turning (w&t)

If you worked the short row as described above, you would create a hole at the junction between the short row and the rest of your knitting. To avoid making a hole, perform an operation called wrapping and turning (abbreviated w&t). Instead of knitting your short row and simply turning, knit your short row, wrap your yarn around the following unworked stitch, and only then turn and work back to the beginning of the row. How you wrap and turn depends on whether you are working on the knit side or the purl side of stockinette stitch fabric.

Wrap and Turn from Knit Side

When working a short row on the knit side of the fabric, knit the required number of stitches, bring the yarn forward to the front of your work, slip the next (unworked) stitch from your left needle to your right needle **(1)**, bring the yarn to the back of your work, and slip the unworked stitch back to your left needle **(2)**. Now turn the knitting and purl back to the beginning **(3)**.

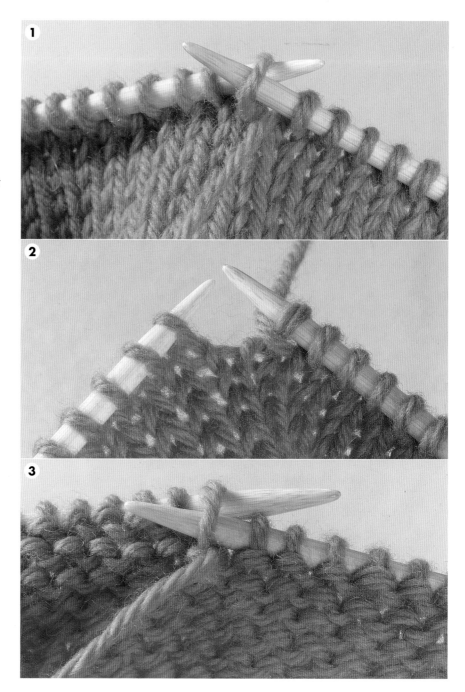

Wrap and Turn from Purl Side

When working a short row on the purl side of the fabric, bring the yarn to the back of the work, slip the next unworked stitch from the left needle to the right needle **(1)**, bring the yarn to the front of the work again, and slip the unworked stitch back to the left needle **(2)**. Then, you're ready to turn and work the next row **(3)**.

Taking Care of Wraps

When you wrap and turn, you are left with some unsightly little bars that highlight where you turned the short row. To make the bar less visible, lift the bar onto the left needle and work it together with the next stitch. Most patterns don't include notes on when you'll be passing these wraps, so you have to watch for them.

Purling Wrap with Stitch

When you pass a wrap on the purl side of the fabric (the wrong side in stockinette stitch), insert your right needle front to back under the wrap **(1)** and place it onto your left needle, allowing it to sit on the right of the stitch around which it was wrapped **(2)**. Then, purl the stitch and its wrap together **(3)**. Though this will produce a bulbous yarn loop on the purl side of the fabric, you'll notice that the wrap will disappear from the knit side of the fabric, leaving an even, neat knit stitch **(4)**.

Knitting Wrap with Stitch

When you pass a wrap on the knit side of the fabric, first insert your right needle front to back under the wrap **(1)**. Then, lift the wrap onto your left needle, up and over the stitch that it was wrapped around **(2)**. Slip first the stitch and then the wrap knitwise **(3)**, and then knit them together **(4)**. Note that this final step of slipping twice and knitting together is nearly identical to the slip-slip-knit (ssk) decrease.

Knitting in the Round

Sometimes it is necessary to knit in a tubular shape, going around in circles. This can be done in different ways: using one circular needle, using four or five double-pointed needles, or using two circular needles. Which method you use depends on how many stitches there are in the circle. If all the stitches fit comfortable (without stretching) on the cable of a circular needle, you can use one circular needle. Tubes with fewer stitches than will fit on the cable of a circular needle can be knit on double pointed needles, dividing the stitches among three or four needles and knitting them consecutively with another needle. You can also knit in the round with two circular needles, dividing the stitches between them and alternating from one needle to the other.

Using Double-Pointed Needles

To begin knitting a tube on double-pointed needles, cast on the required number of stitches that form the initial circumference of your tube onto a single needle. Then divide these stitches evenly onto three or four double-pointed needles **(1)** and arrange the needles in a circle, being careful not to twist your stitches **(2)**. Use an extra needle and the yarn coming from the final stitch that you cast on to begin working the first cast-on stitch, the first stitch of your round. A great way to keep your first stitch firmly attached to your final stitch in your circle is to knit the first three stitches of your round with both your working yarn and the long yarn tail from your cast-on stitches **(3)**. Knit the rest of the stitches from needle one, using only the working yarn. Use the empty needle to continue knitting the stitches on the next needle in your round. Continue in this manner, and you'll soon have a tube-shaped piece of knitting **(4)**.

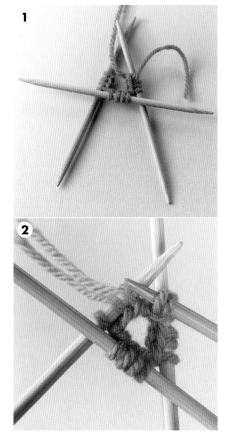

Knitting a Tube with One Circular Needle

Make sure you choose a circular needle with a cable long enough to hold all the stitches. Cast on all the stitches and distribute them along the cable (taking care not to twist your stitches) until the first stitch reaches the opposite point. Hold the tip with the last cast-on stitch in your right hand and the tip with the beginning stitch in your left hand. Use the yarn coming from the final cast-on stitch to begin working the first cast-on stitch, the first stitch of your round. Knit all the stitches in the round, shifting them along the cable as you go. Although the yarn tail indicates where each round begins, you may want to place a stitch marker at the beginning stitch as an extra reminder.

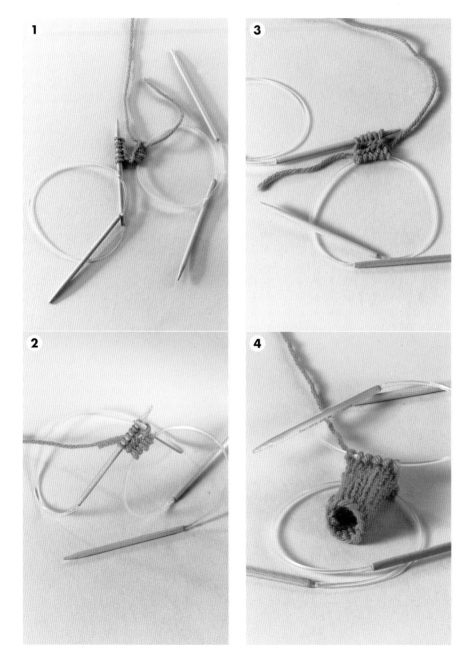

Knitting a Tube on Two Circular Needles

When you knit a tube on two circular needles, you work from only one needle at a time, so you'll always have one working needle and one idle needle. Stitches on the resting circular needle hang loosely on the cable portion of the needle.

To begin, cast on the stitches for the circumference of your tube onto one circular needle. Transfer half the stitches (beginning with the slipknot) onto the second circular needle, and slide these stitches to the opposite tip of that needle (1). Slide the stitches on needle one to the center of the needle cable, and drop needle one. Using the free tip of needle two, join the stitches into a round, working the first three stitches of your round with both the working yarn and the yarn tail from the cast-on end held together (2). Finish knitting the rest of the stitches on that needle, using only the working yarn. Then slide all the stitches on needle two to the center of the needle cable (3). Drop needle two and pick up needle one. Push the stitches from the cable to the tip of the needle. Then, using the opposite end of needle one, knit all the stitches on that needle. Drop needle one and pick up needle two. Continue this process, alternating between needles, until you've finished your tube (4).

I-cord

Some tubes can be knit using only two double-pointed needles. These tubes are known as idiot cord, or merely I-cord. Any tube that has five stitches or fewer in circumference can be worked as I-cord.

Cast on or pick up the required number of stitches on a double-pointed needle. Knit the stitches with another double-pointed needle, but don't turn the work. Slide the stitches to the opposite end of the needle **(1)**. Pull the working yarn tight across the back of the stitches **(2)** and knit another row. Repeat this many times, forming a tiny knitted tube **(3)**. To keep the stitches looking uniform, tug on the tube every few rows.

Checking Your Gauge

Gauge refers to the number of stitches and the number of rows in a given width and length of knitted fabric, usually in 4-inch (10 cm) increments. Before knitting a project, check the gauge to ensure your stitching creates the correct denseness of weave.

Every pattern indicates the exact yarn (or weight of yarn) and size needles to use and the finished measurements of the project shown. Yarn labels also list the needle size and recommended gauge for that yarn. It is important to choose yarn in the weight specified for the project to successfully complete the project. The needle size recommended is the size an average knitter would use to get the correct gauge.

Unfortunately, many knitters don't fall in the average range. Some of us knit tighter, others looser. To check your gauge, use the yarn and needle called for in the instructions to cast on the number of stitches indicated by the gauge in the

pattern plus four more stitches. For example, if the gauge is 16 stitches = 4" (10 cm), cast on 20 stitches. Work the pattern stitch, keeping two stitches at each end in knit, until you have an approximate 4" (10 cm) square. Lay the swatch flat and measure your swatch from side to side between the two edge stitches. If the swatch is 4" (10 cm) wide, you are knitting to the correct gauge. If the swatch is smaller than 4" (10 cm), you need to use a larger needle; if it is larger than 4" (10 cm), you need to use a smaller needle. Don't try to change your personal knitting style; just change your needle size and knit another swatch.

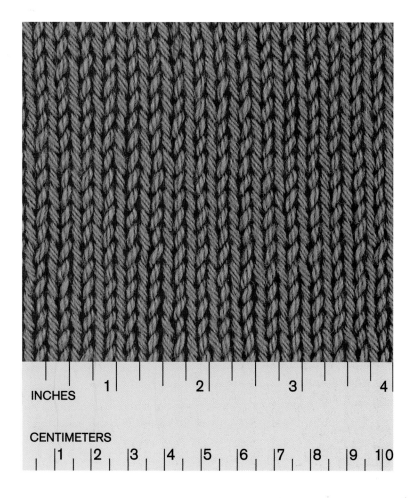

Details and Finishing Techniques

For any project, the quality of the detail work will determine the success of that project. There are various ways to sew seams, pick up stitches, add pockets, or sew in zippers. Here are some techniques for getting the details right every time.

Seaming

Seaming is necessary in nearly any sort of knitting. Different seam methods are used for different circumstances. The following types of seaming are the most common types. For any type of seaming, use a blunt-end yarn or tapestry needle.

Whip Stitch

To whip stitch a seam, hold the pieces with wrong sides facing each other, and push your threaded needle through both pieces. Take the next stitch close to the first one, inserting the needle from the same side as the first stitch. The yarn will wrap over the top of the seam. Repeat to the end of the seam **(1)**.

Mattress Stitch

Mattress stitch is an invisible seaming stitch, useful for attaching two pieces together by their selvages. Lay the pieces edge to edge, right side up. Hook your threaded tapestry needle under the first two running yarns between the selvage and the first column of stitches on one of the pieces. Then, insert your needle under the first two running yarns between the first column of stitches and selvage on the second piece. Zigzag back and forth like this, catching every two rows in turn. Leave the stitches fairly loose. After every few stitches, gently pull the yarn to tighten the seam and bring the edges together **(2)**.

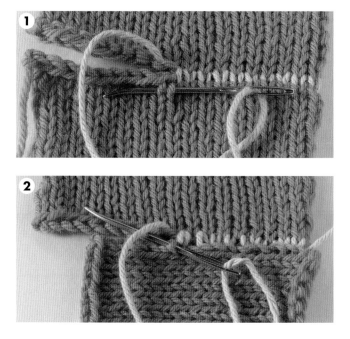

Fake Grafting

Fake grafting allows you to connect cast-on edges to bound-off edges, cast-on edges to other cast-on edges, and bound-off edges to other bound-off edges. To begin, place the pieces edge to edge, right side up. Hook the needle around the first column of stitches in the first piece, then under the first column of stitches in the second piece **(1)**. Continue in this manner. Note that when you hook the needle under a column of stitches, the column must "point" toward the seam itself. In other words, hook the needle around the base of a knit stitch (bottom of the V) rather than around the top of the knit stitch (the top of the V).

Combination Seaming

Pieces do not always align columns to columns or rows to rows. Often you need to seam two pieces together with rows to columns. Use a combination of mattress stitch and fake grafting to attach the pieces together **(2)**.

Kitchener Stitch

Kitchener stitch, also known as grafting, is the seaming method of choice when you need to join a row of live stitches to a second row of live stitches. It produces an invisible seam that's virtually undetectable. Cut the working yarn, leaving a tail about 18" (46 cm) long. Leave the stitches on the needles; there should be the same number of stitches on each. Hold the needles side by side in the left hand, with the right side facing up. Slide the stitches toward the needle tips.

The working yarn will be coming from the first stitch on the back needle. To help demonstrate the steps, a contrasting yarn has been used in the photos. Thread the yarn tail onto a yarn needle. Draw the yarn through the first stitch on the front needle as if to purl, and leave the stitch on the needle **(1)**.

Keeping the yarn under the needles, draw the yarn through the first stitch on the back needle as if to knit, and leave the stitch on the needle **(2)**.

*Draw the yarn through the first stitch on the front needle as if to knit, and slip the stitch off the needle **(3)**. Draw the yarn through the next stitch on the front needle as if to purl, and leave the stitch on the needle.

Draw the yarn through the first stitch on the back needle as if to purl, and slip the stitch off the needle **(4)**. Draw the yarn through the next stitch on the back needle as if to knit, and leave the stitch on the needle.

Repeat from * until all but the last two stitches have been worked off the needles. Insert the tapestry needle knitwise into the stitch on the front needle, and purlwise into the stitch on the back needle, slipping both stitches off their respective needles. Stretch out your seam or use the tip of a needle to adjust stitches a bit to even out the tension in the yarn **(5)**.

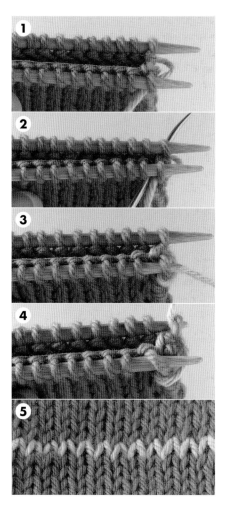

Picking Up Stitches

Picking up stitches from one edge to begin knitting in a new direction is a common technique used in many types of knitting. When knitting a sweater, for example, you might pick up stitches from the neck opening to add a neck band or collar.

To do this, slip your right needle into an available hole along the indicated edge, wrap your yarn around your needle **(1)**, and pull a loop through onto your right needle **(2)**. Now you've picked up one stitch. Continue in this manner across the edge (or middle) of your work until you've picked up the required number of stitches.

The way you pick up stitches also varies slightly depending on where you are picking up your stitches: from a cast-on or bound-off edge, from a selvage, or from the middle of your fabric.

Picking Up Stitches
from a Cast-On Edge

To pick up stitches from a cast-on edge, pick up one stitch per column of stitches. There are two ways to pick up stitches from a cast-on edge. You can pick up stitches invisibly from a cast-on edge by poking your needle between each column directly underneath the yarn strands of the cast-on edge itself **(1)**.

You can also pick up stitches by poking your needle through the loops that are on the other side of the straight edge. This will create a neat line demarcating the edge itself, and is often useful for decorative purposes, where creating a clear line at the edge where you are picking up stitches is an important design element **(2)**.

Picking Up Stitches from a Bound-Off Edge

Picking up stitches from a bound-off edge is almost identical to picking them up from a cast-on edge. Pick up one stitch for every column of stitches on your edge. Pick up stitches invisibly from your edge **(1)**, or pick them up in such a way that you create a clear demarcating line where you've picked up stitches **(2)**.

Picking Up Stitches from a Selvage

When knitting in stockinette, the stitches are wider than they are tall. So, picking up stitches along a selvage requires that you pick up approximately three stitches for every four rows along the edge. How to pick up stitches from your selvage varies, depending on what type of selvage you have. Selvages are either a loose chain selvage **(1)**, created by slipping the first stitch of every row, or a tight garter selvage **(2)**, created by knitting or purling the first stitch of every row. The chain selvage is a nice edge for scarves and shawls.

Chain selvage

Garter selvage

When you're picking up stitches along a chain selvage, you will have two rows of stitches per link in your chain. Pick up your stitches as follows: pick up one stitch in between chains, one stitch at the chain, and another stitch in between chains. Then, skip the next chain and begin again **(1)**. Notice the groups of three. With this method, the picked-up stitches will be tightly attached to your selvage.

Picking up stitches along a chain selvage

In a garter selvage, you have one knot per two rows of knitting. To maintain the three-to-four ratio, pick up one stitch between knots, one stitch at a knot, another stitch between knots, and then skip the next knot **(2)**. The spaces between the knots, as well as the knots themselves, are pretty tight, so as long as you pick up three stitches per four rows of knitting, the junction between your selvage and your new stitches should be relatively hole free.

Picking up stitches along a garter selvage

Inserting a Zipper

Zippers should be inserted into knitted garments by hand. The tricky part of inserting a zipper in a knitted garment is getting the sides to match. Here is one way to insert a zipper.

Baste the two sides of the garment together. Place the zipper face down on the wrong side of the garment, centering the teeth over the basted seam. Pin in place. Hand stitch the zipper to the sweater by stitching along the outer edges of the zipper tape (**1**). After sewing is completed, remove the basting stitches (**2**).

1

2

Pockets

Here is a way to set in patch
pockets that makes them blend
smoothly with the sweater body.

Place the pocket on top of the sweater,
aligning stitch rows, and pin in place.
With a tapestry needle, stitch the pocket
in place using duplicate stitch. This
means you stitch over the knit stitches on
the outer edge of the pocket, echoing
the path of the yarn and going through
the sweater body with each stitch. I find
this easier to do with a needle that has
a curved tip.

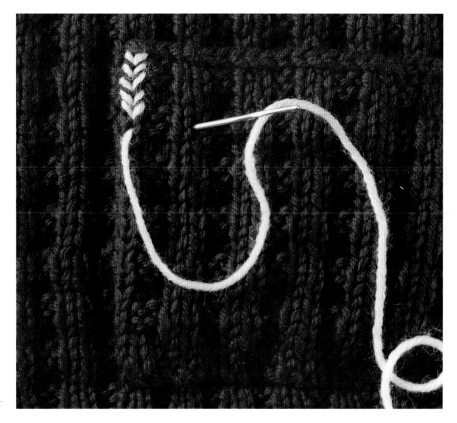

Joining New Yarn

Whenever possible, join new balls of yarn at the beginning or at
the end of a row, which makes it easy to weave ends into seams
when the garment is sewn together.

Sometimes joining the yarn in the middle
of a row is unavoidable. This occurs
in some color-work garments or when
knitting in the round. If joining mid-row
becomes necessary, try joining in an
inconspicuous spot. Loosely tie in the new
yarn and finish the row. Work one more
row, untie the knot, and retie to match the
gauge of stitches in the previous row.

There are ways to avoid running out of
yarn mid-row. If you are near the end of
the ball of yarn, lay your work flat and
fold the remaining yarn back and forth
over the width of your work. If you have
at least four times the width, you will
have enough yarn for simple patterns;
cables or bobbles will require more yarn.

STITCH PATTERNS

Now that you are familiar with knitting, purling, and other basic techniques, you are ready to explore the wide variety of fabrics that you can create. There are hundreds of named stitch patterns from simple to complex, from smooth to highly textured, and from compact and closed to lacy and open. In this section, you'll find 220 stitch patterns grouped by type, some with universally recognized names and others with descriptive names that fit their character. Each stitch pattern is shown in a large swatch with row-by-row instructions.

Basic Stitches

Every knitter begins by learning the knit stitch, and then progresses to learning how to purl. Once these two stitches are mastered, the world of knitting opens up. All other stitch patterns are made by combining knitting and purling in different ways. Some stitches are worked through the back of a stitch, some are crossed or twisted, but all are made up of these two basic stitches. Here are a few of the very basic, beginner stitches.

Garter Stitch

Skill Level: Easy

Cast on any number of stitches.

Knit every row.

Stockinette

Skill Level: Easy

Cast on any number of stitches.

Row 1 (RS): Knit all across row.

Row 2: Purl all across row.

Rep Rows 1 and 2 for pattern.

Reverse Stockinette

Skill Level: Easy

Cast on any number of stitches.

Row 1 (WS): Knit all across row.

Row 2: Purl all across row.

Rep Rows 1 and 2 for pattern.

Twisted Stockinette

Skill Level: Easy

Cast on an odd number of stitches.

Row 1: K1 through the back loop in each stitch.

Row 2: K1, purl across row to last stitch, k1.

Rep Rows 1 and 2 for pattern.

Seed/Moss Stitch

Skill Level: Easy

Cast on an odd number of stitches.

Row 1: K1, *p1, k1, rep from * across row.

Rep Row 1 for pattern.

Seed Stitch II

Skill Level: Easy

Cast on an odd number of stitches.

Row 1: K1, *p1, k1, rep from * across row.

Row 2: P1, *k1, p1, rep from * across row.

Row 3: P1, *k1, p1, rep from * across row.

Row 4: K1, *p1, k1, rep from * across row.

Rep Rows 1–4 for pattern.

Double Seed

Skill Level: Easy

Cast on a multiple of 4 plus 2.

Row 1: K2, *p2, k2, rep from * across row.

Row 2: P2, *k2, p2, rep from * across row.

Row 3: P2, *k2, p2, rep from * across row.

Row 4: K2, *p2, k2, rep from * across row.

Rep Rows 1–4 for pattern.

Nubby Sand

Skill Level: Easy

Cast on an odd number of stitches.

Row 1 (WS): Knit all across row.

Row 2: K1, *p1, k1, rep from * across row.

Rep Rows 1 and 2 for pattern.

Smooth Sand

Skill Level: Easy

Cast on a multiple of 2 plus 1.

Row 1 (RS): Knit all across row.

Row 2: K1, *p1, k1, rep from * across row.

Rep Rows 1 and 2 for pattern.

Knit One, Purl One Rib

Skill Level: Easy

Cast on an odd number of stitches.

Row 1: K1, *p1, k1, rep from * across row.

Row 2: P1, *k1, p1, rep from * across row.

Rep Rows 1 and 2 for pattern.

Twisted Knit One, Purl One Rib

Skill Level: Easy

Cast on an odd number of stitches.

Row 1: K1 through the back loop (tbl), *p1, k1 tbl, rep from * across row.

Row 2: P1 tbl, *k1, p1 tbl, rep from * across row.

Rep Rows 1 and 2 for pattern.

Knit Two, Purl Two Rib

Skill Level: Easy

Cast on a multiple of 4 plus 2.

Row 1: K2, *p2, k2, rep from * across row.

Row 2: P2, *k2, p2, rep from * across row.

Rep Rows 1 and 2 for pattern.

One-Piece Garter Stitch Sweater

This comfortable sweater is easy to knit and easy to wear. Roomy enough to wear over a shirt, the sweater can be worn with the sleeves rolled up or down. The entire sweater is knit in one piece in garter stitch; you will be knitting side to side from one sleeve end to the other.

YOU WILL NEED

Yarn

- Medium weight
- Shown: Patons Canadiana, 100% acrylic, 3.5 oz (100 g)/241 yds (220 m): School Bus Yellow #00432, 5 (5, 6, 7) skeins

Needles

- Size 10 (6 mm) or size to obtain gauge

Notions

- Tapestry needle

Gauge

- 20 sts = 4" (10 cm) in garter st on size 10 needles
- Take time to check gauge.

Sizes

- Small (Medium, Large, X-Large)
- Finished chest: 36 (38, 41, 44)" [91.5 (96.5, 104, 112) cm]

Skill Level: Easy

Note: Entire sweater is knitted side to side in one piece, starting at sleeve edge.

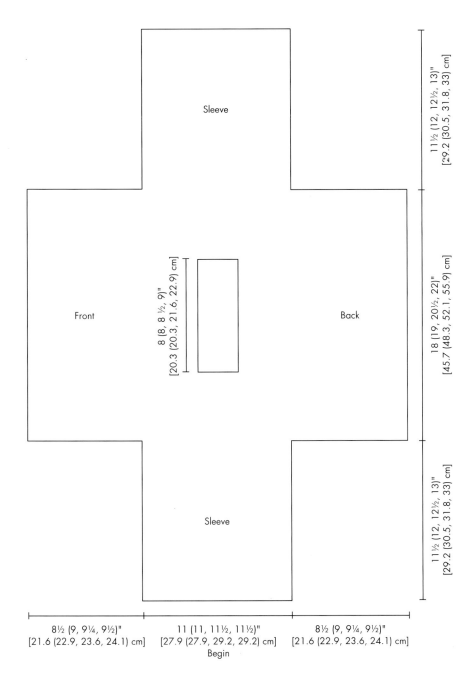

Sleeve

Front

Back

Sleeve

8 (8, 8 ½, 9)"
[20.3 (20.3, 21.6, 22.9) cm]

18 (19, 20½, 22)"
[45.7 (48.3, 52.1, 55.9) cm]

11½ (12, 12½, 13)"
[29.2 (30.5, 31.8, 33) cm]

11½ (12, 12½, 13)"
[29.2 (30.5, 31.8, 33) cm]

8½ (9, 9¼, 9½)"
[21.6 (22.9, 23.6, 24.1) cm]

11 (11, 11½, 11½)"
[27.9 (27.9, 29.2, 29.2) cm]

8½ (9, 9¼, 9½)"
[21.6 (22.9, 23.6, 24.1) cm]

Begin

Body

Starting at left sleeve edge, cast on 56 (56, 58, 58) sts. Work in garter st (knit every row) until piece measures 11½ (12, 12½, 13)" [29 (30.5, 32, 33) cm] from beg.

Next Row: At end of row, using knit or cable cast-on (page 15), cast on 42, (44, 46, 48) sts.

Next Row: K42 (44, 46, 48) cast-on sts, the original 56 (56, 58, 58) sts, then cast on 42 (44, 46, 48) sts. There are now 140 (144, 150, 154) sts on needle. Cont even in garter st for 5 (5½, 6, 6½)" [12.5 (14, 15, 16.5) cm].

Neck Shape

Next Row: Work 61 (62, 64, 65) sts, join a second ball of yarn, bind off next 18, (20, 22, 24) sts, work rem 61 (62, 64, 65) sts.

Work each side of 61 (62, 64, 65) sts with separate balls of yarn for 8 (8, 8½, 9)" [20.5 (20.5, 21.5, 23) cm].

Next Row: K61 (62, 64, 65) sts, using knit or cable cast-on, cast on 18 (20, 22, 24) sts, then cont with this ball of yarn, ending second ball of yarn, and work rem 61 (62, 64, 65) sts. There are now 140 (144, 150, 154) sts on needle. Work even on all sts for 5 (5½, 6, 6½)" [12.5 (14, 15, 16.5) cm].

Bind off 42 (44, 46, 48) sts at beg of next 2 rows. Work even on rem 56 (56, 58, 58) sts for 11½ (12, 12½, 13)" [29 (20.5, 32, 33) cm].

Bind off all sts.

Finishing

Fold sweater in half and pin underarm seams. Sew from sleeve cuff to underarm. Pin side seams, leaving a 4" (10 cm) side vent and sew to underarm. Do not block.

Yarn

- Worsted weight
- Shown: Plymouth Encore Tweed, 75% acrylic, 22% wool, 3% rayon, 3.5 oz (100 g)/200 yds (183 m): Wedgwood White #W515, 3 (3, 4) skeins

Needles

- Sizes 5 (3.75 mm) and 8 (5 mm) or size to obtain gauge

Notions

- Stitch holder
- Tapestry needle

Gauge

- 20 sts and 24 rows = 4" (10 cm) on size 8 needles
- Take time to check gauge.

Sizes

- Child's 2 (4, 6)
- Finished chest: 24 (26, 28)" [61 (66, 71) cm]
- Finished length: 16 (17, 18)" [40.5 (43, 45.5) cm]

Child's Pullover

This cozy, warm sweater works up fast in a Nubby Sand stitch that has great texture. The stitch, shown on page 51 is unusual, as both sides make an interesting pattern. Each sweater follows the same instructions. When finished, choose the side that you want to be the "right" side, before sewing and finishing.

Knit the matching hat (page 58) to complete the ensemble.

Skill Level: Easy

Back

With size 5 needles, cast on 60 (64, 68) sts. Work in k1, p1 ribbing for 2" (5 cm), ending with a RS row and inc 1 st at end of last row—61 (65, 69) sts.

Change to size 8 needles and work patt as follows:

Row 1 (WS): Knit.

Row 2: K1, *p1, k1, rep from * across row.

Rep Rows 1 and 2 for patt until piece measures 10½ (11, 11½)" [26.5 (28, 29) cm] from beg.

Shape Armholes

Bind off 4 (4, 4) sts at beg of the next 2 rows—53 (57, 61) sts. Continue in patt as established until armholes measure 5½ (6, 6½)" [14 (15, 16.5) cm]. Bind off 15 (16, 17) sts at beg of next 2 rows for shoulders. Place remaining 23 (25, 27) sts on holder to be worked later for neckband.

Front

Work same as Back until armholes measure 4 (4½, 5)" [10 (11, 12.5) cm], ending with a WS row.

Shape Neck

Next Row (RS): Work across 17 (18, 19) sts for left neck, turn. Working on these sts only, making sure to keep patt as established, dec 1 st at neck edge every row 2 times. Work even on remaining 15 (16, 17) sts until piece measures same as Back. Bind off.

With RS facing, place center 19 (21, 23) sts on a holder for center neck, join yarn and work remaining 17 (18, 19) sts for right neck. Making sure to keep patt as established, dec 1 st at neck edge every row twice. Work even on remaining 15 (16, 17) sts until piece measures same as Back. Bind off.

Sleeves

With size 5 needles, cast on 37 (39, 41) sts. Work in k1, p1 ribbing for 2 (2¼, 2½)" [5 (5.5, 6) cm]. Change to size 8 needles.

Working patt as on Back, inc 1 st each end of the first row, then repeat inc every 6th row until there are 57 (59, 61) sts. Work even in patt until Sleeve measures 11 (11½, 12)" [28 (29, 30.5) cm] from beg. Bind off all sts loosely.

Finishing

Sew left shoulder seam. With RS facing, using size 5 needles, join yarn at right Back neck, k23 (25, 27) sts from Back neck holder, pick up and k8 (9, 10) sts along left neck edge, k19 (21, 23) sts from front holder, pick up and k8 (9, 10) sts along right neck edge—58 (64, 70) sts. Work in k1, p1 ribbing for 1" (2.5 cm). Change to size 8 needles and continue ribbing until 2¼" (5.5 cm) for all sizes. Bind off loosely.

Sew right shoulder seam and edges of neckband. Fold neckband to inside and sew in place.

Sew in Sleeves: Fold Sleeve in half, mark the center, pin in place, with center of Sleeve at shoulder seam and end of Sleeve at outer edge of bound-off underarm sts, then sew in place. Sew underarm seams.

Blocking is not recommended for this textured patt.

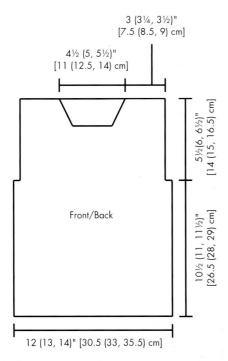

3 (3¼, 3½)"
[7.5 (8.5, 9) cm]

4½ (5, 5½)"
[11 (12.5, 14) cm]

5½ (6, 6½)"
[14 (15, 16.5) cm]

Front/Back

10½ (11, 11½)"
[26.5 (28, 29) cm]

12 (13, 14)" [30.5 (33, 35.5) cm]

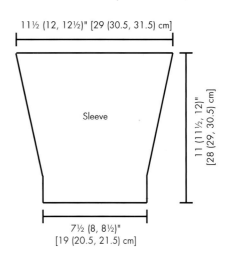

11½ (12, 12½)" [29 (30.5, 31.5) cm]

Sleeve

11 (11½, 12)"
[28 (29, 30.5) cm]

7½ (8, 8½)"
[19 (20.5, 21.5) cm]

Nubby Sand Stitch Hat

Knit an adorable pom-pom beanie to match the sweater (page 56). The ribbed brim and the Nubby Sand stitch body are worked on straight needles, and both stitch patterns are reversible, so decide which side you like best before starting to work the crown in the round.

YOU WILL NEED

Yarn

- Worsted weight
- Shown: Plymouth Encore Tweed, 75% acrylic, 22% wool, 3% rayon, 3.5 oz (100 g)/200 yds (183 m): Wedgwood White #W515, 1 skein

Needles

- Sizes 5 (3.75 mm) and 8 (5 mm) straight needles
- Size 8 (5 mm) double-pointed needles or size to obtain gauge

Notions

- Tapestry needle

Gauge

- 18 sts = 4" (10 cm) in patt st on size 8 needles
- Take time to check gauge.

Sizes

- Small (Medium)
- 16 (18)" [40.5 (45.5) cm]

Skill Level: Easy

Note: Hat stretches slightly.

Brim

With smaller needles cast on 72 (80) sts, work in k1, p1 ribbing for 2½" (6.5 cm). Change to larger needles and work in pattern as for sweater Back until piece measures 6½" (16.5 cm) from beg, ending with a wrong side row:

Shape Crown

Knit 1 row, purl 1 row, change to double-pointed needles, dividing stitches on 3 needles, place a marker at beginning of round.

Rnd 1: *K7 (8), k2tog, rep from * around (64, 72 sts).

Rnd 2 and all even rnds through Rnd 12: Knit.

Rnd 3: *K6 (7), k2tog, rep from * around (56, 64 sts).

Rnd 5: *K5 (6), k2tog, rep from * around (48, 56 sts).

Rnd 7: *K4 (5), k2tog, rep from * around (40, 48 sts).

Rnd 9: *K3 (4), k2tog, rep from * around (32, 40 sts).

Rnd 11: *K2 (3), k2tog, rep from * around (24, 32 sts).

Rnd 13: *K1 (2), k2tog, rep from * around (16, 24 sts).

Rnd 14: *K2tog, rep from * around (8,12 sts).

Cut yarn, leaving an 18" (45.5 cm) end, thread yarn onto a tapestry needle and draw through remaining stitches on needle, gather top fasten securely.

Finishing

Sew Back seam. Blocking is not recommended for this pattern

Pom-Pom

Cut a piece of cardboard 2½" (6.5 cm) wide. Wrap yarn around the cardboard 100 times, slip off cardboard, and tie securely in center. Cut looped ends and trim.

Light Textures

Lightly textured stitches are endlessly versatile and usually easy to knit. They drape well and make comfortable garments. Once you have mastered basic stitches and move on to textured stitches, you will be amazed at the many interesting textures you can achieve with relatively simple techniques.

Star

Skill Level: Intermediate

Cast on a multiple of 4.

Row 1: Knit.

Row 2: K1, *p3tog, hold on needle, yo by wrapping yarn around back to front again, p same 3 sts tog again, sl sts off needle, k1, rep from * across row, end p1, k2.

Row 3: Knit.

Row 4: K1, p1, *k1, p3tog, hold on needle, yo as before, p same 3 sts tog, slip off needle, rep from * across row, end k2.

Rep Rows 1–4 for pattern.

Geometrics

Skill Level: Easy

Cast on a multiple of 10 plus 5.

Row 1: P5 *k5, p5, rep from * across row.

Row 2: *K4, p1, k1, p4, rep from * to last 5 sts, end k4, p1.

Row 3: K2, p3, *k3, p2, k2, p3, rep from * across row.

Row 4: *K2, p3, k3, p2, rep from * to last 5 sts, end k2, p3.

Row 5: K4, p1, *k1, p4, k4, p1, rep from * across row.

Row 6: P5, *k5, p5, rep from * across row.

Row 7: K4, p1, *k1, p4, k4, p1, rep from * across row.

Row 8: *K2, p3, k3, p2, rep from * to last 5 sts, end k2, p3.

Row 9: K2, p3, *k3, p2, k2, p3, rep from * across row.

Row 10: *K4, p1, k1, p4, rep from * to last 5 sts, end k4, p1.

Rep Rows 1–10 for pattern.

Seed Stitch Diamonds

Skill Level: Easy

Cast on a multiple of 10.

Row 1 (RS): *K5, (p1, k1) 2 times, p1, rep from * across row.

Row 2: (P1, k1) 3 times, *p5, (k1, p1) 2 times, k1, rep from * to last 4 sts, end p4.

Row 3: K3, *(p1, k1) 2 times, p1, k5, rep from * to last 7 sts, end (p1, k1) 2 times, p1, k2.

Row 4: P3, *(k1, p1) 2 times, k1, p5, rep from * to last 7 sts, end (k1, p1) 2 times, k1, p2.

Row 5: (K1, p1) 3 times, *k5, (p1, k1) 2 times, p1, rep from * to last 4 sts, end k4.

Row 6: Purl.

Rep Rows 1–6 for pattern.

Trinity

Skill Level: Easy

Cast on a multiple of 4 plus 2.

Row 1 (RS): K1, purl to last st, k1.

Row 2: K1, *(k1, p1, k1) all in next st, p3tog, rep from * across row to last st, end k1.

Row 3: K1, purl to last st, k1.

Row 4: K1,* p3tog, (k1, p1, k1) all in next st, rep from * across row to last st, end k1.

Rep Rows 1–4 for pattern.

Berry

Skill Level: Easy

Cast on a multiple of 4 plus 2.

Row 1 (WS): K1, *(k1, yo, k1) all in same st, p3tog, rep from * across row, end k1.

Row 2: K1, *p1, k3, rep from * across row, end k1.

Row 3: K1, *p3tog, (k1, yo, k1) all in same st, rep from * across row, end k1.

Row 4: K1, *k3, p1, rep from * across row, end k1.

Rep Rows 1–4 for pattern.

Tiny Pebbles

Skill Level: Easy

Cast on an even number of stitches.

Row 1: Knit all across row.

Row 2: K1, purl across to last st, k1.

Row 3: K1, *k2tog, rep from * to last st, end k1.

Row 4: K1, *k1, pick up the horizontal thread before the next st and knit it (inc made), rep from * to last st, end k1.

Rep Rows 1–4 for pattern.

Braids

Skill Level: Intermediate

Cast on a multiple of 10 plus 3.

Row 1: K1, p3, *k5, p5, rep from * to last 9 sts, end k5, p3, k1.

Rows 2 and 4: K4, *p5, k5, rep from *, end last rep k4.

Row 3: K1, *p3, inc 1 by knitting into back loop of the last purl st (to make this increase, place left-hand needle in loop under the last st purled, pick up this loop and leave on the left-hand needle, knit this st from back loop), k1, p3tog, k1, inc 1 by knitting into loop below next st (to make this increase, place right-hand needle in the loop below the next st, and knit it as a st), p2, rep from * across row to last 4 sts, end p3, k1.

Rep Rows 1–4 for pattern.

Crossed Diamonds

Skill Level: Experienced

Cross Two Stitches Left (Cr2L): With right needle behind the left needle, skip next stitch on left needle, knit the second stitch through the back loop, then knit the skipped stitch in the front loop, slip both stitches from the left needle.

Cross Two Stitches Right (Cr2R): Skip the next stitch on left needle, knit the second stitch in front of skipped stitch, then knit the skipped stitch, slip both stitches from left needle.

Cast on a multiple of 6 plus 4.

Row 1: K1, *cross 2 R (Cr2R), k4, rep from * to last 3 sts, end Cr2R, k1.

Row 2 and all even-numbered rows: K1, purl to last st, k1.

Row 3: K2, *cross 2 L (Cr2L), k2, Cr2R, rep from * to last 2 sts, end k2.

Row 5: K3, *Cr2L, Cr2R, k2, rep from * to last st, end k1.

Row 7: K3, *k1, Cr2R, k3, rep from * to last st, end k1.

Row 9: K3, *Cr2R, Cr2L, k2, rep from * to last st, end k1.

Row 11: K2, *Cr2R, k2, Cr2L, rep from * to last 2 sts, end k2.

Row 12: Same as Row 2.

Rep Rows 1–12 for pattern.

Horizontal Nubs

Skill Level: Easy

Cast on a multiple of 3.

Rows 1, 3, 9, and 11: Knit.

Rows 2, 4, 8, and 10: K1, purl across to last st, k1.

Row 5: K2, *p2, k1, rep from *, end last rep k2.

Row 6: K1, *k1, p2, rep from * to last 2 sts, end k2.

Row 7: K1, p1, *k2, p1, rep from *, end k1.

Row 12: Same as Row 2.

Rep Rows 1–12 for pattern.

Airy Garter Stitch

Skill Level: Easy

Cast on an even number of stitches.

Rows 1–4: Knit.

Row 5 (RS): *K1, yo twice, rep from *, end k1.

Row 6: Knit across row, dropping the extra wraps.

Rep Rows 1–6 for pattern.

Diagonal Grain

Skill Level: Easy

Cast on a multiple of 4.

Rows 1 and 3: Knit.

Row 2: K1, *yo, p2, pass yo over both sts, p2, rep from *, end yo, p2, pass yo over both sts, k1.

Row 4: K1, *p2, yo, p2, pass yo over both sts, rep from *, end p2, k1.

Rep Rows 1–4 for pattern.

Stockinette Seed Diamonds I

Skill Level: Easy

Cast on a multiple of 12 plus 1.

Row 1 (RS): K1, *p1, k9, p1, k1, rep from * to end.

Row 2: K1, *p1, k1, p7, k1, p1, k1, rep from * to end.

Row 3: K1, *p1, k1, p1, k5, (p1, k1) twice, rep from * to end.

Row 4: P1, *(p1, k1) twice, p3, k1, p1, k1, p2, rep from * to end.

Row 5: K1, *k2, (p1, k1) 3 times, p1, k3, rep from * to end.

Row 6: P1, *p3, (k1, p1) twice, k1, p4, rep from * to end.

Row 7: K1, *k4, p1, k1, p1, k5, rep from * to end.

Row 8: Same as Row 6.

Row 9: Same as Row 5.

Row 10: Same as Row 4.

Row 11: Same as Row 3.

Row 12: Same as Row 2.

Rep Rows 1–12 for pattern.

Stockinette Seed Diamonds II

Skill Level: Easy

Cast on a multiple of 10 plus 1.

Row 1 (RS): K5, *p1, k9, rep from * to last 6 sts, end p1, k5.

Row 2: K1, p3, *k1, p1, k1, p7, rep from * to last 7 sts, end k1, p1, k1, p3, k1.

Row 3: K3, *(p1, k1) twice, p1, k5, rep from * to last 8 sts, end (p1, k1) twice, p1, k3.

Row 4: K1, (p1, k1) 4 times, *p3, (k1, p1) 3 times, k1, rep from * to last 2 sts, end p1, k1.

Row 5: K1, *p1, k1, rep from * to end.

Row 6: Same as Row 4.

Row 7: Same as Row 3.

Row 8: Same as Row 2.

Row 9: Same as Row 1.

Row 10: K1, purl to last st, k1.

Rep Rows 1–10 for pattern.

Knot Stitch

Skill level: Intermediate

Cast on a multiple of 2 plus 1.

Row 1 (RS): Knit.

Row 2: K2, *p2tog, hold on needle, k same 2 sts tog, rep from * to last st, end k1.

Row 3: Knit.

Row 4: K1, *p2tog, hold on needle, k same 2 sts tog, rep from * to last 2 sts, end k2.

Rep Rows 1–4 for pattern.

Spiny Ridges

Skill Level: Easy

Cast on a multiple of 7 plus 2.

Row 1: K1, *p1, p2tog, yo, k1, yo by wrapping yarn around needle back to front, p2tog, p1, rep from * to last st, end k1.

Row 2: K1, purl to last st, k1.

Row 3: Knit.

Row 4: K1, purl to last st, k1.

Rep Rows 1–4 for pattern.

Hurdles

Skill Level: Easy

Cast on a multiple of 2 plus 1.

Row 1 (RS): Knit.

Row 2: Knit.

Row 3: K2, *p1, k1, rep from * across row, end last rep k2.

Row 4: K1, *p1, k1, rep from * across row.

Rep Rows 1–4 for pattern.

Climbing Leaf

Skill Level: Experienced

Note: Pattern worked on 29 stitches. Sample shows border stitches to set off pattern.

Knit 2 rows, then begin pattern as follows:

Row 1: K3, p2, k4, k2tog, k3, yo, k1, yo, k3, sl 1, k1, psso (skp), k4, p2, k3.

Row 2: K5, p5, k3, p3, k3, p5, k5.

Row 3: K3, p2, k3, k2tog, k4, yo, k1, yo, k4, skp, k3, p2, k3.

Row 4: K5, p4, k3, p5, k3, p4, k5.

Row 5: K3, p2, k2, k2tog, k5, yo, k1, yo, k5, skp, k2, p2, k3.

Row 6: K5, p3, k3, p7, k3, p3, k5.

Row 7: K3, p2, k1, k2tog, k6, yo, k1, yo, k6, skp, k1, p2, k3.

Row 8: K5, p2, k3, p9, k3, p2, k5.

Row 9: K3, p2, k2tog, k7, yo, k1, yo, k7, skp, p2, k3.

Row 10: K5, p1, k3, p11, k3, p1, k5.

Row 11: K3, p2, k1, yo, k3, skp, k7, k2tog, k3, yo, k1, p2, k3.

Row 12: K5, p2, k3, p9, k3, p2, k5.

Row 13: K3, p2, k2, yo, k3, skp, k5, k2tog, k3, yo, k2, p2, k3.

Row 14: K5, p3, k3, p7, k3, p3, k5.

Row 15: K3, p2, k3, yo, k3, skp, k3, k2tog, k3, yo, k3, p2, k3.

Row 16: K5, p4, k3, p5, k3, p4, k5.

Row 17: K3, p2, k4, yo, k3, skp, k1, k2tog, k3, yo, k4, p2, k3.

Row 18: K5, p5, k3, p3, k3, p5, k5.

Row 19: K3, p2, k5, yo, k3, sl 1, k2tog, psso, k3, yo, k5, p2, k3.

Row 20: K5, p6, k7, p6, k5.

Rep Rows 1–20 for pattern.

Herringbone

Skill Level: Easy

Note: All increases for this stitch are made by knitting one stitch in the yarn between the last stitch worked and the next stitch.

Cast on a multiple of 15 plus 2.

Row 1 (RS): P2, *inc 1 st in yarn between 2 sts (M1), k3, p2, p3tog, p2, k3, M1, p2, rep from across row.

Row 2: K2, *p4, k5, p4, k2, rep from * across row.

Row 3: P2, *M1, k4, p1, p3tog, p1, k4, M1, p2, rep from * across row.

Row 4: K2, *p5, k3, p5, k2, rep from * across row.

Row 5: P2, *M1, k5, p3tog, k5, M1, p2, rep from * across row.

Row 6: K2, *p6, k1, p6, k2, rep from * across row.

Rep Rows 1–6 for pattern.

Diagonal Columns

Skill Level: Intermediate

Right Twist (RT): Skip one stitch, insert right needle into front loop of second stitch on left needle, knit this stitch but do not slip stitch off needle. Knit the skipped stitch through the front loop, and slip both stitches from left needle.

Cast on a multiple of 7 plus 1.

Rows 1 and 3 (WS): *K1, p6, rep from * across to last st, end k1.

Row 2: P1, *(RT) 3 times, p1, rep from * across row.

Row 4: P1, *k1, (RT) twice, k1, p1, rep from * across row.

Rep Rows 1–4 for pattern.

Raised Trellis Stitch

Skill Level: Intermediate

Cast on a multiple of 6 plus 2.

Row 1: K1, p2, k2, *p4, k2, rep from * to last 3 sts, end p2, k1.

Rows 2 and 4: K3, p2, *k4, p2, rep from * to last 3 sts, end k3.

Row 3: Same as Row 1.

Row 5: K1, *sl 2 sts onto a cable needle and hold to back of work, k1, p2 from cable needle, sl 1 st onto cable needle and hold to front of work, p2, k1 from cable needle, rep from *, end k1.

Rows 6, 8, and 10: K1, p1, *k4, p2, rep from *, end k4, p1, k1.

Rows 7 and 9: K2, *p4, k2, rep from * to end.

Row 11: K1, *sl 1 st onto cable needle and hold to front of work, p2, k1 from cable needle, sl 2 sts on cable needle and hold to back of work, k1, p2, from cable needle, rep from *, end k1.

Row 12: Same as Row 2.

Rep Rows 1–12 for pattern.

Flagon Stitch

Skill Level: Intermediate

Cast on a multiple of 6 plus 4.

Row 1 and all wrong side rows: K1, *p2, k1, rep from * across row.

Rows 2, 4, 6, and 8: *P1, k2, p1, yarn front (yf) sl 1 pwise, p1, wrap yarn over needle back to front, pass the sl st over the p1 and the wrap, rep from * to last 4 sts, end p1, k2, p1.

Rows 10, 12, 14, and 16: *P1, (yf), sl 1 pwise, p1, wrap yarn over needle back to front, pass the sl st over the p1 and the wrap, p1, **k2, rep from * ending last rep at **.

Rep Rows 1–16 for pattern.

Bell Flower Stitch

Skill Level: Intermediate

Note: When making a yarn over before a purl stitch, wrap yarn around needle from front to back to front.

Cast on a multiple of 5 plus 4.

Row 1: K1, p2 *k3, p2, rep from * to last st, end k1.

Rows 2 and 4: K3, *p3, k2, rep from *, end last rep k3.

Row 3: Same as Row 1.

Row 5: K1, p2, *yo, sl 1, k2tog, psso, yo, p2, rep from *, end k1.

Row 6: Same as Row 2.

Rep Rows 1–6 for pattern.

Harebell

Skill Level: Moderate.

Note: When making a yarn over before a purl stitch, wrap yarn around needle from front to back to front.

Cast on a multiple of 6 plus 5.

Rows 1, 3, and 5 (WS): K1, p3, *k3, p3, rep from * to last st, k1.

Row 2: K4, *p2tog, yo, p1, k3, rep from * to last st, k1.

Row 4: K4, *p1, yo, p2tog, k3, rep from * to last st, k1.

Row 6: K2, k2tog, *(p1, yo) twice, p1, yarn back (yb), sl 1, k2tog, psso, rep from *, ending last rep yb, k2tog through the back loop, k2 (instead of sl 1, k2tog, psso, k1).

Rows 7, 9, and 11: K4, *p3, k3, rep from * to last st, k1.

Row 8: K1, p1, yo, p2tog, *k3, p1, yo, p2tog, rep from * to last st, k1.

Row 10: K1, p2tog, yo, p1, *k3, p2tog, yo, p1, rep from * to last st, k1.

Row 12: K1, p2, yo, p1, yb, *sl 1, k2tog, psso, (p1, yo) twice, p1, rep from * to last 7 sts, yb, sl 1, k2tog, psso, p1, yo, p2, k1.

Rep Rows 1–12 for pattern.

Diagonal Waffle Stitch

Skill Level: Experienced

Notes: When making a yarn over before a purl stitch, wrap yarn around needle from front to back to front.

Cross Two Right (Cr2R): Skip the next stitch on left needle, knit the second stitch in front of skipped stitch, then knit the skipped stitch, slip both stitches from left needle.

If through back loop (tbl) is stated, knit or purl through the back loop of the stitch.

Cast on a multiple of 4 plus 2.

Row 1 (RS): K1, yo, *skp, k2tog, yo (twice), rep from * to last 5 sts, skp, k2tog, yo, k1.

Row 2: K1, k the yo st, p2, *k the first yo tbl, then k the 2nd yo, p2, rep from * to last 2 sts, k the yo, k1.

Row 3: K1, p1, *Cr2R, p2, rep from * to last 4 sts, Cr2R, p1, k1.

Row 4: *K2, p2, rep from * to last 2 sts, k2.

Row 5: K1, *k2tog, yo (twice), skp, rep from * to last st, k1.

Row 6: K1, p1, *k the first yo tbl, then k the 2nd yo, p2, rep from * to last 4 sts, k the first yo tbl, then k the 2nd yo, p1, k1.

Row 7: K2, p2, *Cr2R, p2, rep from * to last 2 sts, k2.

Row 8: K1, p1, k2, *p2, k2, rep from * to last 2 sts, p1, k1.

Rep Rows 1–8 for pattern.

Garter Stitch Sweater with Trim

Dress up a plain sweater by knitting a lightly textured trim around the neck and cuffs using a trinity stitch. Follow the instructions for the One-Piece Garter Stitch Sweater on page 54. Then, pick up stitches at the neck and sleeve ends to finish with trinity stitches.

YOU WILL NEED

- Same as on page 54 with additional needles: size 8 (5 mm) circular knitting needle, 29" (73.5 cm) long

Note: Even though you will be working back and forth, a circular needle is needed because neck opening is closed.

Trinity Stitch pattern (multiple of 4 plus 2)

Row 1 (RS): K1, purl to last st, k1.

Row 2: K1, *(k1, p1, k1) all in next st, p3tog, rep from * across row to last st, end k1.

Row 3: K1, purl to last st, k1.

Row 4: K1, *p3tog, (k1, p1, k1) all in next st, rep from * across row to last st, end k1.

Rep Rows 1–4 for pattern.

Neck Trim

Starting at center of right shoulder, with RS facing, pick up and k11 (11, 12, 12) sts from mid shoulder to beg of front neckline, 25 (25, 27, 27) sts along front neckline, 11 (11, 12, 12) sts from front neckline to mid left shoulder, 11 (11, 12, 12) sts from mid shoulder to beg of back neckline, 25 (25, 27, 27) sts along back neckline, 11 (11, 12, 12) sts from back neckline to mid right shoulder. There are now 94 (94, 102, 102) sts on needle. Do not join; working back and forth, work as follows:

(WS) Purl 1 row.

Work back and forth in Trinity St patt for 6 rows. Bind off in purl, from RS.

Sleeve Trim

Starting at underarm seam, with RS facing, pick up and k58 (58, 62, 62) sts, do not join. Working back and forth, work as follows:

(WS) Purl 1 row.

Work back and forth in Trinity St patt for 6 rows. Bind off in purl from RS.

Sew underarm seams as for sweater.

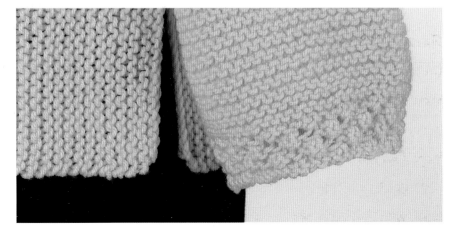

Spiny Ridges Socks

Knitting your first pair of socks is quite a learning experience. You might perform several knitting procedures you've never done before, and you will learn a lot about shaping. Once you've knit socks, you'll want to knit more. They are so much fun to knit! These socks are knit in the round from the top down on double-pointed needles.

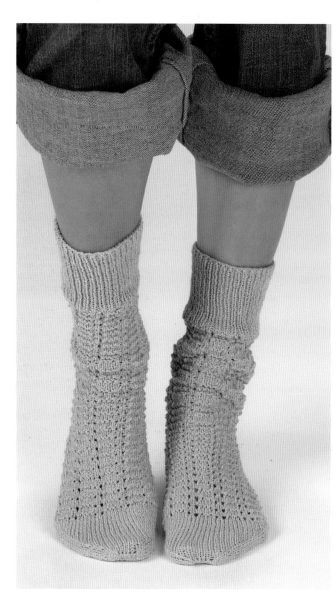

YOU WILL NEED

Yarn

- Super fine

- Shown: Crystal Palace Maizy, 82% corn, 18% elastic, 3.5 oz (50 g)/204 yds (188.5 m): Cactus #1206, 2 skeins

Needles

- Size 2 (2.75 mm) double-pointed needles or size to obtain gauge

Notions

- Stitch marker

Gauge

- 32 sts = 4" (10 cm) in Spiny Ridges patt on size 2 (2.75 mm) needles

- Take time to check gauge.

Sizes

- Woman's Small (Medium, Large) shoe sizes 5/6 (7/8, 9/10)

- Finished foot length: 9 (9½, 10)" [23 (24, 25.5) cm]; yarn does stretch to fit a few sizes.

Skill Level: Intermediate

Note: For this pattern, when making a yarn over before the purl 2 together, it is necessary to wrap yarn around needle from front to back to front again.

Socks (make 2)

Cast on 72 sts; divide into 24 sts on 3 needles. Join, being careful not to twist; place marker here to mark as beg of rnds (center back).

Work in k1, p1 ribbing for 3" (7.5 cm). Beg Spiny Ridges patt as follows:

Rnd 1: K1, *p1, p2tog, yo, k1, yo, p2tog, p1, rep from * around, end with k1.

Rnds 2, 3, and 4: Knit.

Rep Rnds 1–4 for patt until 8½" (21.5 cm) from beg, ending with patt Row 1.

Note: You will be at marker, which will become center back of heel.

Arrange sts to beg heel as follows:

K12 on first needle (half heel), k24 on 2nd needle (half instep), k24 on 3rd needle (other half instep), which is the 2nd rnd of Spiny Ridges patt, sl rem 12 sts onto first needle and k them, along with 12 sts already on first needle (heel sts complete).

Leave the 48 instep sts on 2nd and 3rd needles and work on 24 heel sts only as follows:

Next Row (WS): Sl 1, p10, p2tog, p11 (23 sts).

Heel Pattern

Row 1 (RS): *Sl 1, k1, rep from * to last st, k1.

Row 2: Sl 1, p to end of row.

Rep Rows 1 and 2 of Heel Patt for 2½" (6.5 cm), ending with Row 1.

Turn Heel

Row 1: Sl 1, p12, p2tog, p1, turn.

Row 2: Sl 1, k4, sl 1, k1, psso, k1, turn.

Row 3: Sl 1, p5, p2tog, p1, turn.

Row 4: Sl 1, k6, sl 1, k1, psso, k1, turn.

Row 5: Sl 1, p7, p2tog, p1, turn.

Row 6: Sl 1, k8, sl 1, k1, psso, k1, turn.

Row 7: Sl 1, p9, p2tog, p1, turn.

Row 8: Sl 1, k10, sl 1, k1, psso, k1, turn.

Row 9: Sl 1, p11, p2tog, turn.

Row 10: Sl 1, k11, sl 1, k1, psso (13 sts).

Shape Instep

With first needle, pick up 15 sts along side of heel, k2tog at beg of 2nd needle, cont knitting across 2nd and 3rd needle of instep (this will be Rnd 3 of Spiny Ridges patt), k2tog at end of 3rd needle (23 sts each on 2nd and 3rd needles), pick up 16 sts along other side of heel, k7 from heel needle (you are now at center back of heel) and your sts are divided as follows: 22 sts on first needle, 23 sts on 2nd needle, 23 sts on 3rd needle and 22 sts on 4th needle. In order to cont, slide the 23 sts of 3rd needle, onto 2nd needle, freeing up this needle to cont working; be sure that you are at center back of heel. You now have 22 sts on first needle, 46 sts on 2nd needle, and 22 sts on 3rd needle.

Next rnd: K to last 3 sts on first needle, k2tog, k1; on 2nd needle k2tog, k to last 2 sts, k2tog (you now have 44 sts on instep and have completed Rnd 4 of Spiny Ridges patt); on 3rd needle k1, sl 1, psso, k to end of rnd.

Next rnd: On first needle k; on 2nd needle work Rnd 1 of Spiny Ridges patt; on 3rd needle k.

Next rnd: On first needle, k to last 3 sts, k2tog, k1; on 2nd needle work Rnd 2 of Spiny Ridges patt; on 3rd needle k1, sl 1, k1, psso, k to end of rnd.

Cont in this manner to dec 1 st at end of first needle and beg of 3rd needle every other row, keeping Spiny Ridges patt as established on 44 sts of 2nd needle, until you have 14 sts on first and 3rd needles (72 sts).

Work even, keeping instep in patt until 6½ (7, 7½)" [16.5 (18, 19) cm] from heel.

Shape Toe

It is necessary to rearrange sts on needle before beg toe shaping; remainder of sock is finished in St st (knit every rnd).

Sl 6 sts from beg of 2nd needle onto end of first needle; sl 6 sts from end of 2nd needle onto beg of 3rd needle. Sts are now divided as follows: 18 sts on first and 3rd needles, 36 sts on 2nd needle.

Rnd 1: On first needle to last 3 sts, k2tog, k1; on 2nd needle k1, sl 1, k1, psso, k to last 3 sts, k2tog, k1; on 3rd needle k1, sl 1, k1, psso, k to end of rnd.

Rnd 2: Knit.

Rep last 2 rnds until 16 sts rem. K sts of first needle onto end of 3rd needle; end yarn, leaving about 10" (25.5 cm) for joining at toe.

Graft toe stitches together with Kitchener stitch (page 39).

Note: Blocking is not recommended for elastic yarns.

YOU WILL NEED

Yarn

- Lightweight
- Shown: Ann Geddes Baby Yarn, 80% acrylic, 20% nylon, 3 oz (85 g)/340 yds (310 m): Jam #556, 2 (3, 3) skeins

Needles

- Sizes 4 (3.5 mm) and 6 (4 mm) or size to obtain gauge

Notions

- Stitch markers
- Tapestry needle

Gauge

- 4 Harebell patt repeats = 6" (15 cm) on size 6 (4 mm) needles
- Take time to check gauge.

Sizes

- Teen 12 (14, 16)
- Finished chest: 30 (32, 34)" [76 (81, 86) cm]
- Finished length: 17½ (18½, 19½)" [44.5 (47, 49.5) cm]

Teen Topper

Young teens will love the loose, casual fit of this cropped sweater. It can be worn over jeans, shorts, or a skirt. The tie at the neck allows them to adjust the neckline to pull up close or wear draped over one shoulder.

Note: For Harebell stitch, when making a yarn over before a purl stitch, wrap yarn around needle from front to back to front.

Harbell Stitch (Back and Front patt)

(multiples of 6 plus 5)

Rows 1, 3, and 5 (WS): K1, p3, *k3, p3, rep from * to last st, k1.

Row 2: K4, *p2tog, yo, p1, k3, rep from * to last st, k1.

Row 4: K4, *p1, yo, p2tog, k3, rep from * to last st, k1.

Row 6: K2, k2tog, *(p1, yo) twice, p1, yarn back (yb), sl 1, k2tog, psso, rep from *, ending last rep yb, k2tog through the back loop, k2 (instead of sl 1, k2, psso, k1).

Rows 7, 9, and 11: K4, *p3, k3, rep from * to last st, k1.

Row 8: K1, p1, yo, p2tog, *k3, p1, yo, p2tog, rep from * to last st, k1.

Row 10: K1, p2tog, yo, p1, *k3, p2tog, yo, p1, rep from * to last st, k1.

Row 12: K1, p2, yo, p1, yb, *sl 1, k2tog, psso, (p1, yo) twice, p1, rep from * to last 7 sts, yb, sl 1, k2tog, psso, p1, yo, p2, k1.

Rep Rows 1–12 for patt.

Easy Eyelets (Sleeve patt)

Multiple of 2 sts

Row 1 (WS): K1, purl to last st, k1.

Row 2: K1, purl to last st, k1.

Row 3: K1, purl to last st, k1.

Row 4: K1, *yo, sl 1 pwise, k1, psso, rep from * to last st, k1.

Rep Rows 1–4 for patt.

Skill Level: Intermediate

Back

With size 6 needles, cast on 83 (89, 95) sts. Work in Harebell stitch until piece measures 11 (11½, 12)" [28 (29, 30.5) cm] from beg. Place a marker on each side to be used for sleeve placement. Cont in patt until piece measures 16 (17, 18)" [38 (39, 40.5) cm] from beg, ending with patt Row 3.

Shape Neck

Next row: Cont in patt across first 16 (18, 20) sts, do not fasten off, join a new ball of yarn, bind off center 51 (53, 55)

sts, work remaining 16 (18, 20) sts. Working both sides at once, each with separate yarn, cont in patt as est until piece measures 17½ (18½, 19½)" [47 (48, 49.5) cm] from beg. Fasten off.

Front

Work same as Back, except start neck shaping at 15 (15½, 16)" [35.5 (36.5, 38) cm] from beg.

Sleeve (make 2)

Notes: Sleeves are worked by picking up at armhole and working down toward wrist.

Sew shoulder seams. With RS facing, starting at underarm marker, with size 6 needles, pick up and k27 (29, 31) sts from marker to shoulder seam, then pick up and k27 (29, 31) sts from shoulder to second marker—54 (58, 62) sts. Work in Easy Eyelet patt until piece measures 14½ (15, 15½)" [36.5 (38, 39) cm] from beg. Change to size 4 needles. Knit 1 row, dec 4 sts evenly spaced across row—50 (54, 58) sts. Knit 4 more rows. Bind off.

Finishing

Sew underarm and side seams. Weave in ends.

Blocking: Lay garment flat on a padded surface, spritz lightly with water, pat into shape, allow to dry.

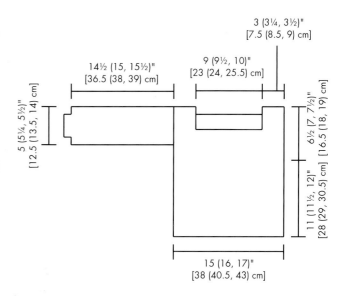

Medium and Heavy Textures

The stitch patterns included in this section are suitable for knitting heavier garments, such as jackets, hats, and outerwear. They also make great blankets, bags, and other accessories. It's fun to experiment with some of these stitches; by using a larger needle than the yarn usually calls for, you can create different effects.

Bells

Skill Level: Intermediate

Cast on a multiple of 8.

Row 1 (RS): Knit.

Row 2: K2, purl to last 2 sts, end k2.

Row 3: K2, p4, *cast on 5 sts, p4, rep from *, end k2.

Row 4: K6, *p5 cast-on sts, k4, rep from *, end last rep k6.

Row 5: K2, p4, *k5, p4, rep from *, end k2.

Row 6: K6, *p5, k4, rep from *, end last rep k6.

Row 7: K2, p4, *ssk, k1, k2tog, p4, rep from *, end k2.

Row 8: K6, *p3, k4, rep from *, end last rep k6.

Row 9: K2, p4, *sl 2 sts, k1, pass both sl sts over the k st, p4, rep from *, end k2.

Row 10: Knit.

Rep Rows 1–10 for pattern.

Tulips

Skill Level: Experienced

Cast on a multiple of 13 plus 2.

Row 1 (RS): K1, p to last st, k1.

Row 2: K across row.

Row 3: K1, p6, *(p1, k1, p1, k1, p1, k1) in next st, p12, repeat from * to last 8 sts, end (p1, k1, p1, k1, p1, k1) in next st, p6, k1.

Row 4: K7, *p6, k12, rep from * to last 13 sts, end p6, k7.

Row 5: K1, p6, *k6, p12, rep from * to last 13 sts, end k6, p6, k1.

Row 6: Same as Row 4.

Row 7: K1, p2tog (twice), p2, *k2, yo, k2, yo, k2, p2, (p2tog) 4 times, p2, rep from * to last 13 sts, end k2, yo, k2, yo, k2, p2, (p2tog) twice, k1.

Row 8: K5, *p8, k8, rep from * to last 13 sts, end p8, k5.

Row 9: K1, (p2tog) twice *(k2tog, yo, k1, yo) twice, k2tog, (p2tog) 4 times, rep from * to last 5 sts, end last rep (p2tog) twice, k1.

Row 10: K3, *p9, k4, rep from * to last 12 sts, end p9, k3.

Rep Rows 1–10 for pattern.

Clam Stitch

Skill Level: Experienced

Cast on a multiple of 6 plus 3.

Rows 1 and 5: Knit.

Row 2: K1, *p1, p5, winding yarn twice around the needle for each st, rep from * to last 2 sts, end p1, k1.

Row 3: K2, *sl next 5 sts onto right needle, dropping extra loop of each st, pass the sts back onto left needle and work them tog as follows: (once kwise, once pwise, once kwise, once pwise, once kwise, each time winding yarn twice around needle), k1, rep from * across row to last st, k1.

Row 4: K1, *p1, k5, dropping extra loops off needle, rep from * to last 2 sts, p1, k1.

Row 6: K1, p4, *p5, winding yarn twice around needle for each st, p1, rep from * to last 4 sts, p3, k1.

Row 7: K4, *k1, sl next 5 sts onto right needle, dropping extras off needle, pass the sts back onto left needle and work them tog as follows: (once kwise, once pwise, once kwise, once pwise, once kwise, each time winding yarn twice around needle), rep from * to last 5 sts, k5.

Row 8: K1, p4, *k5, dropping extra loops off needle, p1, rep from * to last 4 sts, p3, k1.

Rep Rows 1–8 for pattern.

Basket Weave

Skill Level: Easy

Cast on a multiple of 8 plus 3.

Row 1 (RS): Knit.

Row 2: K4, p3, *k5, p3, rep from * to last 4 sts, end k4.

Row 3: P4, k3, *p5, k3, rep from * to last 4 sts, end p4.

Row 4: Same as Row 2.

Row 5: Knit.

Row 6: P3, *k5, p3, rep from * across row.

Row 7: K3, *p5, k3, rep from * across row.

Row 8: Same as Row 6.

Rep Rows 1–8 for pattern.

Fence Posts Blocked

Skill Level: Easy

Cast on a multiple of 6 plus 3.

Rows 1 and 3: Knit.

Rows 2 and 4: Purl.

Row 5: K3, *p3, k3, rep from * across row.

Row 6: Purl.

Row 7: Same as Row 5.

Row 8: Purl.

Row 9: Same as Row 5.

Row 10: Purl.

Row 11: Knit.

Row 12: Purl.

Row 13: Knit.

Row 14: Same as Row 5.

Row 15: Knit.

Row 16: Same as Row 5.

Row 17: Knit.

Row 18: Same as Row 5.

Rep Rows 1–18 for pattern.

Fence Posts Not Blocked

Skill Level: Easy

Cast on a multiple of 6 plus 3.

Rows 1 and 3: Knit.

Rows 2 and 4: Purl.

Row 5: K3, *p3, k3, rep from * across row.

Row 6: Purl.

Row 7: Same as Row 5.

Row 8: Purl.

Row 9: Same as Row 5.

Row 10: Purl.

Row 11: Knit.

Row 12: Purl.

Row 13: Knit.

Row 14: Same as Row 5.

Row 15: Knit.

Row 16: Same as Row 5.

Row 17: Knit.

Row 18: Same as Row 5.

Rep Rows 1–18 for pattern.

Garden Fence

Skill Level: Easy

Cast on a multiple of 5 plus 1.

Row 1 (RS): K1 through the back loop (tbl), *p1, k2, p1, k1 tbl, rep from * across row.

Row 2: P1, *k1, p2, k1, p1, rep from * across row.

Row 3: K1 tbl, *p4, k1 tbl, rep from * across row.

Row 4: P1, *k4, p1, rep from * across row.

Rep Rows 1–4 for pattern.

Seed Checks

Skill Level: Easy

Cast on a multiple of 4 plus 3.

Row 1: K3, *p1, k3, rep from * across row.

Row 2: K1, *p1, k3, rep from *, end p1, k1.

Rows 3 and 5: Same as Row 1.

Rows 4 and 6: Same as Row 2.

Rows 7, 9, and 11: Same as Row 2.

Rows 8, 10, and 12: Same as Row 1.

Rep Rows 1–12 for pattern.

Arrow Heads

Skill Level: Intermediate

Note: A cable needle is used to form this unusual stitch.

Cast on a multiple of 3 plus 2.

Row 1: K1, *sl 1 st to a cable needle and hold to front of work, k2, then k1 st from the cable needle, rep from * to last st, end k1.

Rows 2 and 4: K1, purl to last st, k1.

Row 3: K1, *sl 2 sts to cable needle and hold to back of work, k1, then k2 from cable needle, rep from * to last st, end k1.

Row 5: Knit.

Row 6: K1, purl to last st, k1.

Rep Rows 1–6 for pattern.

Lace Medallions

Skill Level: Intermediate

Cast on a multiple of 8 plus 2.

Rows 1 and 3 (RS): K1, p3, *k2, p6, rep from * to last 6 sts, end k2, p3, k1.

Rows 2 and 4: K4, p2, *k6, p2, rep from *, end k4.

Row 5: K1, p2, *k2tog, yo, ssk, p4, rep from *, end last rep p3.

Row 6: K3, *p1, k into front and back of next st, p1, k4, rep from *, end last rep k3.

Row 7: K1, p1, *k2tog, yo, k2, yo, ssk, p2, rep from * across row.

Row 8: K2, *p6, k2, rep from * across row.

Row 9: K1 *(k2tog, yo) twice, ssk, yo, ssk, rep from *, end k1.

Row 10: K1, p3, *k into front and back of next st, p6, rep from * end last rep p4.

Row 11: K1, *(yo, ssk) twice, k2tog, yo, k2tog, rep from *, end yo, k1.

Row 12: K1, k1 from back, p6, *k into front and back of next st, p6, rep from * to last 2 sts, k1 from back, k1.

Row 13: K1, p1, * yo, sl 1, k2tog, psso, yo, k3tog, yo, p2, rep from * across row.

Row 14: K2, *k1 from back, p1, k into front and back of next st, p1, k1 from back, k2, rep from * across row.

Row 15: K1, p2 *yo, ssk, k2tog, yo, p4, rep from *, end last rep p2, k1 instead of p4.

Row 16: K3, *k1 from back, p2, k1 from back, k4, rep from *, end last rep k3.

Rep Rows 3–16 for pattern.

Leaf Clusters

Skill Level: Experienced

Note: This stitch is made by an unusual placement of the needle between stitches to pick up a long loop and is a little tricky to complete.

Cast on a multiple of 12 plus 3.

Row 1: K1, *k1, yo, k4, sl 1, k2tog, psso, k4, yo, rep from *, end k2.

Rows 2, 4, 6, 8, and 10: K1, purl to last st, k1.

Row 3: K3, *yo, k3, sl 1, k2tog, psso, k3, yo, k3, rep from * across row.

Row 5: K4, *yo, count the next 7 sts on needle, skipping them, and insert the right-hand needle between the 7th and 8th st, draw up a long loop, k this loop with the first of the 7 skipped sts, work the next 6 sts as follows: k1, sl 1, k2tog, psso, k2, yo, k5, rep from *, end last rep k4.

Row 7: K1, k2tog, *k4, yo, k1, yo, k4, sl 1, k2tog, psso, rep from * to last 12 sts, end k4, yo, k1, yo, k4, sl 1, k1, psso, k1.

Row 9: K1, k2tog, *k3, yo, k3, yo, k3, sl 1, k2tog, psso, rep from * across to last 3 sts, end skp, k1.

Row 11: K1, k2tog, k2, *yo, k5, yo, count the next 7 sts on needle and insert the right-hand needle between the 7th and 8th sts, draw up a long loop, k this loop with the first of the 7 sts, work the next 6 sts as follows: k1, sl 1, k2tog, psso, k2, rep from * to last 10 sts, end yo, k5, yo, k2tog, k3.

Row 12: Same as Row 2.

Rep Rows 1–12 for pattern.

Mosaics

Skill Level: Intermediate

Cast on a multiple of 20 plus 12.

Row 1 (WS): K1, *(p2, k2) twice, p4, (k2, p2) twice, rep from * to last 11 sts, end (p2, k2) twice, p2, k1.

Row 2: K1, *(k2, p2) twice, k4, (p2, k2) twice, rep from * to last 11 sts, end k2, (p2, k2) twice, k1.

Row 3: K1, *p2, k2, rep from * to last 3 sts, end p2, k1.

Row 4: K1, *k2, p2, rep from * to last 3 sts, end k3.

Row 5: K1, *(p2, k2) twice, p4, (k2, p2) twice, rep from * to last 11 sts, end (p2, k2) twice, p2, k1.

Row 6: K1, *(k2, p2) twice, k4, (p2, k2) twice, rep from * to last 11 sts, end (k2, p2) twice, k3.

Row 7: Same as Row 3.

Row 8: Same as Row 4.

Row 9: Same as Row 5.

Row 10: Same as Row 6.

Row 11: K1, *(k2, p2) twice, k4, (p2, k2) twice, rep from * to last 11 sts, end (k2, p2) twice, k3.

Row 12: K1, *(p2, k2) twice, p4, (k2, p2) twice, rep from * to last 11 sts, end (p2, k2) twice, p2, k1.

Row 13: Same as Row 3.

Row 14: Same as Row 4.

Row 15: Same as Row 11.

Row 16: Same as Row 12.

Row 17: Same as Row 13.

Row 18: Same as Row 14.

Row 19: Same as Row 2.

Row 20: Same as Row 1.

Rep Rows 1–20 for pattern.

Vertical Bobbles

Skill Level: Intermediate

Cast on a multiple of 8 plus 5.

Row 1: K4, *p2, (p1, k1) twice in next st, p2, k3, rep from *, end last rep k4.

Row 2: K1, p3, *k8, p3, rep from * to last st, end k1.

Row 3: K4, *p2, k4, pass the 4th st on right-hand needle over 3, then the 3rd st over 2, 2nd over the first, p2, k3, rep from *, end k1.

Row 4: K1, p3, *k2, p1, k2, p3, rep from *, end k1.

Rep Rows 1–4 for pattern.

Hazel Nut

Skill Level: Intermediate

Cast on a multiple of 4 plus 1.

Row 1: K1, *p3, (k1, yo, k1) all in next st, rep from * until last 4 sts, end p3, k1.

Row 2: K4, *p3, k3, rep from *, end last rep k4.

Row 3: K1, *p3, k3, rep from * until last 4 sts, end p3, k1.

Row 4: K4, *p3tog, k3, rep from *, end last rep k4.

Row 5: K1, purl to last st, k1.

Row 6: Knit.

Row 7: K1, p1, *(k1, yo, k1) all in next st, p3, rep from * until last 3 sts, end (k1, yo, k1) all in next st, p1, k1.

Row 8: K2, *p3, k3, rep from * to last 5 sts, end p3, k2.

Row 9: K1, p1, *k3, p3, rep from * to last 5 sts, k3, p1, k1.

Row 10: K2, *p3tog, k3, rep from * to last 5 sts, p3tog, k2.

Row 11: Same as Row 5.

Row 12: Same as Row 6.

Rep Rows 1–12 for pattern.

Almonds

Skill Level: Easy

Cast on a multiple of 4 plus 3.

Row 1: K1, p2, *(k1, p1, k1) all in next st, p3, rep from *, end last rep p2, k1 instead of p3.

Rows 2, 4, 6, 8 and 10: K1, purl to last st, k1.

Rows 3 and 5: K1, p2, *k3, p3, rep from *, end last rep p2, k1 instead of p3.

Row 7: K1, p2, *k3tog through the back loop (tbl), p3, rep from *, end last rep p2 instead of p3.

Row 9: Knit.

Row 11: Knit.

Row 12: K1, purl to last st, k1.

Rep Rows 1–12 for pattern.

Bell Pulls

Skill Level: Intermediate

Cast on a multiple of 8 plus 4.

Foundation Row (RS): K1, *p2, k1, yo, k1, p2, k2, rep from *, end p2, k1.

Rows 1, 3, and 5: P1, *k2, p2, k2, p3, rep from *, end k2, p1.

Rows 2 and 4: K1, *p2, k3, p2, k2, rep from *, end p2, k1.

Row 6: K1, *p2, k1, drop next st off needle and unravel down to the yo 6 rows below, k1, p2, k1, yo, k1, rep from *, end p2, k1.

Rows 7, 9, and 11: P1, *k2, p3, k2, p2, rep from *, end k2, p1.

Rows 8 and 10: K1, *p2, k2, p2, k3, rep from *, end p2, k1.

Row 12: K1, *p2, k1, yo, k1, p2, k1, drop next st off needle and unravel to the yo 6 rows below, k1, rep from *, end p2, k1.

Rep Rows 1–12 for pattern.

Stamen Stitch

Skill Level: Easy

Cast on an even number of stitches.

Row 1: Knit.

Row 2: K1, *k1, sl 1 as to purl, rep from * to last 3 sts, end k3.

Row 3: Knit.

Row 4: K3, *sl 1 as to purl, k1, rep from *, end last rep k2.

Rep Rows 1–4 for pattern.

Garter and Rib

Skill Level: Easy

Cast on a multiple of 2 plus 1.

Rows 1, 2, 3, and 4: Knit.

Row 5: K1, *p1, k1, rep from * across row.

Row 6: K1, *k1, p1, rep from * across row to last 2 sts, end k2.

Rep Rows 1–6 for pattern.

Triangles and Pleats

Skill Level: Easy

Cast on a multiple of 10 plus 2.

Row 1: K1, *p2, k8, rep from * to last st, end k1.

Row 2: K1, *p7, k3, rep from * to last st, end k1.

Row 3: K1, *p4, k6, rep from * to last st, end k1.

Row 4: K1, *p5, k5, rep from * to last st, end k1.

Row 5: K1, *p6, k4, rep from * to last st, end k1.

Row 6: K1, *p3, k7, rep from * to last st, end k1.

Row 7: K1, *p8, k2, rep from * to last st, end k1.

Row 8: Same as Row 6.

Row 9: Same as Row 5.

Row 10: Same as Row 4.

Row 11: Same as Row 3.

Row 12: Same as Row 2.

Rep Rows 1–12 for pattern.

Diagonal Knots

Skill Level: Easy

Cast on a multiple of 4.

Row 1 (RS): K3, *p2, k2, rep from *, end k1.

Row 2: K1, p2, *k2, p2, rep from *, end k1.

Row 3: K3, *p1, k1 in the yarn between the st just worked and the next st (M1), p1, k2, rep from *, end k1.

Row 4: K1, p2, *k3, pass first st of 3 over next 2, p2, rep from *, end k1.

Row 5: K1, p2, *k2, p2, rep from *, end k1.

Row 6: K3, *p2, k2, rep from *, end last rep k3.

Row 7: K1, p1, M1, p1, *k2, p1, M1, p1, rep from *, end k1.

Row 8: K1, *k3, pass first st over 2, p2, rep from * to last 4 sts, end k3, pass first st over 2, k1.

Rep Rows 1–8 for pattern.

Double Leaf

Skill Level: Experienced

Notes: This is a panel that can be repeated with a multiple of 23 plus 6 sts or used as an insert on 29 sts.

When making a yarn over before a purl stitch it is necessary to wrap yarn around needle from front to back and front again.

Cast on a multiple of 23 plus 6.

Row 1 (RS): K11, k2tog, yo, k1, p1, k1, yo, sl 1, k1, psso, k11.

Row 2: K3, p7, p2tog through the back loop (tbl), p2, yo, k1, yo, p2, p2tog, p7, k3.

Row 3: K9, k2tog, k1, yo, k2, p1, k2, yo, k1, sl 1, k1, psso, k9.

Row 4: K3, p5, p2tog tbl, p3, yo, p1, k1, p1, yo, p3, p2tog, p5, k3.

Row 5: K7, k2tog, k2, yo, k3, p1, k3, yo, k2, sl 1, k1, psso, k7.

Row 6: K3, p3, p2tog tbl, p4, yo, p2, k1, p2, yo, p4, p2tog, p3, k3.

Row 7: K5, k2tog, k3, yo, k4, p1, k4, yo, k3, sl 1, k1, psso, k5.

Row 8: K3, p1, p2tog tbl, p5, yo, p3, k1, p3, yo, p5, p2tog, p1, k3.

Row 9: K3, k2tog, k4, yo, k5, p1, k5, yo, k4, sl 1, k1, psso, k3.

Row 10: K3, p11, k1, p11, k3.

Row 11: K14, p1, k14.

Row 12: K3, p11, k1, p11, k3.

Rep Rows 1–12 for pattern.

Reversible Ridges

Skill Level: Intermediate

Cast on a multiple of 4 plus 3.

Row 1: K2, *yo, p3tog, yo, k1, rep from * to last st, end k1.

Row 2: K1, p2tog, yo, k1, yo, *p3tog, yo, k1, yo, rep from * to last 3 sts, end p2tog, k1.

Rep Rows 1 and 2 for pattern.

Woven Blocks

Skill Level: Easy

Cast on a multiple of 9 plus 8.

Row 1: K1, *p6, k3, rep from *, end p6, k1.

Row 2: K1, *k6, p3, rep from *, end k7.

Row 3: Same as Row 1.

Row 4: Same as Row 2

Row 5: Same as Row 1.

Row 6: Same as Row 2.

Row 7: K1, *k6, p3, rep from *, end k7.

Row 8: K1, p6, k3, rep from *, end p6, k1.

Row 9: Same as Row 7.

Row 10: Same as Row 8.

Rep Rows 1–10 for pattern.

Shell Puffs

Skill Level: Experienced

Cast on a multiple of 4 plus 2.

Rows 1–4: Knit.

Row 5 (RS): K1, *k1 wrapping yarn around needle twice, rep from *, end k1.

Row 6: K1, *sl 4 sts to right-hand needle, dropping extra wraps, sl same 4 sts back to left-hand needle, k same 4 sts together without dropping from left-hand needle, p1, k1, p1, into same 4 sts, sl them off needle, rep from *, end k1.

Rep Rows 1–6 for pattern.

Boxed Cables

Skill Level: Intermediate

Cast on a multiple of 12.

Row 1 (RS): K3, p6, *k6, p6, rep from * to last 3 sts, end k3.

Row 2: P3, k6, *p6, k6, rep from *, end p3.

Rows 3 and 4: Same as Rows 1 and 2.

Row 5: K3, p6, *twist next 6 sts as follows: sl 3 sts onto a cable needle and hold to back of work, k3, k3 from cable needle, p6, rep from *, end k3.

Row 6: Same as Row 2.

Row 7: Same as Row 3.

Row 8: Same as Row 4.

Row 9: K9, p6, *k6, p6, rep from *, end k9.

Row 10: P9, k6, *p6, k6, rep from *, end p9.

Row 11 and 12: Same as Rows 9 and 10.

Row 13: K3, twist next 6 sts as follows: sl 3 sts onto a cable needle and hold to back of work, k3, k3 from cable needle, *p6, sl 3 sts onto a cable needle and hold to back of work, k3, k3 from cable needle, rep from *, end k3.

Rows 14–16: Same as Rows 10–12.

Rep Rows 1–16 for pattern.

Blue Bells

Skill Level: Intermediate

Note: To make a double yarn over, insert right-hand needle into next st, wrap yarn twice around, complete st.

Cast on a multiple of 10 plus 1.

Rows 1 and 3 (RS): Knit.

Rows 2 and 4: Purl.

Rows 5 and 6: Knit.

Row 7: *K1, (yo, k1) twice, k5 with double yo, (k1, yo) twice, rep from *, end k1.

Row 8: *K5, yarn forward (yf) sl 5 as to purl, dropping extra wraps, k4, rep from *, end k1.

Row 9: *K5, yarn back (yb) sl 5 as to purl, k4, rep from *, end k1.

Row 10: *P5, p5tog, p4, rep from *, end k1.

Rep Rows 1–10 for pattern.

Goldenrod

Skill Level: Intermediate

Cast on a multiple of 7.

Row 1 (RS): K1, k2tog, yo, k1, yo, sl 1, k1, psso, *k2, k2tog, yo, k1, yo, sl 1, k1, psso, rep from *, end k1.

Row 2: *P2tog through the back loop, yo, p3, yo, p2tog, rep from * across row.

Row 3: K1, yo, sl 1, k1, psso, k1, k2tog, yo, *k2, yo, sl 1, k1, psso, k1, k2tog, yo, rep from *, end k1.

Row 4: P2, yo, p3tog, yo, *p4, yo, p3tog, yo, rep from *, end p2.

Rep Rows 1–4 for pattern.

Butterflies and Buds

Skill Level: Experienced

Notes: To make a bobble, k into the front and back of next stitch two times, slip 4 stitches back to left-hand needle, k2tog two times, slip second stitch on right-hand needle over the first stitch.

Cast on a multiple of 12 plus 7.

Rows 1, 3, and 5 (RS): K1, *yarn front (yf), sl 5, k7, rep from *, end last rep k1.

Row 2 and all even-numbered rows: Purl.

Row 7: K3, *insert right-hand needle from below under the 3 loose strands on RS of work and k next st, catching all 3 strands as you knit, k11, rep from *, end last rep k3.

Row 9: K3, *make bobble, k11, rep from *, end last rep k3.

Row 11: K2, *(make bobble, k1) twice, k8, rep from *, end last rep k1.

Row 13: K1, *(make bobble, k1) 3 times, yf, sl 5, k1, rep from *, end (make bobble, k1) 3 times.

Row 15: K2, *(make bobble, k1) twice, k1, yf, sl 5, k2, rep from *, end (make bobble, k1) twice, k1.

Row 17: K3, *make bobble, k3, yf, sl 5, k3, rep from *, end make bobble, k3.

Row 19: K9, *insert right-hand needle from below under the 3 loose strands and knit as in Row 7, k11, rep from *, end last rep k9.

Row 21: K9, *make bobble, k11, rep from *, end last rep k9.

Row 23: K8, *(make bobble, k1) twice, k8, rep from *, end last rep k7.

Row 25: K7, *(make bobble, k1) 3 times, k6, rep from *, to end.

Row 27: Same as Row 23.

Row 29: Same as Row 21.

Row 30: Purl.

Rep Rows 1–30 for pattern.

Bobble Bouquet

Skill Level: Experienced

Notes: Bobble Bouquet is worked on center panel of 16 stitches, mark these stitches, slip markers as you come to them.

Left Twist (LT): Skip 1 stitch, insert right needle and knit second stitch through the back loop, insert right needle into backs of both stitches, k2tog through the back loop.

Left Purl Twist (LPT): Slip 1 stitch to a cable needle, hold to front of work, p1, k1, from the cable needle.

Right Twist (RT): K2tog leaving stitches on left-hand needle, k the first stitch again, slip both stitches from needle.

Right Purl Twist (RPT): Slip 1 stitch to a cable needle and hold to back of work, k1, p1 from the cable needle.

Make Bobble (MB): (K1, p1) twice into the next stitch, turn, p4, turn, k4, turn, (p2tog) twice, turn, k2tog.

Cast on 36.

Foundation row (WS): K10, place marker, k7, p2, k7, place marker, k10.

Row 1: K3, p7, p6, RT, LT, p6, p7, k3.

Row 2: K10, k5, LPT, p2, RPT, k5, k10.

Row 3: K3, p7, p4, RPT, RT, LT, LPT, p4, p7, k3.

Row 4: K10, k3, LPT, k1, p4, k1, RPT, k3, k10.

Row 5: K3, p7, p2, RPT, p1, RPT, k2, LPT, p1, LPT, p2, p7, k3.

Row 6: K10, (k2, p1) twice, k1, p2, k1, (p1, k2) twice, k10.

Row 7: K3, p7, p2, MB, p1, RPT, p1, k2, p1, LPT, p1, MB, p2, p7, k3.

Row 8: K10, k4, p1, k2, p2, k2, p1, k4, k10.

Row 9: K3, p7, p4, MB, p2, k2, p2, MB, p4, p7, k3.

Row 10: K10, k7, p2, k7, k10.

Rep Rows 1–10 for pattern.

Hyacinth Stitch

Skill Level: Experienced

Cast on a multiple of 6 plus 2.

Row 1 (WS): K1 *p3tog, p2tog, pass the p3tog st over the p2tog st, (k1, p1, k1, p1, k1) into the next st, rep from * to last st, end k1.

Rows 2 and 4: K1, p to last st, k1.

Row 3: K1, *(k1, p1, k1, p1, k1) into the next st, p3tog, p2tog, pass the p3tog st over the p2tog st, rep from * to last st, end k1.

Row 5: K1, k across, wrapping yarn 3 times around needle for each st to last st, end k1.

Row 6: K1, p across row, dropping extra loops off needle to last st, end k1.

Rep Rows 1–6 for pattern.

Grape Clusters

Skill Level: Experienced

To make a bobble: (K1, yo, k1, yo, k1) into the same stitch, turn, p5, turn, k5, then pass the 4th, 3rd, 2nd, and 1st stitches over the last knit stitch to complete bobble.

P1-b: Purl one from back.

Cast on a multiple of 20 plus 1.

Row 1 (RS): K1, *(p4, k1) twice, p4, make a bobble (MB), p4, k1, rep from * across.

Row 2: P1, *k4, p1, rep from * across.

Row 3: K1, *(p4, k1) twice, p3, MB, p1, MB, p3, k1, rep from * across.

Row 4: P1, *k3, p1-b, k1, p1-b, k3, p1, (k4, p1) twice, rep from * across.

Row 5: K1, *(p4, k1) twice, p2, MB, (p1, MB) twice, p2, k1, rep from * across.

Row 6: P1, *k2, p1-b, (k1, p1-b) twice, k2, p1, (k4, p1) twice, rep from * across.

Row 7: K1, *p4, MB, (p4, k1) 3 times, rep from * across.

Row 8: P1, *k4, p1, rep from * across.

Row 9: K1, *p3, MB, p1, MB, p3, k1, (p4, k1) twice, rep from * across.

Row 10: P1, *(k4, p1) twice, k3, p1-b, k1, p1-b, k3, p1, rep from * across.

Row 11: K1, *p2, MB, (p1, MB) twice, p2, k1, (p4, k1) twice, rep from * across.

Row 12: P1, *(k4, p1) twice, k2, (p1-b, k1) twice, p1-b, k2, p1, rep from * across.

Rep Rows 1–12 for pattern.

Seed Checks Baby Sweater

Knit this adorable sweater for a precious baby. The Seed Checks pattern (page 84) is a small-scale design that gives the sweater enough texture to make it cozy and cute. This sweater can be worn either by a girl or boy.

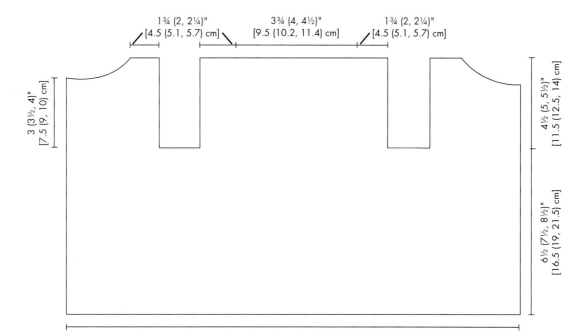

1 ¾ (2, 2¼)"
[4.5 (5.1, 5.7) cm]

3 ¾ (4, 4½)"
[9.5 (10.2, 11.4) cm]

1 ¾ (2, 2¼)"
[4.5 (5.1, 5.7) cm]

3 (3½, 4)"
[7.5 (9, 10) cm]

4½ (5, 5½)"
[11.5 (12.5, 14) cm]

6½ (7½, 8½)"
[16.5 (19, 21.5) cm]

24 (26¾, 29½)" [61 (68, 74.9) cm]

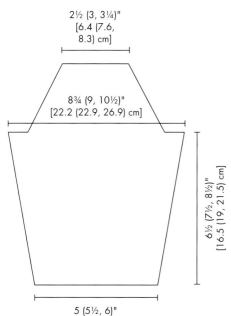

2½ (3, 3¼)"
[6.4 (7.6, 8.3) cm]

8¾ (9, 10½)"
[22.2 (22.9, 26.9) cm]

6½ (7½, 8½)"
[16.5 (19, 21.5) cm]

5 (5½, 6)"
[12.7, 14, 15.2) cm]

YOU WILL NEED

Yarn

- Lightweight
- Shown: Cascade Cherub Collection D K , 55% nylon, 45% acrylic, 1.75 oz (50 g)/190 yds (174 m): Rose #4088, 2 (3, 3) skeins

Needles

- Size 6 (4 mm) or size to obtain gauge

Notions

- Five ½" (1.3 cm) buttons
- Three stitch holders
- Tapestry needle

Gauge

- 22 sts = 4" (10 cm) in Seed Checks pattern on size 6 needles
- Take time to check gauge.

Sizes

- Child's 1 (2, 3)
- Finished chest: 26 (29, 32)" [66 (73.5, 81.5) cm]

(continued)

Skill Level: Intermediate

Note: Body is worked in one piece to armhole.

Front

With size 6 needles, cast on 131 (147, 163) sts.

Bottom Picot Hem Border

Row 1 (WS): Purl.

Row 2: Knit.

Row 3: Purl.

Row 4 (Picot Row): K1, *yo, k2tog, rep from * across row, end k2.

Row 5: Purl.

Row 6: Knit.

Row 7: Purl.

Beg Seed Checks patt (multiple of 4 plus 3) as follows:

Row 1 (RS): K3, *p1, k3, rep from * across row.

Row 2: K1, *p1, k3, rep from *, end p1, k1.

Rows 3 and 5: Rep Row 1.

Rows 4 and 6: Rep Row 2.

Rows 7, 9, and 11: Rep Row 2.

Rows 8, 10, and 12: Rep Row 1.

Rep Rows 1–12 of Seed Checks patt until Body measures 6½ (7½, 8½)" [16.5 (19, 21.5) cm] from Picot Row, ending on a RS row.

Dec row (WS): P4 (2, 0), p2tog, *p3, p2tog, rep from * to last 5 (3, 1) sts, p5 (3, 1)—106 (118, 130) sts.

Yoke

Yoke is worked in St st throughout.

Dividing row (RS): K22 (25, 28) and sl these sts onto a holder for right front, bind off next 6 sts (underarm), k until 50 (56, 62) sts are on right needle and sl these sts on to another holder for back, bind off 6 sts (underarm), k rem 22 (25, 28) for left front. Note: You will be working on last 22 (25, 28) sts only for left front as follows.

Left Front Armhole Shape

Next row (WS): Purl.

Cont in St st, dec 1 st at armhole edge every row 3 times, then every other row 2 (3, 4) times—17, (19, 21) sts.

Cont in St st until armhole measures 3 (3½, 4)" [7.5 (9, 10) cm], ending at front edge.

Neck Shape

Next row (WS): Bind off 2 (3, 3) sts at beg of row, finish row.

Cont in patt as est, dec 1 st at neck edge every row 3 times, then every other row 2 (2, 3) times—10 (11, 12) sts. Cont until armhole measures 4½ (5, 5½)" [11.5 (12.5, 14) cm], ending at armhole edge.

Shoulder Shape

Bind off rem 10 (11, 12) sts.

Back

With WS facing, rejoin yarn to 50 (56, 62) back sts on holder and purl 1 row. Cont in St st, dec 1 st each side every row 3 times, then every other row 2 (3, 4) times—40 (44, 48) sts. Keeping patt as est, work even until Back is same length as Front to shoulder. Bind off 10 (11, 12) sts at beg of next 2 rows. Place rem 20 (22, 24) sts onto holder to be worked later for back of neck.

Right Front Armhole Shape

With WS facing, rejoin yarn to 22 (25, 28) sts on holder and purl across.

Cont in St st, dec 1 st at armhole edge every row 3 times, then every other row 2 (3, 4) times—17, (19, 21) sts.

Cont in St st until armhole measures 3 (3½, 4)" [7.5, (9, 10) cm], ending at front edge.

Neck Shape

Next row (RS): Bind off 2 (3, 3) sts at beg of row, finish row.

Cont in patt as est, dec 1 st at neck edge every row 3 times, then every other row 2 (2, 3) times—10 (11, 12) sts. Cont until armhole measures 4½ (5, 5½)" [11.5 (12.5, 14) cm], ending at armhole edge.

Shoulder Shape

Bind off rem 10 (11, 12) sts.

Sleeves (make 2)

With size 6 needles, cast on 28 (30, 32) sts.

Bottom Picot Hem Border

Row 1 (WS): Purl.

Row 2: Knit.

Row 3: Purl.

Row 4 (Picot Row): K1, *yo, k2tog, rep from * across row, ending k1.

Row 5: Purl.

Row 6: Knit.

Row 7: Purl.

Cont in St st, inc 1 st each side of next row, every other row 7 (7, 7) times, then every 4th row 2 (4, 5) times—48 (54, 58) sts.

Cont even until sleeve measures 6½ (7½, 8½)" [16.5 (19, 21.5) cm] from Picot Row, end with a WS row.

Cap Shape

Bind off 3 sts at beg of next 2 rows—42 (48, 52) sts.

Dec 1 st at beg and end of every row 3 times, then every other row 4 (4, 5) times, then every row 7 (9, 9) times, ending with a WS row. Bind off rem 14 (16, 18) sts.

Finishing

Sew shoulder seams.

Neck Picot Hem Border: With RS facing, pick up and k2 (3, 3) sts in bound-off sts at front edge, pick up and k15 (17, 19) sts along right side of neck, k20 (22, 24) sts on back holder, pick up and k15 (17, 19) along left side of neck, then pick up and k2 (3, 3) sts in bound-off sts at front edge—54 (62, 68) sts.

Row 1 (WS): Purl.

Row 2: Knit.

Row 3: Purl.

Row 4 (Picot row): K1, *yo, k2tog, rep from * across row, end k1.

Row 5: Purl.

Row 6: Knit.

Row 7: Purl.

Bind off in knit.

Fold Picot Hem borders at neck and bottom in half and sew to inside, forming little points.

Left Front Button Band

With RS facing, starting at left front neck edge (not including Picot Hem Neck border), pick up and k50 (52, 54) sts down to bottom left front, including Picot Hem border at bottom.

Knit 6 rows. Bind off in knit on WS.

Right Front Button Band

With RS facing, starting at bottom right front including Picot Hem, pick up and k50 (52, 54) sts along right front up to but not including Picot Hem Neck border.

Work buttonholes as follows:

Row 1 (WS): Knit.

Row 2 (RS): Knit.

Row 3 (WS): K2, yo, k2tog, *k9, yo, k2tog, rep from * 3 times more (5 buttonholes), end k2 (4, 6).

Rows 4, 5, and 6: Knit.

Bind off in knit on WS.

Sew Picot Hem on sleeve to inside. Mark center of sleeve cap. Pin to shoulder seam, then pin sleeve cap in place and sew. Sew underarm seams. Sew on buttons.

Blocking: If blocking is required, lay on padded surface, spritz lightly with water, pat into place. Do not press this pattern or texture will be lost.

YOU WILL NEED

Yarn

- Extra fine

- Shown: Lucci Yarns Galaxy, 80% extra fine merino, 14% kid mohair, 6% nylon, 1.5 oz (41 g) 110 yd (101m): #11, 3 skeins for Scarf, 2 skeins for Hat

Needles

- Size 7 (4.5 mm) straight needles or size to obtain gauge

- Size 7 (4.5 mm) double-pointed needles

Notions

- Stitch markers

- Tapestry needle

Gauge

- 4 patt reps = 4" (10 cm)

- Take time to check gauge.

Size

- Finished Scarf: 8" x 54" (20.5 x 137 cm)

- Finished Hat: 20" (50.5 cm)

Hyacinth Hat and Scarf

Combining a luxurious, soft yarn with a fun stitch that resembles hyacinths and berries, this lovely hat and scarf set is challenging, but worth the effort.

Shape Crown

Rnd 1: *K10, k2tog, rep from * around—110 sts.

Rnds 2, 3, 5, 6, 8, 9, 11, 12, and 14: Knit.

Rnd 4: *K9, k2tog, rep from * around—100 sts.

Rnd 7: K8, k2tog, rep from * around—90 sts.

Rnd 10: *K7, k2tog, rep from * around—80 sts.

Rnd 13: *K6, k2tog, rep from * around—70 sts.

Cont in this manner, dec every other rnd, always having 1 st less between decs, until 20 sts remain.

Fasten off yarn, leaving a long end. Thread this end of yarn onto a tapestry needle, draw through the remaining 20 sts, draw together, bring through a second time, and fasten off. Weave in end.

Blocking is not recommended for this pattern stitch.

Skill Level: Experienced

Scarf

Cast on 44 sts.

Knit 2 rows.

Work in Hyacinth patt (page 97) for 54" (137 cm), ending with patt Row 4. Bind off.

Hat

Note: Hat is worked back and forth until crown. Crown is worked in the round on double-pointed needles.

Cast on 122 sts.

Work in Hyacinth patt (page 97) for 5" (12.5 cm).

Knit 1 row, dec 1 st each side—120 sts. Purl 1 row.

Place sts, divided evenly, on 3 dpns. Before joining, pm to denote beg of rnds.

Laces

Lace and other openwork patterns are some of the most loved of all the knitting patterns. Their delicate, intricate look and wonderful drape make them a favorite for tops, shawls, and baby items. While some of the lace patterns may look complex, they are not difficult to master.

Cascades

Skill Level: Experienced

Cast on a multiple of 34 plus 2.

Row 1 (RS): K1, *k3, k2tog, k4, yo, p2, (k2, yo, ssk) 3 times, p2, yo k4, ssk, k3, rep from *, end k1.

Row 2: K1, *p2, p2tog through back loop (tbl), p4, yo, p1, k2, (p2, yo, p2tog) 3 times, k2, p1, yo, p4, p2tog, p2, rep from *, end k1.

Row 3: K1, *k1, k2tog, k4, yo, k2, p2, (k2, yo, ssk) 3 times, p2, k2, yo, k4, ssk, k1, rep from *, end k1.

Row 4: K1, *p2tog tbl, p4, yo, p3, k2, (p2, yo, p2tog) 3 times, k2, p3, yo, p4, p2tog, rep from *, end k1.

Rows 5–12: Rep Rows 1–4, twice more.

Row 13: K1, *yo, ssk, k2, yo, ssk, p2, yo, k4, ssk, k6, k2tog, k4, yo, p2, k2, yo, ssk, k2, rep from *, end k1.

Row 14: K1, *yo, p2tog, p2, yo, p2tog, k2, p1, yo, p4, p2tog, p4, p2tog tbl, p4, yo, p1, k2, p2, yo, p2tog, p2, rep from *, end k1.

Row 15: K1, *yo, ssk, k2, yo, ssk, p2, k2, yo, k4, ssk, k2, k2tog, k4, yo, k2, p2, k2, yo, ssk, k2, rep from *, end k1.

Row 16: K1, *yo, p2tog, p2, yo, p2tog, k2, p3, yo, p4, p2tog, p2tog tbl, p4, yo, p3, k2, p2, yo, p2tog, p2, rep from *, end k1.

Rows 17–24: Rep Rows 13–16, twice more.

Rep Rows 1–24 for pattern.

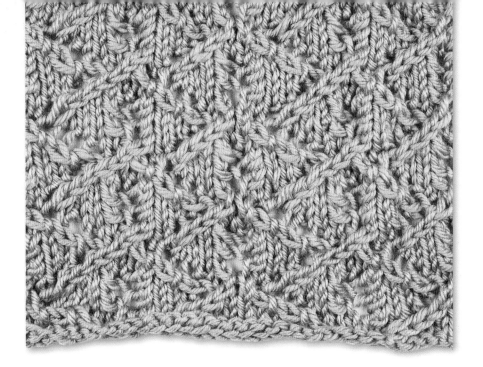

Dutch Lace

Skill Level: Intermediate

Note: When making a yarn over before a purl stitch, wrap yarn around needle from front to back to front.

Cross 2 Stitches Right (Cr2R): Skip the next stitch on left needle, knit the second stitch in front of skipped stitch, then knit the skipped stitch, slip both stitches from left needle.

Cast on a multiple of 16 plus 2.

Row 1: K1, *k5, k2tog, yo, k2, yo, skp, k5, rep from * to last st, end k1.

Row 2: K1, *p4, p2tog, yo, p4, yo, p2tog, p4, rep from * to last st, end k1.

Row 3: K1, *k3, k2tog, yo, k6, yo, skp, k3, rep from * to last st, end k1.

Row 4: K1, *p2, p2tog, yo, p4, yo, p2tog, p2, yo, p2tog, p2, rep from * to last st, end k1.

Row 5: K1, *k1, k2tog, yo, k5, yo, skp, k3, yo, skp, k1, rep from * to last st, end k1.

Row 6: K1, *p2tog, yo, p6, yo, p2tog, p4, yo, p2tog, rep from * to last st, end k1.

Row 7: K1, *sl 1 pwise, k1, yo, skp, k4, yo, skp, k2, k2tog, yo, k1, sl 1 pwise, rep from * to last st, end k1.

Row 8: K1, *p3, yo, p2tog, p3, yo, p2tog, p1, p2tog, yo, p3, rep from * to last st, end k1.

Row 9: K1, *yo, skp, k2, yo, skp, k4, k2tog, yo, k4, rep from * to last st, end k1.

Row 10: K1, *yo, p2tog, p3, yo, p2tog, p2, p2tog, yo, p5, rep from * to last st, end k1.

Row 11: K1, *yo, skp, k4, yo, skp, k2tog, yo, k6, rep from * to last st, end k1.

Row 12: K1, *yo, p2tog, p2, p2tog, yo, p1, sl 2 pwise, p1, yo, p2tog, p4, rep from * to last st, end k1.

Row 13: K1, *yo, skp, k1, k2tog, yo, k2, Cr2R, k2, yo, skp, k3, rep from * to last st, end k1.

Row 14: K1, *p2, p2tog, yo, p4, yo, p2tog, p2, yo, p2tog, p2, rep from * to last st, end k1.

Row 15: K1, *k1, k2tog, yo, k5, yo, skp, k3, yo, skp, k1, rep from * to last st, end k1.

Row 16: K1, *p2tog, yo, p6, yo, p2tog, p4, yo, p2tog, rep from * to last st, end k1.

Rep Rows 7–16 for pattern.

Lacy Diamonds

Skill Level: Intermediate

Cast on a multiple of 11 plus 6.

Row 1: *K6, k2tog, yo, k1, yo, sl 1, k1, psso, rep from *, end k6.

Row 2 and all even-numbered rows: Purl.

Row 3: K5, *k2tog, yo, k3, yo, sl 1, k1, psso, k4, rep from *, end last rep k5.

Row 5: K4, *k2tog, yo, k5, yo, sl 1 k1, psso, k 2, rep from *, end last rep k4.

Row 7: K5, *yo, sl 1, k1, psso, k3, k2tog, yo, k4, rep from *, end last rep k5.

Row 9: K6, *yo, sl 1, k1, psso, k1, k2tog, yo, k6, rep from * across row.

Row 11: K7, *yo, sl 1, k2tog, psso, yo, k8, rep from *, end last rep k7.

Row 12: Purl.

Rep Rows 1–12 for pattern.

Lacy V's

Skill Level: Intermediate

Cast on a multiple of 10 plus 2.

Row 1: K1, *yo, sl 1, k1, psso, k8, rep from * to last st, end k1.

Row 2 and all even-numbered rows: K1, purl to last st, k1.

Row 3: K1, *k1, yo, sl 1, k1 psso, k5, k2tog, yo, rep from * to last st, end k1.

Row 5: K1, *k2, yo, sl 1, k1, psso, k3, k2tog, yo, k1, rep from * to last st, end k1.

Row 7: K1, *k5, yo, sl 1, k1, psso, k3, rep from * to last st, k1.

Row 9: K1, *k3, k2tog, yo, k1, yo, sl 1, k1, psso, k2, rep from * to last st, end k1.

Row 11: K1, *k2, k2tog, yo, k3, yo, sl 1, k1, psso, k1, rep from * to last st, end k1.

Row 12: Same as Row 2.

Rep Rows 1–12 for pattern.

Lily of the Valley

Skill Level: Intermediate

Note: This pattern makes a large scallop at bottom edge.

Cast on a multiple of 29 plus 2.

Row 1: K1, *k1, sl 1, k2tog, psso, k9, yo, k1, yo, p2, yo, k1, yo, k9, sl 1, k2tog, psso, rep from *, end k1.

Row 2 and all even-numbered rows: K1, *p13, k2, p14, rep from *, end k1.

Row 3: K1, *k1, sl 1, k2tog, psso, k8, (yo, k1) twice, p2, (k1, yo) twice, k8, sl 1, k2tog, psso, rep from *, end k1.

Row 5: K1, *k1, sl 1, k2tog, psso, k7, yo, k1, yo, k2, p2, k2, yo, k1, yo, k7, sl 1, k2tog, psso, rep from *, end k1.

Row 7: K1, *k1, sl 1, k2tog, psso, k6, yo , k1, yo, k3, p2, k3, yo, k1, yo, k6, sl 1, k2tog, psso, rep from *, end k1.

Row 9: K1, *k1, sl 1, k2tog, psso, k5, yo, k1, yo, k4, p2, k4, yo, k1, yo, k5, sl 1, k2tog, psso, rep from * across row, end k1.

Row 10: Same as Row 2.

Rep Rows 1–10 for pattern.

Small Shells

Skill Level: Experienced

Cast on a multiple of 6 plus 1.

Rows 1 and 2: Knit.

Row 3: Sl 1, k2, (k1, yo, k1) in next st, *(wrapping yarn twice , k1) 5 times, (k1, yo, k1, yo, k1) in next st, rep from * to last 9 sts, end (wrapping yarn twice , k1) 5 times, (k1, yo, k1) in next st, k3.

Row 4: Sl 1, k5, *holding yarn to front, sl 5 sts dropping extra wraps, then insert left-hand needle into these 5 long sts and p5tog, k5, rep from *, end last rep k6 instead of k5 (13 shells).

Rows 5 and 6: Knit.

Row 7: Sl 1, k2, (wrapping yarn twice, k1) 3 times, *(k1, yo, k1, yo, k1) in next st, (wrapping yarn twice, k1) 5 times, rep from *, end (k1, yo, k1, yo, k1) in next st, (wrapping yarn twice, k1) 3 times, k3.

Row 8: Sl 1, k2, holding yarn to front, sl 3 sts dropping extra wraps, then insert left-hand needle into these 3 long sts and p3tog, *k5, holding yarn to front, sl 5 sts dropping extra wraps, then insert left-hand needle into these 5 long sts and p5tog, rep from *, end k5, holding yarn to front, sl 3 sts dropping extra wraps, then insert needle into these 3 sts and p3tog, k3.

Rep Rows 1–8 for pattern.

Large Shells

Skill Level: Experienced

Cast on a multiple of 19.

Notes: *To make a yarn over before a purl stitch, it is necessary to wrap yarn from front to back and front again before purling.*

To make a yarn over before a knit stitch, yarn should be in front as if to purl, then knit with the yarn in this position.

Rows 1 and 2: Knit.

Row 3: *K1, yo, p2tog, k13, p2tog, yo, k1, rep from * across row.

Row 4: *K1, (k1, p1) into yo st, k15, (p1, k1) into yo st, k1, rep from * across row.

Row 5 and 6: Knit.

Row 7: *K1, (yo, p2tog) twice, k11, (p2tog, yo) twice, k1, rep from * across row.

Row 8: *K1, (k1, p1, into yo st, k1) twice, k up to next yo, (p1, k1 into yo st, k1) twice, rep from * across row.

Row 9: Knit.

Row 10: *K6, (yo, k1) 14 times, k5, rep from * across row.

Row 11: *K1, (yo, p2tog) twice, yo, sl next 15 sts to right-hand needle, allowing the wraps to drop forming long sts, then sl all the long sts back onto left-hand needle and p all of them together forming a shell, (yo, p2tog) twice, yo, k1, rep from * across row.

Row 12: *K1, (p1, k1 into yo st) 3 times, k1, (k1, p1 into yo st, k1) 3 times, rep from * across row.

Rep Rows 1–12 for pattern.

Trellis I

Skill Level: Experienced

Note: *When working yarn over stitches on purl rows, wrap yarn by bringing yarn to front, back, to front again.*

Cast on a multiple of 7 plus 2.

Row 1: K1, *k2, k2tog, yo, k3, rep from * to last st, end k1.

Row 2: K1, *p1, p2tog through the back loop (tbl), yo, p1, yo, p2tog, p1, rep from * to last st, end k1.

Row 3: K1, *k2tog, yo, k3, yo, sl 1, k1, psso, rep from * to last st, end k1.

Row 4: K1, purl across to last st, k1.

Row 5: K1, *yo, sl 1, k1, psso, k5, rep from * to last st, end k1.

Row 6: K1, *yo, p2tog, p2, p2tog tbl, yo, p1, rep from * to last st, end k1.

Row 7: K1, *k2, yo, sl 1, k1, psso, k2tog, yo, k1, rep from * to last st, end k1.

Row 8: Same as Row 4.

Rep Rows 1–8 for pattern.

Trellis II

Skill Level: Intermediate

Cast on a multiple of 6 plus 2.

Row 1 (RS): K1, p1, *yo, k2tog tbl, k2tog, yo, p2, rep from * to last 6 sts, end yo, k2tog tbl, k2tog, yo, p1, k1.

Row 2: K2, *p4, k2, rep from * across row.

Row 3: K1, p1, *k2tog, yo twice (wrap yarn twice around needle), k2tog tbl, p2, rep from * to last 6 sts, end k2tog, yo twice, k2tog tbl, p1, k1.

Row 4: K2, *p1, (k1, p1) into the double yo of previous row, p1, k2, rep from * across row.

Row 5: K1, *k2tog, yo, p2, yo, k2tog tbl, rep from * to last st, end k1.

Row 6: K1, p2, *k2, p4, rep from * to last 5 sts, end k2, p2, k1.

Row 7: K1, yo, *k2tog tbl, p2, k2tog, yo twice, rep from * to last 7 sts, end k2tog tbl, p2, k2tog, yo, k1.

Row 8: K1, p2, k2, p1, *(k1, p1) into the double yo of previous row, p1, k2, p1, rep from * to last 2 sts, p1, k1.

Rep Rows 1–8 for pattern.

Vertical I

Skill Level: Intermediate

Cast on a multiple of 7 plus 2.

Rows 1, 3, and 5: K1, purl to last st, k1.

Row 2: K1, *k1, k2tog, yo, k1, yo, ssk, k1, rep from * to last st, k1.

Row 4: K1, *k2tog, yo, k3, yo, ssk, rep from * to last st, k1.

Row 6: K1, *k2, yo, sl 1, k2tog, psso, yo, k2, rep from * to last st, k1.

Rep Rows 1–6 for pattern.

Vertical II

Skill Level: Easy

Cast on a multiple of 7 plus 2.

Rows 1 and 3 (WS): K1, purl to last st, k1.

Row 2: *K2, k2tog, yo, k1, yo, ssk, rep from * to last 2 sts, k2.

Row 4: K1, *k2tog, yo, k3, yo, ssk, rep from * to last st, k1.

Rep Rows 1–4 for pattern.

Vertical III

Skill Level: Easy

Cast on a multiple of 9 plus 4.

Row 1 (WS): Purl.

Row 2: K3, *yo, k2, ssk, k2tog, k2, yo, k1, rep from *, end k1.

Row 3: Purl.

Row 4: K2, *yo, k2, ssk, k2tog, k2, yo, k1, rep from *, end k2.

Rep Rows 1–4 for pattern.

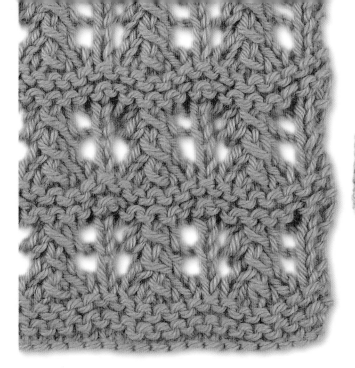

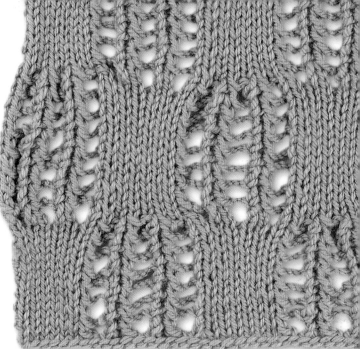

Window Boxes

Skill Level: Intermediate

Note: To increase in this pattern, knit in front and back of the same stitch.

Cast on a multiple of 6 plus 3.

Rows 1, 2, 3, 4, and 5: Knit.

Rows 6, 8, and 10: K1, purl to last st, k1.

Rows 7 and 9: K1, *k1, yo, k1, sl 1, k2tog, psso, k1, yo, rep from *, end last rep k2.

Row 11: K1, *k1, inc 1 st, k1, sl 1, k2tog, psso, k1, inc 1 st, rep from *, end last rep k2.

Row 12: Knit.

Rep Rows 1–12 for pattern.

Peaks and Valleys

Skill Level: Experienced

Note: In this pattern, because of the placement of yarn overs, some rows will have a different number of stitches than the previous row.

Cast on a multiple of 10 plus 8.

Foundation row (WS): Purl.

Row 1 (RS): K1, *k6, [(k2tog, yo) twice, sl 1, k1, psso] 3 times, rep from * to last 7 sts, end k7.

Row 2: Purl across row working (p1, k1) into each double yo from previous row.

Rows 3–14: Rep Rows 1 and 2, 6 times more.

Row 15: K2, (yo twice, k2) twice, k1, *(k2tog, sl 1, k1, psso) 3 times, k1, (yo twice, k2) twice, k1, rep from * to last st, end k1.

Row 16: Rep Row 2.

Row 17: K1, (k2tog, yo twice, sl 1, k1, psso) 3 times, *k6, [(k2tog, yo) twice, sl 1, k1, psso] 3 times, rep from * to last st, end k1.

Row 18: Rep Row 2.

Rows 19–30: Rep Rows 17 and 18, 6 times more.

Row 31: K1, (k2tog, sl 1, k1, psso) 3 times, *k1, (yo twice, k2) twice, k1, (k2tog, sl 1, k1, psso) 3 times, rep from * to last st, end k1.

Row 32: Rep Row 2.

Rep Rows 1–32 for pattern.

Small Fern

Skill Level: Intermediate

Cast on a multiple of 6 plus 3.

Row 1 and all odd-numbered rows (WS): K1, purl to last st, end k1.

Row 2: K2, *yo, ssk, k1, k2tog, yo, k1, rep from * to last st, end k1.

Row 4: K2, *yo, k1, sl 1, k2tog, psso, k1, yo, k1, rep from * to last st, end k1.

Row 6: K2, *k2tog, yo, k1, yo, ssk, k1, rep from * to last st, end k1.

Row 8: K1, k2tog, *(k1, yo) twice, k1, sl 1, k2tog, psso, rep from * to last 6 sts, end (k1, yo) twice, k1, ssk, k1.

Rep Rows 1–8 for pattern.

Keyhole Lace

Skill Level: Experienced

Cast on a multiple of 12 plus 4.

Row 1 (RS): K3, *k2, k2tog, yo, k2tog but do not slip off needle, knit first of these 2 sts again, then sl both off, yo, sl 1, k1, psso, k4, rep from * to last st, end k1.

Row 2: K1, purl to last st, k1.

Row 3: K3, *k1, k2tog, yo, k4, yo, sl 1, k1, psso, k3, rep from * to last st, end k1.

Row 4: K1, purl to last st, k1.

Row 5: K3, *k2tog, yo, k1, k2tog, yo twice, sl 1, k1, psso, k1, yo, sl 1, k1, psso, rep from * to last st, end k1.

Row 6: K1, p2, *p4, (k1, p1) into the double yo from back loop, p6, rep from * to last st, end k1.

Row 7: K3, *k2, yo, sl 1, k1, psso, k2, k2tog, yo, k4, rep from * to last st, end k1.

Row 8: K1, purl to last st, k1.

Row 9: K3, *k3, yo, sl 1, k1, psso, k2tog, yo, k5, rep from * to last st, end k1.

Row 10: K1, purl to last st, k1.

Rep Rows 1–10 for pattern.

Beehive

Skill Level: Experienced

Notes: When knitting in the stitch 3 rows below, after stitch is completed, drop original stitch off needle and allow to run down.

When knitting 2 stitches in the yarn overs, first knit in the front, then in the back of the same yarn over.

Cast on a multiple of 10 plus 3.

Row 1: K1, *p1, k9, rep from *, end p1, k1.

Row 2: K1, *k1, p9, rep from *, end k2.

Row 3: Same as Row 1.

Row 4: Same as Row 2.

Row 5: K1, *p1, k2tog, k5, sl 1, k1, psso, rep from *, end p1, k1.

Row 6: K1, purl to last st, k1.

Row 7: K1, *k1, k2tog, k3, sl 1, k1, psso, rep from *, end k2.

Row 8: K1, purl to last st, k1.

Row 9: K1, k1 inserting needle into corresponding st 3 rows below, *yo, k5, yo, k1 inserting needle into corresponding st 3 rows below, rep from *, end k1.

Row 10: K2, k2 sts into the yo, *p5, k2 sts in the yo, k1, k2 in yo, rep from *, end p5, k2 in yo, k2.

Row 11: K6, *p1, k9, rep from *, end p1, k6.

Row 12: K3, p3, *k1, p3, k3, p3, rep from * to last 7 sts, end k1, p3, k3.

Row 13: K6, *p1, k9, rep from * to last 7 sts, end p1, k6.

Row 14: K1, *k1, p4, rep from * to last 2 sts, end k2.

Row 15: K1, *k3, sl 1, k1, psso, p1, k2tog, k2, rep from * to last 2 sts, end k2.

Row 16: K1, purl to last st, k1.

Row 17: K1, *k2, sl 1, k1, psso, k1, k2tog, k1, rep from * to last 2 sts, end k2.

Row 18: K1, purl to last st, k1.

Row 19: K1, *k3, yo, k1 in st 3 rows below, yo, k2, rep from * to last 2 sts, end k2.

Row 20: K1, *p3, k2 sts in yo, k1, k2 sts in yo, p2, rep from * to last 2 sts, end p1, k1.

Row 21: Same as Row 1.

Row 22: K1, *k1, p3, k3, p3, rep from * to last 2 sts, end k2.

Row 23: Same as Row 1.

Row 24: Same as Row 14.

Rep Rows 5–24 for pattern.

Traveling Vines

Skill Level: Intermediate

Notes: If through back loop (tbl) is stated, knit or purl through the back loop of the stitch; however, if through back loop is not stated, knit or purl in usual manner.

All slip stitches are slipped pwise.

Cast on a multiple of 8 plus 2.

Row 1: K1, *yo, k1 tbl, yo skp, k5, rep from * to last st, k1.

Row 2: K1, *p4, p2tog tbl, p3, rep from * across to last st, k1.

Row 3: K1, *yo, k1 tbl, yo, k2, skp, k3, rep from * to last st, k1.

Row 4: K1, *p2, p2tog tbl, p5, rep from * to last st, k1.

Row 5: K1, *k1 tbl, yo, k4, skp, k1, yo, rep from * to last st, k1.

Row 6: K1, *p1, p2tog tbl, p6, rep from * to last st, k1.

Row 7: K1, *k5, k2tog, yo, k1 tbl, yo, rep from * to last st, k1.

Row 8: K1, *p3, p2tog, p4, rep from * to last st, k1.

Row 9: K1, *k3, k2tog, k2, yo, k1 tbl, yo, rep from * to last st, k1.

Row 10: K1, *p5, p2tog, p2, rep from * to last st, k1.

Row 11: K1, *yo, k1, k2tog, k4, yo, k1 tbl, rep from * to last st, k1.

Row 12: K1, *p6, p2tog, p1, rep from * to last st, k1.

Rep Rows 1–12 for pattern.

Spanish Lace

Skill Level: Experienced

Note: Due to the nature of the pattern increases and decreases, the stitch count fluctuates on Rows 6, 7, 8, and 9.

P2tog-b: Purl 2 together from back loop.

Cast on a multiple of 15 plus 2.

Row 1 (RS): K1, *k5, k2tog, yo, k1, yo, ssk, k5, rep from * across row, end k1.

Row 2: K1, *p4, p2tog-b, yo, p3, yo, p2tog, p4, rep from * across row, end k1.

Row 3: K1, *k3, k2tog, yo, k5, yo, ssk, k3, rep from * across row, end k1.

Row 4: K1, *p2, p2tog-b, yo, p1, yo, p2tog, p1, p2tog-b, yo, p1, yo, p2tog, p2, rep from * across, end k1.

Row 5: K1, *k1, k2tog, yo, k3, yo, k3tog, yo, k3, yo, ssk, k1, rep from * across row, end k1.

Row 6: K1, *p2, yo, p5, yo, p1, yo, p5, yo, p2, rep from * across row, end k1.

Row 7: K1, *(k3, yo, ssk, k1, k2tog, yo) twice, k3, rep from * across row, end k1.

Row 8: K1, *p4, p3tog, yo, p5, yo, p3tog, p4, rep from * across row, end k1.

Row 9: K1, *k6, yo, ssk, k1, k2tog, yo, k6, rep from * across row, end k1.

Row 10: K1, *p3, p2tog-b, p2, yo, p3tog, yo, p2, p2tog, p3, rep from * across row, end k1.

Rep Rows 1–10 for pattern.

Lacy Sweater

Soft and feminine, this dressy little short sleeve sweater is knit from baby alpaca yarn that feels like a gentle, warm hug. Three buttons at the top allows the sweater to fall gently and swing freely to show off the lacy stitch pattern.

YOU WILL NEED

Yarn

- Lightweight
- Shown: Plymouth Baby Alpaca DK, 100% baby alpaca, 1.75 oz (50 g)/125 yds (114 m): Lavender #1830, 6 (6, 7, 7) skeins

Needles

- Size 6 (4 mm) or size to obtain gauge

Notions

- Three ½" (1.3 cm) buttons
- Tapestry needle

Gauge

- 22 sts = 4" (10 cm) in patt on size 6 needles
- Take time to check gauge.

Sizes

- Small (Medium, Large, X-Large)
- Finished chest: 33 (37, 41, 45)" [84 (94, 104, 114.5) cm]

Skill Level: Easy

Note: Pattern is multiple of 9 plus 4 (Large and X-Large sizes have added sts on sides).

 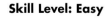

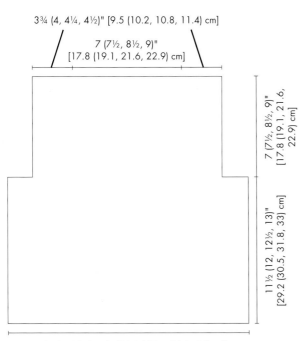

3¾ (4, 4¼, 4½)" [9.5 (10.2, 10.8, 11.4) cm]

7 (7½, 8½, 9)" [17.8 (19.1, 21.6, 22.9) cm]

7 (7½, 8½, 9)" [17.8 (19.1, 21.6, 22.9) cm]

11½ (12, 12½, 13)" [29.2 (30.5, 31.8, 33) cm]

17 (18¾, 20, 21¼)" [43.2 (47.6, 50.8, 54) cm]

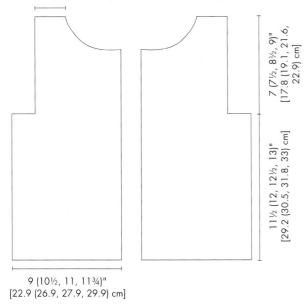

3¾ (4, 4¼, 4½)" [9.5 (10.2, 10.8, 11.4) cm]

7 (7½, 8½, 9)" [17.8 (19.1, 21.6, 22.9) cm]

11½ (12, 12½, 13)" [29.2 (30.5, 31.8, 33) cm]

9 (10½, 11, 11¾)" [22.9 (26.9, 27.9, 29.9) cm]

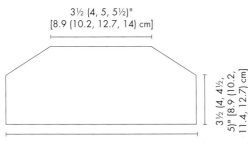

3½ (4, 5, 5½)" [8.9 (10.2, 12.7, 14) cm]

3½ (4, 4½, 5)" [8.9 (10.2, 11.4, 12.7) cm]

12 (13¾, 14¾, 16)" [30.5 (34.9, 37.5, 40.6) cm]

Back

With size 6 needles, cast on 94 (103, 109, 117 sts).

Row 1 (WS): Purl.

Row 2: K3 (3, 6, 10), *yo, k2, ssk, k2tog, k2, yo, k1, rep from * 9 (10, 10, 10) times more, end k1 (1, 4, 8).

Row 3: Purl.

Row 4: K2 (2, 5, 9), *yo, k2, ssk, k2tog, k2, yo, k1, rep from *, end k2 (2, 5, 9).

Rep Rows 1–4 for patt until piece measures 11½ (12, 12½, 13)" [29 (30.5, 32, 33) cm] from beg.

Armhole Shape

Bind off 9 (9, 9, 9) sts at beg of next 2 rows. Cont on 76 (85, 91, 99) sts in patt as est until armhole is 7 (7½, 8½, 9)" [18 (19, 21.5, 23) cm].

Shoulder Shape

Bind off 21 (22, 23, 24) sts at beg of next 2 rows.

Bind off rem 34 (41, 45, 51) sts.

Left Front

With size 6 needles, cast on 49 (58, 61, 65) sts.

Row 1 (WS): Purl.

Row 2: K3 (3, 6, 10), *yo, k2, ssk, k2tog, k2, yo, k1, rep from * 4 (5, 5, 5) times more, end k1 (1, 1, 1).

Row 3: Purl.

Row 4: K2 (2, 5, 9), *yo, k2, ssk, k2tog, k2, yo, k1, rep from *, end k2 (2, 2, 2).

Rep Rows 1–4 for patt until piece measures 11½ (12, 12½, 13)" [29 (30.5, 32, 33) cm] from beg, ending at arm side.

Armhole Shape

Next row (RS): Bind off 9 sts at beg of row, finish row.

Keeping front edge even, cont in patt as est until armhole is 5 (5½, 6½, 7)" [12.5 (14, 16.5, 18) cm], ending at front edge.

(continued)

Lacy Sweater (continued)

Neck and Shoulder Shape

Next Row (WS): Bind off 14 (18, l9, 21) sts at beg of row, finish row.

Being sure to keep patt as est, dec 1 st neck edge every row 5 (9, 10, 11) times. Work even until same as back to shoulder.

Bind off rem 21 (22, 23, 24) sts.

Right Front

With size 6 needles, cast on 49 (58, 61, 65 sts).

Row 1 (WS): Purl.

Row 2: K1 (1, 1, 1), *yo, k2, ssk, k2tog, k2, yo, k1, rep from * 4 (5, 5, 5) times more, end k3 (3, 6, 10).

Row 3: Purl.

Row 4: K2 (2, 2, 2), *yo, k2, ssk, k2tog, k2, yo, k1, rep from *, end k2 (2, 5, 9).

Rep Rows 1–4 for patt until 11½ (12, 12½, 13)" [29 (30.5, 32, 33) cm] from beg, ending at arm side.

Armhole Shape

Next Row (WS): Bind off 9 sts at beg of row, finish row.

Keeping front edge even, cont in patt as est until armhole is 5 (5½, 6½, 7)" [12.5 (14, 16.5, 18) cm], ending at front edge.

Neck and Shoulder Shape

Next Row (RS): Bind off 14 (18, l9, 21) sts at beg of row, finish row.

Being sure to keep patt as est, dec 1 st neck edge every row 5 (9, 10, 11) times. Work even until same as Back to shoulder.

Bind off rem 21 (22, 23, 24) sts.

Sleeves (make 2)

With size 6 needles, cast on 67 (76, 81, 90) sts.

Row 1 (WS): Purl.

Row 2: K3 (3, 6, 10), *yo, k2, ssk, k2tog, k2, yo, k1, rep from *, end k1 (1, 4, 8).

Row 3: Purl.

Row 4: K2 (2, 5, 9), *yo, k2, ssk, k2tog, k2, yo, k1, rep from *, end k2 (2, 5, 9).

Rep Rows 1–4 for patt until 3½ (4, 4½, 5)" [9 (10, 11.5, 12.5) cm] from beg.

Cap Shape

Being sure to keep patt as est, bind off 8 (9, 9, 10) sts at beg of next 6 rows.

Bind off rem 19 (22, 27, 30) sts.

Finishing

Sew shoulder seams. Set in Sleeves, pinning center of Sleeve to shoulder seam and bottom to armhole. Sew Sleeves in place. Sew underarm seams.

Neckband

With RS facing, pick up and k26 (27, 28, 29) sts along right front neck edge, 34 (41, 45, 51) sts along back neck edge, 26 (27, 28, 29) sts along left front—86 (95, 101, 109) sts.

Row 1: Knit, dec 1 (1, 1, 1) in center of row [85 (94, 100, 108) sts].

Row 2: Knit.

Row 3: *K1, yo, k2tog, rep from *, end k1.

Row 4: Knit.

Row 5: Knit.

Bind off in knit.

Sew three buttons, evenly spaced on Left Front, using yo spaces on Right Front as buttonholes.

Blocking: Do not press with iron, lay flat on padded surface, sprinkle lightly with water, gentle pat into shape, allow to dry.

Traveling Vines Pullover

This dainty pullover, made with lovely silk and alpaca yarn, has softness, drape, and shimmer. In addition to all the wonderful qualities of the yarn, there is very little finishing to do.

YOU WILL NEED

Yarn

• Worsted weight

• Shown: Hampden Hills Alpacas, Alpaca Silk, 70% baby alpaca, 30% silk, 3.5 oz (100 g)/245 yds (224 m): Brilliant Blue, 3 (3, 4, 4) skeins

Needles

• Sizes 5 (3.75 mm) and 6 (4 mm) or size to obtain gauge

Notions

• Stitch holder

• Tapestry needle

Gauge

• 3 patt repeats = 4" (10 cm) on size 6 needles

• Take time to check gauge.

Sizes

• Women's S (M, L, XL)

• Finished bust: 32 (34, 36, 38)" [81 (86, 91, 96.5) cm]

• Finished length: 18½ (19½, 20½, 21½)" [47 (49.5, 52, 54.5) cm]

• This is a close-fitting garment.

(continued)

Skill Level: Intermediate

Back

With size 6 needles, cast on 90 (98, 106, 114) sts. Work in the Traveling Vines patt on page 114 until piece measures 11½ (12, 12½, 13)" [29 (30.5, 31.5, 33) cm] from beg.

Shape Armholes

Bind off 8 (8, 8, 8) sts at beg of next 2 rows [74 (82, 90, 98) sts]. Continue in patt as established until armholes measure 7 (7½, 8, 8½)" [18 (19, 20.5, 21.5) cm].

Bind off 18 (20, 22, 24) sts at beg of next 2 rows. Place remaining 38 (42, 46, 50) sts on holder to be worked later for neckband.

Front

Work same as Back until armholes measure 5 (5½, 6, 6½)" [12.5 (14, 15, 16.5) cm], ending with a WS row.

Shape Neck

Next Row (RS): Work across 18 (20, 22, 24) sts for left neck, turn. Work on these sts only, making sure to keep patt as established, until armholes measure same as Back. Bind off.

With RS facing, place center 38 (42, 46, 50) sts on holder for center neck, join yarn, and work rem 18 (20, 22, 24) sts for right neck until piece measures same as Back. Bind off.

Sleeves (make 2)

With size 6 needles, cast on 74 (82, 90, 98) sts. Work patt same as Back until Sleeve measures 5 (5½, 6, 6½)" [12.5 (14, 15, 16.5) cm] from beg. Bind off loosely.

Finishing

Sew left shoulder. With RS facing, using size 5 needles, join yarn at right Back neck, k38 (42, 46, 50) sts from Back neck holder, pick up and k7 (8, 9, 10) sts along left neck edge, k38 (42, 46, 50) sts from Front holder, pick up and k7 (8, 9, 10) sts along right neck edge—90 (100, 110, 120) sts. Work in St st (purl 1 row, knit 1 row) for 5 rows. Using size 6 needles, bind off loosely in knit.

Sew right shoulder seam and edges of neckband. Allow neckband to roll naturally to Front.

Sew in sleeves: Fold Sleeve in half, mark the center, pin in place with center of Sleeve at shoulder seam and end of Sleeve at outer edge of bound-off underarm sts, easing into place if necessary, then sew in place. Sew underarm seams. Weave in ends.

Blocking: Place garment on a padded surface, spritz with water, pat into shape, pinning points of patt. Allow to dry.

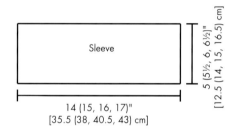

Sleeve

5 (5½, 6, 6½)" [12.5 (14, 15, 16.5) cm]

14 (15, 16, 17)" [35.5 (38, 40.5, 43) cm]

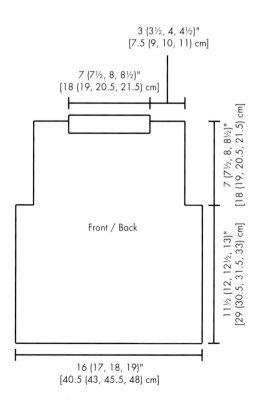

3 (3½, 4, 4½)" [7.5 (9, 10, 11) cm]

7 (7½, 8, 8½)" [18 (19, 20.5, 21.5) cm]

7 (7½, 8, 8½)" [18 (19, 20.5, 21.5) cm]

Front / Back

11½ (12, 12½, 13)" [29 (30.5, 31.5, 33) cm]

16 (17, 18, 19)" [40.5 (43, 45.5, 48) cm]

Fanciful Feet Socks

Socks are such fun to knit, and they incorporate several knitting procedures that you may not have encountered before. Once you make your first pair, you will definitely want to make more. This pair is worked from the top down on double-pointed needles, with a lacy pattern added for interest.

Skill Level: Intermediate

Note: Yarn does stretch to fit a few sizes.

YOU WILL NEED

Yarn

- Fingering weight
- Shown: On-Line Supersocke 100, 75% wool, 25% polyamide, 3.5 oz (100 g)/460 yds (420 m): Florida, 1 skein

Needles

- Size 2 (2.75 mm) double-pointed needles or size to obtain gauge

Notions

- Stitch marker
- Tapestry needle

Gauge

- 34 sts = 4" (10 cm) in Lacy Patt
- Take time to check gauge.

Sizes

- Women's Small (Medium, Large); shoe sizes 5/6 (7/8, 9/10)
- Finished foot length: 9 (9½, 10)" [23 (24, 25.5) cm]

Lacy Patt

Rnds 1 and 3: Knit

Rnd 2: *K2, k2tog, yo, k1, yo, ssk, rep from * to last 2 sts, k 2.

Rnd 4: K1, *k2tog, yo, k3, yo, ssk, rep from * to last st, k1.

Rep Rows 1–4 for patt.

Work Lacey Patt until 8½" (21.5 cm) beg.

(continued)

Socks (make 2)

Cast on 68 sts and divide between 3 needles (22 sts on first needle, 24 sts on 2nd needle, 22 sts on 3rd needle). Join, being careful not to twist; place marker at beg of rnds (center back).

Work in k1, p1 ribbing for 3" (7.5) cm.

K one rnd, inc 4 sts evenly spaced—72 sts; divide 24 sts on each of 3 needles.

Note: You will be at marker, which will become center back of heel.

Making sure to cont Lacy Patt as established, k12 sts on first needle (half heel), k24 sts on 2nd needle (half instep), k24 sts on 3rd needle (other half of instep), slip rem 12 sts onto first needle and k them along with 12 sts already on first needle (heel sts complete).

Leave the 48 instep sts on 2nd and 3rd needles and work on 24 heel sts only as follows:

Next row (WS): Sl 1, p10, p2tog, p11—23 sts.

Heel Patt

Row 1 (RS): *Sl 1, k1, rep from * to last st, k1.

Row 2: Sl 1, p to end of row.

Rep rows 1 and 2 of heel patt for 2½" (6.5 cm), ending with Row 1.

Turn Heel

Row 1: Sl 1, p12, p2tog, p1, turn.

Row 2: Sl 1, k4, sl 1, k1, psso, k1, turn.

Row 3: Sl 1, p5, p2tog, p1, turn.

Row 4: Sl 1, k6, sl 1, k1, psso, k1, turn.

Row 5: Sl 1, p7, p2tog, p1, turn.

Row 6: Sl 1, k8, sl 1, k1, psso, k1, turn.

Row 7: Sl 1, p9, p2tog, p1, turn.

Row 8: Sl 1, k10, sl 1, k1, psso, k1, turn.

Row 9: Sl 1, p11, p2tog, turn.

Row 10: Sl 1, k11, sl 1, k1, psso—13 sts.

Shape Instep

With first needle, pick up 15 sts along side of heel, k2tog at beg of 2nd needle, cont knitting across 2nd and 3rd needles of instep (making sure to keep Lacy Patt as established now and throughout), k2tog at end of 3rd needle (23 sts each on 2nd and 3rd needles), pick up 16 sts along other side of heel, k7 from heel needle (you are now at center back of heel), and divide sts as follows: 22 sts on first needle, 23 sts on 2nd needle, 23 sts on 3rd needle, and 22 sts on 4th needle. In order to cont, slide the 23 sts of 3rd needle onto 2nd needle, freeing up this needle to cont working; make sure that you are at center back of heel. You now have 22 sts on first needle, 46 sts on 2nd needle, and 22 sts on 3rd needle.

Next rnd: K to last 3 sts on first needle, k2tog, k1; on second needle, k2tog, k to last 2 sts, k2tog (you now have 44 sts on instep); on 3rd needle, k1, sl 1, k1, psso, k to end of rnd.

Next rnd: On first needle k; on 2nd needle cont Lacy Patt; on 3rd needle k.

Next rnd: On first needle, k to last 3 sts, k2tog, k1; on 2nd needle cont Lacy Patt; on 3rd needle k1, sl 1, k1, psso, k to end of rnd.

Cont in this manner to dec 1 st at end of first needle and beg of 3rd needle every other rnd, keeping Lacy Patt as established on 44 sts of 2nd needle until you have 14 sts on first and 3rd needles—72 sts.

Work even, still keeping instep in patt until 6½ (7, 7½)" [16.5 (18, 19) cm] from heel.

Shape Toe

Rearrange sts on needle before beg toe shaping; remainder of sock is finished in St st (k every rnd).

Sl 6 sts from beg of 2nd needle onto end of first needle; sl 6 sts from end of 2nd needle onto beg of 3rd needle. Sts are now divided as follows: 18 sts on first and 3rd needles, 36 sts on 2nd needle.

Rnd 1: K to last 3 sts, k2tog, k1; on 2nd needle k1, sl 1, k1, psso, k to last 3 sts, k2tog, k1; on 3rd needle k1, sl 1, k1, psso, k to end of rnd.

Rnd 2: Knit.

Rep last 2 rnds until 24 sts rem. K sts of first needle onto end of 3rd needle; end yarn, leaving about 10" (25.5 cm) for joining toe.

Graft toe sts together with Kitchener stitch (page 39).

Weave in ends.

Blocking: Lay finished socks on a padded surface, spritz lightly with water, pin into shape, allow to dry.

Ribs

Rib stitch patterns have side-to-side elasticity that makes them very useful for creating borders on sweaters, socks, and hats. Their stretchiness also causes them to pull in a little, which is desirable for yokes of sweaters or waistlines and when you want to give a garment a little shaping. Many of the following rib stitches can be substituted for more ordinary rib stitches used in most sweater patterns; by using the rib stitches in this section, you can entirely change the look of a sweater.

Mistake Rib

Skill Level: Easy

Note: This pattern is called Mistake Stitch because it doesn't follow the expected rib procedure. When the pattern begins to emerge, you will see it clearly.

Cast on a multiple of 4 plus 3.

Row 1: *K2, p2, rep from * to last 3 sts, end k2, p1.

Rep Row 1 for pattern.

Fancy Rib

Skill Level: Intermediate

Cast on a multiple of 5 plus 2.

Row 1 (RS): P2, *yo, k2tog tbl, k1, p2, rep from * across row.

Row 2: K2, *yo, k2tog tbl, p1 in the yo from previous row, k2, rep from *across row.

Row 3: P2, *yo, k2tog tbl, k1 in yo from previous row, p2, rep from * across row.

Rep Rows 2 and 3 for pattern.

Bamboo Reed

Skill Level: Easy

Cast on an even number of stitches.

Row 1: K1, *yo, k2, pass the yarn over st over both knit sts, rep from * across row to last st, k1.

Row 2: K1, purl across to last st, k1.

Rep Rows 1 and 2 for pattern.

Little Puffs

Skill Level: Easy

Cast on a multiple of 4 plus 3.

Row 1 (RS): K2, *p3tog, keeping the sts on left-hand needle, k them tog tbl, then p them tog again, k1, rep from *, end last rep k2 instead of k1.

Row 2: K1, purl to last st, k1.

Rep Rows 1 and 2 for pattern.

Little Puffs Reverse

Skill Level: Easy

Cast on a multiple of 4 plus 3.

Row 1 (WS): K2, *p3tog, keeping the sts on left-hand needle, k them tog tbl, then p them tog again, k1, rep from *, end last rep k2 instead of k1.

Row 2: K1, purl to last st, k1.

Rep Rows 1 and 2 for pattern.

Twisted Rib

Skill Level: Easy

Note: To make a twisted stitch, skip one stitch, knit the next stitch, knit the skipped stitch, drop both stitches off needle.

Cast on a multiple of 10 plus 4.

Row 1 (RS): P4, *twist 2, p2, twist 2, p4, rep from * across row.

Row 2: K4, *p2, k2, p2, k4, rep from * across row.

Rep Rows 1 and 2 for pattern.

Twisted Rib II

Skill Level: Easy

Note: To make an increase for this pattern, knit in front and back of same stitch.

Cast on an even number of stitches.

Row 1 (WS): Purl.

Row 2: K1, *sl 1, k and increase 1 st in next st, psso both the knit st and the increase, rep from * to last st, end k1.

Rep Rows 1 and 2 for pattern.

Eyelet Rib

Skill Level: Easy

Note: To make yarn over when purling the next stitch, wrap yarn from front, to back, to front again.

Cast on a multiple of 8 plus 6.

Rows 1 and 3 (WS): K6, *p2, k6, rep from * across row.

Row 2: P6, *yo, ssk, p6, rep from * across row.

Row 4: P6, *k2tog, yo, p6, rep from * across row.

Rep Rows 1–4 for pattern.

Lacy Rib

Skill Level: Intermediate

Cast on a multiple of 4 plus 2.

Rows 1 and 2: Knit.

Row 3: K4, *yo, k2tog, k2, rep from * across row, end last rep k4 instead of k2.

Rep Row 3 for pattern.

Lacy Raised Rib

Skill Level: Intermediate

Notes: The yarn over in this pattern requires an extra wrap around the needle. When purling the yarn over stitches, make one stitch in the yarn over space and drop extra wrap off needle.

Cast on a multiple of 3 plus 2.

Row 1 (RS): K1, *p2, yo by wrapping yarn over needle from front to back to front again, k1, yo by wrapping yarn from back to front, back over needle to front again, rep from * to last 3 sts, end p2, k1.

Row 2: K3, *p3, k2, rep from *, end last rep k3.

Row 3: K1, *p2, k3, rep from * to last 3 sts, end p2, k1.

Row 4: K3, *p3tog, k2, rep from *, end last rep k3.

Rep Rows 1–4 for pattern.

Mock Cable

Skill Level: Easy

Cast on a multiple of 4 plus 2.

Row 1 (WS): K2, *p2, k2, rep from * across row.

Row 2: P2, *k1, yo, k1, p2, rep from * across row.

Row 3: K2, *p3, k2, rep from * across row.

Row 4: P2, *sl 1, k2, psso both k sts, p2, rep from * across row.

Rep Rows 1–4 for pattern.

Mock Rib

Skill Level: Easy

Cast on an even number of stitches.

Row 1 (RS): K1, *p1, yarn back, sl 1 as to purl, yarn front, rep from * to last 3 sts, yarn front, p1, yarn back, sl 1, end k1.

Row 2: K1, purl across row to last st, k1.

Rep Rows 1 and 2 for pattern.

Mock Rib Reverse

Skill Level: Easy

Cast on an even number of stitches.

Row 1 (WS): K1, *p1, yarn back, sl 1 as to purl, yarn front, rep from * to last 3 sts, yarn front, p1, yarn back sl 1, end k1.

Row 2: K1, purl across row to last st, k1.

Rep Rows 1 and 2 for pattern.

Rib Stitch IV

Skill Level: Easy

Cast on a multiple of 4 plus 2.

Row 1 (WS): Purl.

Row 2 (RS): Knit.

Row 3: P2, *k2, p2, rep from * across row.

Row 4: K2, *p2, k2, rep from * across row.

Rep Rows 1–4 for pattern.

Slip Stitch Rib

Skill Level: Easy

Cast on a multiple of 5 plus 4.

Row 1: K1, p2, *k1, sl 1, k1, p2, rep from * to last st, end k1.

Row 2: K1, *k2, p3, rep from * to last 3 sts, end k3.

Rep Rows 1 and 2 for pattern.

Twisted Bars

Skill Level: Intermediate

Cast on a multiple of 6 plus 3.

Row 1 (RS): K2, *yo, k1, k3tog, k1, yo, k1, rep from *, end last rep k2.

Row 2: K1, p1, *k5, p1, rep from *, end k1.

Rep Rows 1 and 2 for pattern.

Little Puffs Ribbed Hat

This hat is made with a soft cotton yarn that would be great for a chemo cap, but it can also be made with any worsted weight yarn. The pattern is Little Puffs (page 125). When the cuff is turned up, the reverse side of the pattern shows. For this hat, the puff pattern is altered slightly so that it can be worked in the round.

(continued)

YOU WILL NEED

Yarn

- Medium weight
- Shown: Universal Yarns Cotton Supreme, 100% cotton, 3.5 oz (100 g)/180 yds (165 m): Magenta #510 , 1 skein

Needles

- Size 8 (5 mm) double-pointed needles or size to obtain gauge

Notions

- Stitch marker
- Tapestry needle

Gauge

- 5 Little Puff patts = 4" (10 cm)
- Take time to check gauge.

Size

- Adult Medium
- Finished hat: 22" (55.5 cm)

Skill Level: Easy

Hat

Cast on 91 sts and divide equally among 3 double-pointed needles, being careful not to twist, placing marker before joining to mark beg of rnds.

Rnd 1: K2, *p3tog, keeping the sts on left-hand needle, k them tog tbl, then p them tog again, k1, rep from *, at end of last rep k2 instead of k1.

Rnd 2: Knit.

Rep Rnds 1 and 2 until piece measures 7" (18 cm) from beg.

Shape Crown

Rnd 1: Knit, dec 1 st at end of rnd—90 sts.

Rnds 2 and 3: Knit.

Rnd 4: *K7, k2tog, rep from * around—80 sts.

Rnd 5: Knit.

Rnd 6: *K6, k2tog, rep from * around—70 sts.

Rnd 7: Knit.

Rnd 8: *K5, k2tog, rep from * around—60 sts.

Rnd 9: Knit.

Rnd 10: *K4, k2tog, rep from * around—50 sts.

Rnd 11: Knit.

Rnd 12: *K3, k2tog, rep from * around—40 sts.

Rnd 13: Knit.

Rnd 14: *K2, k2tog, rep from * around—30 sts.

Rnd 15: Knit.

Rnd 16: *K1, k2tog, rep from * around—20 sts.

Rnd 17: *K2tog, rep from * around—10 sts.

Cut yarn, leaving 36" (91 cm) for sewing. Thread a tapestry needle onto the cut end, draw yarn through the rem sts and gather up, go through these sts again and fasten off securely. Weave in ends.

Blocking is not recommended for this pattern stitch.

Child's Patchwork Sweater

This sweater gives the knitter an opportunity to try several textured stitches in one garment. We use Double Seed stitch (page 50), Berry stitch (page 62), Mock Cable stitch (page 128), and Rib stitch IV (page 130).

Skill Level: Intermediate

Note: Always change colors from wrong side, and always twist colors by picking up new color from underneath color that you are dropping.

Back

With size 3 needles and A, cast on 76 (84, 92) sts. Work in k1, p1 ribbing for 10 (10, 12) rows, pm on last row after 38 (42, 46) sts.

Change to size 6 needles and work as follows:

First Patt Tier

Row 1 (WS): With A, k1, *(k1, yo, k1) all in same st, p3tog, rep from * until 1 st before marker, k1, sm, join B, k2, **p2, k2, rep from ** to end of row.

Row 2: With B, p2, *k2, p2, rep from * to marker, drop B, pick up A, k1, **p1, k3, rep from ** to last st, end k1.

Row 3: With A, k1, *p3tog, (k1, yo, k1) all in the same st, rep from * to 1 st before marker, k1, drop A, pick up B, p2, **k2, p2, rep from ** to end of row.

Row 4: With B, k2, *p2, k2, rep from * to marker, drop B, pick up A, k1, **k3, p1, rep from ** to last st, k1.

Rep Rows 1–4 until piece measures 6½ (7, 7½)" [16.5 (18, 19) cm] above ribbing, ending with a RS row.

Fasten off A and B.

Next row (WS): Rejoin B at beg of row, purl across to marker; join C, purl to end of row.

Next row: With C, p to marker, drop C, pick up B, p to end of row.

Second Patt Tier

Row 1 (WS): With B, purl to marker, drop B, pick up C, k2, *p2, k2, rep from * to end of row.

Row 2: With C, p2, *k1, yo, k1, p2, rep from * to marker, drop C, pick up B, k to end of row.

Row 3: With B, p2, *k2, p2, rep from * to marker, drop B, pick up C, k2, **p3, k2, rep from ** to end of row.

YOU WILL NEED

Yarn

- Lightweight
- Shown: Ann Geddes Baby Yarn, 80% acrylic, 20% nylon, 3 oz (85 g)/340 yds (310 m): Posy #591 (A), 1 (1, 2) skeins; Rocking Horse #936 (B), 1 (1, 1) skein; Robin #504 (C), 1 (1, 1) skein

Needles

- Sizes 3 (3.25 mm) and 6 (4 mm) or size to obtain gauge

Notions

- Stitch markers
- Tapestry needle
- Six decorative buttons (optional)

Gauge

- 23 sts = 4" (10 cm) in stockinette stitch on size 6 needles
- Although each patt has the same multiple, the gauge varies slightly with each patt; all evens out with blocking.
- Take time to check gauge.

Sizes

- Child's 2 (4, 6)
- Finished chest: 24 (26, 28)" [61 (66, 71) cm]
- Finished length: 13½ (14½, 15½)" [34 (37, 39.5) cm]

(continued)

Child's Patchwork Sweater (continued)

Row 4: With C, p2, *yarn back (yb), sl 1, k2, psso both k sts, p2, rep from * to marker, drop C, pick up B, k2, **p2, k2, rep from ** to end of row.

Rep Rows 1–4 for patt until Second patt Tier measures 5½ (6, 6½)" [12.5 (15, 16.5) cm], ending with patt Row 4.

Right Neck Shape

Next row (WS): P 23 (24, 25), turn, leaving rem sts unworked.

Cont patt as established, dec 1 st at neck edge every row 3 (3, 3) times. Bind off rem 20 (21, 22) sts.

Left Neck Shape

Place center 30 (36, 42) sts on holder. Rejoin C at neck edge and work rem 23 (24, 25) sts making sure to keep patt as established, dec 1 st at neck edge, every row 3 (3, 3) times. Bind off rem 20 (21, 22) sts.

Front

Work same as Back except start neck shaping at 5 (5½, 6)" [12.5 (14, 15) cm].

Sleeves (make 2)

With A and size 3 needles, cast on 42 (42, 44) sts. Work in k1, p1 ribbing for 10 rows. Knit 1 row, inc 4 (4, 6) sts evenly spaced across row—46 (46, 50) sts. Change to size 6 needles. Work in Double Seed patt as on Front and Back, inc 1 st each side every 8th row, 9 (10, 10) times, making sure to keep patt as established as sts are inc'd—64 (66, 70) sts. Work even in patt until Sleeve measures 10½ (11, 11½)" [26.5 (28, 29) cm] from beg. Bind off loosely.

Neckband

Sew left shoulder seam. With RS facing, using size 3 needles and A, starting at right shoulder, pick up and k5 (5, 5) sts along right side of Back neck, k30 (36, 42) sts from Back holder, pick up and k5 (5, 5) sts along left side of Back neck, pick up and k10 (10, 10) sts along left side of Front neck, k30 (36, 42) sts from Front holder, pick up and k10 sts along right side of Front neck—90 (102, 114) sts. Work in k1, p1 ribbing for 12 rows. Change to size 6 needles. Work 2 more rows in ribbing. Bind off loosely in ribbing.

Finishing

Sew right shoulder and neckband seam. Fold neckband in half and sew to inside. Mark center of Sleeve, pin in place with center of Sleeve top matching shoulder seam (edges of Sleeve top should reach top of first patt group). Sew Sleeve in place. Sew side and underarm seams. Weave in ends.

Blocking: Thoroughly wet garment in cold water, place on a padded surface, using rust-proof pins, pin into shape, allow to dry.

Sew on decorative buttons, if desired.

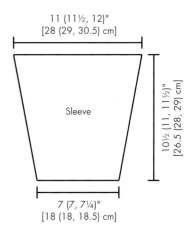

11 (11½, 12)"
[28 (29, 30.5) cm]

Sleeve

10½ (11, 11½)"
[26.5 (28, 29) cm]

7 (7, 7¼)"
[18 (18, 18.5) cm]

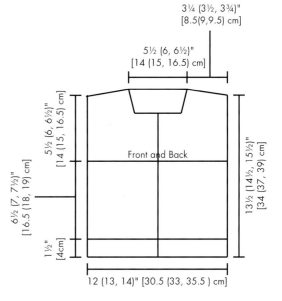

3¼ (3½, 3¾)"
[8.5 (9, 9.5) cm]

5½ (6, 6½)"
[14 (15, 16.5) cm]

5½ (6, 6½)"
[14 (15, 16.5) cm]

Front and Back

6½ (7, 7½)"
[16.5 (18, 19) cm]

1½"
[4cm]

13½ (14½, 15½)"
[34 (37, 39) cm]

12 (13, 14)" [30.5 (33, 35.5) cm]

Honeycomb and Brioche Stitches

Honeycomb and brioche stitch patterns make interesting, thick fabric. However, they can be very tricky to work and are difficult to fix if you make a mistake while knitting. Many honeycomb patterns are worked by knitting a stitch in the row below the next stitch on the needle, and this can be confusing if you are not acquainted with the maneuver. Before using any of these stitch patterns in a project, perfect your technique by making a practice swatch. The inviting texture of these stitches makes them well worth learning.

Piqué

Skill Level: Intermediate

Note: To knit stitch two rows below, follow stitch down two rows, place point of needle in that stitch, knit as usual, allow original stitch to fall off needle.

Cast on a multiple of 4 plus 1.

Row 1: K1, purl across row to last st, k1.

Row 2 and all even-numbered rows: Knit.

Row 3: K1, p3, *k1 st 2 rows below, p3, rep from * to last st, end k 1.

Row 5: K1, purl to last st, k1.

Row 7: K1, p1, k1 st 2 rows below, *p3, k1 st 2 rows below, rep from * to last 2 sts, end p1, k1.

Row 8: Knit.

Rep Rows 1–8 for pattern.

Brioche

Skill Level: Experienced

Note: All the slipped stitches are slipped as to knit with yarn to back.

Cast on a multiple of 3 plus 2.

Row 1 (WS): K1, *yo, sl 1, k2tog tbl, rep from *, end k1.

(Note: After initial row, the k2tog will be worked in the yo from previous row and the next st.)

Row 2: K3, *sl 1 (all the sl sts will be the yo's from previous row), k2, rep from *, end sl 1, k1.

Row 3: K1, *k2tog tbl, (k2tog is worked in the yo from previous row and the next st), yo, sl 1, rep from *, end k1.

Row 4: K2, *sl 1 (all the sl sts will be the yo's from previous row), k2, rep from * across row.

Rep Rows 1–4 for pattern.

Brioche Rib

Skill Level: Intermediate

Cast on an even number of stitches.

Row 1: Knit across row.

Row 2: K1, *k1, k1 in row below, rep from * to last 3 sts, end k3.

Rep Row 2 for pattern.

Slip Stitch Honeycomb

Skill Level: Experienced

Note: To make a yarn over for this stitch, it is necessary to bring yarn from back to front over the right needle, then between two needles and to the back again, so that yarn is in back as you slip the stitches.

All slipped stitches are slipped as to purl.

This pattern has a foundation row, which is not repeated again.

Cast on an even number of stitches.

Foundation row (WS): K1, *k1, yo, sl 1, rep from *, end k1.

Row 1: K2, *sl the yo st, k2, rep from * across row.

Row 2: K1, *yo, sl 1, k the yo and the next st tog, rep from *, end k1.

Row 3: K1, *k2, sl the yo st, rep from *, end k1.

Row 4: K1, *k the yo and the next st tog, yo, sl 1, rep from *, end k1.

Rep Rows 1–4 for pattern.

Alternating Wasp

Skill Level: Intermediate

Cast on a multiple of 4 plus 2.

Rows 1, 2, 5, 6, 8, 11, and 12: K1, *p2, k2, rep from *, end k1.

Rows 3 and 9: K1, *p2, yarn front, sl 2, rep from *, end k1.

Rows 4 and 10: K1, *yarn back (yb), sl 2, k2, rep from *, end k1.

Row 7: K1, *p2, k tog the 2 loops of previous 2 rows and the next st, k1, rep from *, end k1.

Row 13: K1, *p 2, k1, k tog the 2 loops of previous 2 rows, rep from *, end k1.

Row 14: Same as Row 1.

Rep Rows 3–14 for pattern.

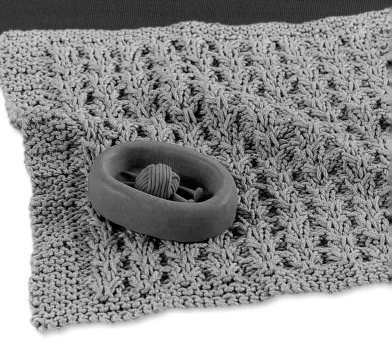

Honeycomb Washcloth

Washcloths are fun to knit because they allow you to try out new stitch patterns and can be completed quickly. Textured stitches like these honeycomb patterns, knitted in natural fibers like cotton or linen, make a washcloth extra absorbent. Useful in the bathroom or kitchen, washcloths also make great gifts.

YOU WILL NEED

Yarn

- Medium weight
- Shown: Tahki Cotton Classic, 100% mercerized cotton, 1.75 oz (50 g)/108 yds (100 m): Lime Green #3760, 1 skein

Needles

- Size 6 (4 mm) or size to obtain gauge

Gauge

- 20 sts = 4" (10 cm) in patt st
- Take time to check gauge.

Sizes

- Approximately: 10" × 10" (25.5 × 25.5 cm)

Skill Level: Easy

Note: When knitting the two loops from previous rows, together with the next stitch, insert right-hand needle under both loops, insert into next stitch, knit off all together.

Washcloth

Cast on 50 sts.

Knit 4 rows.

Beg patt as follows:

Row 1 (RS): K4, *p2, k2, rep from * to last 6 sts, p2, k4.

Row 2: K4, *k2, pk2, rep from * to last 6 sts, k6.

Row 3: K4, *p2, yarn front (yf) sl 2, rep from * to last 6 sts, p2, k4.

Row 4: K4, *k2, yarn back (yb) sl 2; rep from * to last 6 sts, k6.

Row 5: K4, *p2, k2, rep from * to last 6 sts, p2, k4.

Row 6: K4, *k2, p2, rep from * to last 6 sts, k6.

Row 7: K4, *p2, k the 2 loops of Rows 3 and 4 and the next st together, k1, rep from * to last 6 sts, p2, k4.

Row 8: K4, *k2, p2, rep from * to last 6 sts, k6.

Row 9: Same as Row 3.

Row 10: Same as Row 4.

Row 11: K4, p2, *k2, p2, rep from * to last 4 sts, k4.

Row 12: K4, *k2, p2, rep from * to last 6 sts, k6.

Row 13: K4, *p2, k1, k the 2 loops of Rows 9 and 10 and the next st together, rep from * to last 6 sts, p2, k4.

Row 14: K4, *k2, p2, rep from * to last 6 sts, k6.

Rep Rows 3–14 for pattern.

Work patt for 9½" (24 cm).

Knit 4 rows.

Bind off in knit.

Finishing

If blocking is necessary, pin into 10" × 10" (25.5 × 25.5 cm) square, spritz with water, allow to dry. Do not press with iron.

YOU WILL NEED

Yarn

- Medium weight
- Shown: Lily Sugar 'n Cream, 100% cotton, 2.5 oz (70 g), 20 yds (109 m): #270659 Hot Pink, 1 skein; #270656 Hot Purple, 1 skein; #270660 Hot Blue, 1 skein

Needles

- Size 6 (4 mm) needles or size to obtain gauge.

Notions

- Stitch markers

Gauge

- 18 sts = 4" (10 cm) in patt for A and B.
- 15 sts = 4" (10 cm) in patt for C.
- Take time to check gauge.

Size

- Approximately 10" x 10" (25.5 cm x 25.5 cm)

Set of Three Hot Pads

The honeycomb and brioche stitches are a little tricky to master, so practice your skill on this set of hot pads. The heavy woven textures and the 100% worsted weight cotton yarn are a perfect choice for this project.

Skill Level: Intermediate

A: Piqué Stitch

Cast on 43 sts.

Work in Seed/Moss St (page 49) for 6 rows.

Place a marker 5 sts in from each end. Cont as follows: Keeping the 5 sts on each end in Seed/Moss St and center 33 sts in Pique St (page 135), work until 9" (23 cm) from beg.

Work 6 rows Seed/Moss St. Bind off in patt.

B: Alternating Wasp Stitch

Cast on 44 sts.

Work in Seed/Moss St (page 49) for 6 rows.

Place a marker 5 sts in from each end. Cont as follows: Keeping the 5 sts on each end in Seed/Moss St and center 34 sts in Alternating Wasp Stitch (page 137), work until 9" (23 cm) from beg. .

Work 6 rows seed st. Bind off in patt.

C: Brioche Rib Stitch

Cast on 44 sts.

Work in Seed/Moss St (page 49) for 6 rows.

Place a marker 5 sts in from each end. Cont as follows: Keeping the 5 sts on each end in Seed/Moss St and center 34 sts in Brioce Rib (page 136), work until 9" (23 cm) from beg.

Work 6 rows Seed/Moss St. Bind off in patt.

Eyelets

Eyelet patterns are similar to lace patterns, but most are not quite as airy as lace. These patterns have little holes (usually made by making yarn overs) spaced at different intervals to create interesting designs. Very versatile, eyelets work wonderfully for a variety of projects, from baby sweaters to blankets. By changing the size of your knitting needles and yarn, you can dramatically change the look of the stitches.

Boxed Eyelets I

Skill Level: Easy

Note: When making a yarn over, before purling the next st, bring yarn forward around needle and back to front.

Cast on a multiple of 8 plus 3.

Row 1 (RS): K2, *p3, k5, rep from * to last st, end k1.

Row 2: P1, *p5, k3, rep from * to last 2 sts, end p2.

Row 3: K2, *p1, yo, p2tog, k5, rep from * to last st, end k1.

Row 4: P1, *p5, k3, rep from * to last 2 sts, end p2.

Row 5: K2, *p3, k5, rep from * to last st, end k1.

Row 6: Purl.

Row 7: K1, *k5, p3, rep from * to last 2 sts, end k2.

Row 8: P2, *k3, p5, rep from * to last st, end p1.

Row 9: K1, *k5, p1, yo, p2tog, rep from * to last 2 sts, end k2.

Row 10: P2, *k3, p5, rep from * to last st, end p1.

Row 11: K1, *k5, p3, rep from * to last 2 sts, end k2.

Row 12: Purl.

Rep Rows 1–12 for pattern.

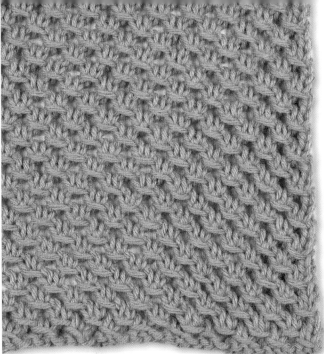

Diagonal Cross Stitch

Skill Level: Intermediate

Cast on a multiple of 3 plus 2.

Row 1: K1, *sl 1, k2, psso both k sts, yo, rep from * across row (making sure to work last yo before end), end k1.

Row 2: K1, p to last st, k1.

Row 3: K2, *yo, sl 1, k2, psso both k sts, rep from * to last 3 sts, end k3.

Row 4: K1, p to last st, k1.

Rep Rows 1–4 for pattern.

Easy Eyelets

Skill Level: Easy

Cast on an even number of stitches.

Row 1 (WS): K1, p to last st, k1.

Row 2: K1, p to last st, k1.

Row 3: K1, p to last st, k1.

Row 4: K1, *yo, sl 1 pwise, k1, psso, rep from * to last st, k1.

Rep Rows 1–4 for pattern.

Boxed Eyelets I Reverse

Skill Level: Easy

Note: When making a yarn over, before purling the next st, bring yarn forward around needle and back to front.

Cast on a multiple of 8 plus 3.

Row 1 (WS): K2, *p3, k5, rep from * to last st, end k1.

Row 2: P1, *p5, k3, rep from * to last 2 sts, end p2.

Row 3: K2, *p1, yo, p2tog, k5, rep from * to last st, end k1.

Row 4: P1, *p5, k3, rep from * to last 2 sts, end p2.

Row 5: K2, *p3, k5, rep from * to last st, end k1.

Row 6: Purl.

Row 7: K1, *k5, p3, rep from * to last 2 sts, end k2.

Row 8: P2, *k3, p5, rep from * to last st, end p1.

Row 9: K1, *k5, p1, yo, p2tog, rep from * to last 2 sts, end k2.

Row 10: P2, *k3, p5, rep from * to last st, end p1.

Row 11: K1, *k5, p3, rep from * to last 2 sts, end k2.

Row 12: Purl.

Rep Rows 1–12 for pattern.

Boxed Eyelets II

Skill Level: Intermediate

Psso: Pass the slipped stitch over the knit stitch.

P2sso: Pass both slipped stitches over the knit stitch.

Cast on a multiple of 8 plus 7.

Row 1 (WS): Purl.

Row 2: K5, sl 1, k1, psso, yo, k1, yo, k2tog, *k3, sl 1, k1, psso, yo, k1, yo, k2tog, rep from *, end k5.

Row 3 and all WS rows: Purl.

Row 4: K6, yo, sl 2, k1, p2sso, yo, *k5, yo, sl 2, k1, p2sso, yo, rep from *, end k6.

Row 6: Same as Row 2.

Row 8: K1, sl 1, k1, psso, yo, k1, yo, k2tog, *k3, sl 1, k1, psso, yo, k1, yo, k2tog, rep from *, end k1.

Row 10: K2, yo, sl 2, k1, p2sso, yo, *k5, yo, sl 2, k1, p2sso, yo, rep from *, end k2.

Row 12: Same as Row 8.

Rep Rows 1–12 for pattern.

Boxed Eyelets III

Skill Level: Intermediate

Cast on a multiple of 6 plus 5.

Row 1 (RS): K1, *yo, sl 1, k2tog, psso, yo, k3, rep from * to last 4 sts, end yo, sl 1, k2tog, psso, yo, k1.

Row 2 and all WS rows: Purl.

Row 3: Same as Row 1.

Row 5: Knit.

Row 7: K4, *yo, sl 1, k2tog, psso, yo, k3, rep from *, end k1.

Row 9: Same as Row 7.

Row 11: Knit.

Row 12: Purl.

Rep Rows 1–12 for pattern.

Petite Bells

Skill Level: Intermediate

Note: To slip two stitches together as to knit, place right-hand needle as you would to knit next two stitches together, slip them to left-hand needle without knitting them.

To pass both the slipped stitches over the next knit stitch, place left-hand needle in both stitches together, and bring over the knit stitch.

Cast on an even number of stitches.

Row 1 (RS): K1, *p1, sl2tog as to k, k1, pass 2 slipped sts over the k st, p1, rep from *, end k1.

Row 2: K1, *(k1, p1, k1) in same st, k1, rep from * across row, end k1.

Row 3: K1, *p1, k3, p1, rep from * across row, end k1.

Row 4: K1, *k1, p3, k1, rep from * across row, end k1.

Rep Rows 1–4 for pattern.

Little Bells

Skill Level: Experienced

Cast on a multiple of 8 plus 7.

Row 1 (WS): K3, *p1 through the back loop (tbl), k3, rep from * across row.

Row 2: P3, *k1 tbl, p3, rep from * across row.

Row 3: K3, p1 tbl, k3, *(k1, p1, k1, p1, k1) in next st, k3, p1 tbl, k3, rep from * across row.

Row 4: P3, k1 tbl, p3, *k5, p3, k1 tbl, p3, rep from * across row.

Row 5: K3, p1 tbl, k3, *p5, k3, p1 tbl, k3, rep from * across row.

Row 6: P3, k1 tbl, p3, *ssk, k1, k2tog, p3, k1 tbl, p3, rep from * across row.

Row 7: K3, p1 tbl, k3, *p3, k3, p1 tbl, k3, rep from * across row.

Row 8: P3, k1 tbl, p3, *sl 1, k2tog, psso, p3, k1 tbl, p3, rep from * across row.

Rows 9 and 10: Same as Rows 1 and 2.

Row 11: K3, (k1, p1, k1, p1, k1) in next st, k3, *p1 tbl, (k1, p1, k1, p1, k1) in next st, k3, rep from * across row.

Row 12: P3, k5, p3, *k1 tbl, p3, k5, p3, rep from * across row.

Row 13: K3, p5, k3, *p1 tbl, k3, p5, k3, rep from * across row.

Row 14: P3, ssk, k1, k2tog, p3, *k1 tbl, p3, ssk, k1, k2tog, p3, rep from * across row.

Row 15: K3, p3, k3, *p1 tbl, k3, p3, k3, rep from * row.

Row 16: P3, sl 1, k2tog, psso, p3, *k1 tbl, p3, sl 1, k2tog, psso, p3, rep from * across row.

Rep Rows 1–16 for pattern.

Little Shells I

Skill Level: Easy

Cast on a multiple of 6 plus 3.

Row 1: K2, *yo by wrapping yarn over needle to back then to front again, p1, p3tog, p1, yo, k1, rep from * to last st, end k1.

Row 2: K1, purl to last st, k1.

Row 3: Knit.

Row 4: K1, purl to last st, k1.

Rep Rows 1–4 for pattern.

Little Shells II

Skill Level: Easy

Cast on a multiple of 7 plus 2.

Row 1: Knit.

Row 2: Purl.

Row 3: K2, *yo by wrapping yarn over needle to back then to front again, p1, p3tog, p1, yo, k2, rep from * across row.

Row 4: Purl.

Rep Rows 1–4 for pattern.

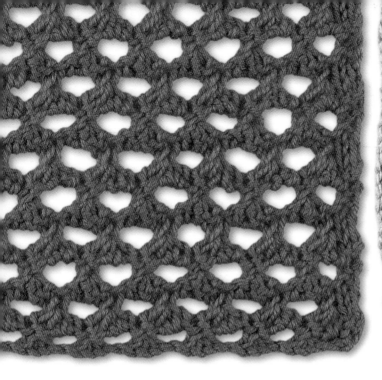

Eyelet Lace

Skill Level: Easy

Note: For this pattern, yarn overs are made by wrapping yarn from front, back over needle, to front again.

Cast on a multiple of 4.

Row 1: P2, *yo, p4tog, rep from *, end p2.

Row 2: K2, *work (k1, p1, k1) into the yo space, rep from *, end k2.

Row 3: Knit.

Rep Rows 1–3 for pattern.

Eyelet Ferns

Skill Level: Easy

Cast on a multiple of 10 plus 2.

Rows 1, 3, 5, 7, 9, 11, 13, and 15 (WS): Purl.

Rows 2, 4, 6, and 8: K2, *yo, k2tog, k4, ssk, yo, k2, rep from * across row.

Rows 10, 12, 14, and 16: K3, *ssk, yo, k2, yo, k2tog, k4, rep from *, end last rep k3.

Rep Rows 1–16 for pattern.

Diagonal Eyelets

Skill Level: Easy

Cast on a multiple of 4.

Row 1 (WS): K3, *p2, k2, rep from *, end k1.

Row 2: K1, p2, *k2, p2, rep *, end k1.

Row 3: K3, *p1, k1 in the yarn between the st just worked and the next st (M1), p1, k2, rep from *, end k1.

Row 4: K1, p2, *k3, pass first st of 3 over next 2, p2, rep from *, end k1.

Row 5: K1, p2, *k2, p2, rep from *, end k1.

Row 6: K3, *p2, k2, rep from *, end last rep k3.

Row 7: K1, p1, M1, p1, *k2, p1, M1, p1, rep from *, end k1.

Row 8: K1, *k3, pass first st of 3 over 2, p2, rep from * to last 4 sts, end k3, pass first st of 3 over 2, k1.

Rep Rows 1–8 for pattern.

Eyelet Towers

Skill Level: Easy

Note: For this pattern always yarn over by wrapping yarn toward back and around before purling two together.

Cast on a multiple of 8 plus 5.

Row 1: K1, p1, *yo, p2tog, p6, rep from * to last 3 sts, end yo, p2tog, k1.

Rows 2, 4, and 6: K2, p1, *k7, p1, rep from * to last 2 sts, end k2.

Rows 3, 5, and 7: K1, p1, *k1, p7, rep from * to last 3 sts, end k1, p1, k1.

Row 8: K1, purl across row to last st, k1.

Row 9: K1, p5, *yo, p2tog, p6, rep from * to last 7 sts, end yo, p2tog, p4, k1.

Rows 10, 12, and 14: K6, p1, *k7, p1, rep from * to last 6 sts, end k6.

Rows 11, 13, and 15: K1, p5, *k1, p7, rep from * to last 7 sts, end k1, p5, k1.

Row 16: K1, purl across row to last st, k1.

Rep Rows 1–16 for pattern.

Fancy Eyelets

Skill Level: Easy

Cast on a multiple of 5.

Row 1 (RS): K4, *p2, k3, rep from * to last st, end k1.

Row 2: K1, *p3, k1, yo, k1, rep from * to last 4 sts, end p3, k1.

Row 3: K4, *p1, k1, p1, k3, rep from * to last st, end k1.

Row 4: K1, *p3 tog, (k1, yo) twice, k1, rep from * to last 4 sts, end p3tog, k1.

Row 5: K1, (k1, yo, k1) in next st, *p1, p3tog, p1, (k1, yo, k1) in next st, rep from * to last st, end k1.

Row 6: K1, *p3, yarn back, sl 1, k the next st and leave on left-hand needle, psso the st just worked, then knit the st that was left on the left-hand needle together with the next st, rep from * to last 4 sts, end p3, k1.

Rep Rows 1–6 for pattern.

Fancy Eyelets Reverse

Skill Level: Easy

Cast on a multiple of 5.

Row 1 (WS): K4, *p2, k3, rep from * to last st, end k1.

Row 2: K1, *p3, k1, yo, k1, rep from * to last 4 sts, end p3, k1.

Row 3: K4, *p1, k1, p1, k3, rep from * to last st, end k1.

Row 4: K1, *p3tog, (k1, yo) twice, k1, rep from * to last 4 sts, end p3tog, k1.

Row 5: K1, (k1, yo, k1) in next st, *p1, p3tog, p1, (k1, yo, k1) in next st, rep from * to last st, end k1.

Row 6: K1, *p3, yarn back, sl 1, k the next st and leave on left-hand needle, psso the st just worked, then knit the st that was left on the left-hand needle together with the next st, rep from * to last 4 sts, end p3, k1.

Rep Rows 1–6 for pattern.

Eyelet Mesh

Skill Level: Easy

Cast on an even number of stitches.

Row 1: K1, *yo, p2tog, rep from * to last st, end yarn back (yb), k1.

Row 2: K1 *yo, p next st and yo tog, rep from * to last st, end yb, k1.

Rep Row 2 for pattern.

Eyelet Rib

Skill Level: Easy

Cast on a multiple of 4 plus 3.

Rows 1 and 3: K1, *k1, p3, rep from *, end k2.

Rows 2 and 4: K1, p1, *k3, p1, rep from *, end k1.

Row 5: K1, *k1, p1, yo by wrapping yarn around needle, p2tog, rep from *, end k2.

Row 6: Same as Row 2.

Rep Rows 1–6 for pattern.

Eyelets and Pleats

Skill Level: Intermediate

Note: When making a yarn over before a purl stitch, wrap yarn around needle front to back to front.

Cast on a multiple of 8 plus 2.

Row 1 (RS): K1, *k6, k2tog, yo, rep from * to last st, end k1.

Row 2: K1, *k1, p7, rep from * to last st, end k1.

Row 3: K1, *k5, k2tog, yo, p1, rep from * to last st, end k1.

Row 4: K1, *k2, p6, rep from * to last st, end k1.

Row 5: K1, *k4, k2tog, yo, p2, rep from * to last st, end k1.

Row 6: K1, *k3, p5, rep from * to last st, end k1.

Row 7: K1, *k3, k2tog, yo, p3, rep from * to last st, end k1.

Row 8: K1, *k4, p4, rep from * to last st, end k1.

Row 9: K1, *k2, k2tog, yo, p4, rep from * to last st, end k1.

Row 10: K1, *k5, p3, rep from * to last st, end k1.

Row 11: K1,* k1, k2tog, yo, p5, rep from * to last st, end k1.

Row 12: K1, *k6, p2, rep from * to last st, end k1.

Row 13: K1, *k2tog, yo, p6, rep from * to last st, end k1.

Row 14: K1, *k7, p1, rep from * to last st, end k1.

Rep Rows 1–14 for pattern.

Textured Eyelets

Skill Level: Intermediate

Cast on a multiple of 3 plus 2.

Row 1 (WS): K1, *k1, p2, rep from * to last st, end k1.

Row 2: K1, *k1, yo, k2tog, rep from * to last st, end k1.

Row 3: K1, *p1, k1 in the yo, p1, rep from * to last st, end k1.

Row 4: K1, *k1, k2tog, yo, rep from * to last st, end k1.

Row 5: K1, *k1 in the yo, p2, rep from * to last st, end k1.

Rep Rows 2–5 for pattern.

Zigzag Eyelets

Skill Level: Intermediate

Cast on a multiple of 3 plus 2.

Row 1 (RS): K1, *k1, p2, rep from * to last st, end k1.

Row 2: K1, *k1, yo, k2tog, rep from * to last st, end k1.

Row 3: K1, *p1, k1 in the yo, p1, rep from * to last st, end k1.

Row 4: K1, *k1, k2tog, yo, rep from * to last st, end k1.

Row 5: K1, *k1 in the yo, p2, rep from * to last st, end k1.

Rep Rows 2–5 for pattern.

Spiral Eyelets

Skill Level: Intermediate

Note: When making a yarn over before a purl stitch, it is necessary to wind yarn around needle from front to back to front.

Cast on a multiple of 6 plus 5.

Row 1 (RS): K4, p3, *k3, yo, p3, rep from * to last 4 sts, k4.

Row 2: K3, p1, k3, *p4, k3, rep from * to last 4 sts, p1, k3.

Row 3: K4, p3, *k1, k2tog, yo, k1, p3, rep from * to last 4 sts, k4.

Row 4: K3, p1, k3, *p2, p2tog, k3, rep from * to last 4 sts, p1, k3.

Row 5: K4, p3, *k1, yo, k2tog, p3, rep from * to last 4 sts, k4.

Row 6: K3, p1, k3, *p3, k3, rep from * to last 4 sts, p1, k3.

Rep Rows 1–6 for pattern.

Honeycomb Eyelets

Skill Level: Intermediate

P2tog-b: Purl two together from back loop

Cast on a multiple of 4.

Row 1 (RS): Knit.

Row 2: P2, *p2tog-b, yo, p2tog, rep from *, end p2.

Row 3: K3, *(k1, p1) into the yo of previous row, k2, rep from *, end k1.

Row 4: Purl.

Row 5: *K2tog, yo, ssk, rep from * across row.

Row 6: P1, *(k1, p1) into yo of previous row, p2, rep from *, end last rep p1.

Rep Rows 1–6 for pattern.

Eyelet Cloche

An open, airy eyelet stitch pattern is the perfect choice for a close-fitting cap. This cloche, sporting a sassy flower-and-leaf motif over one temple, is a nod to the Roaring Twenties. Isn't it fun to watch fashions recycle?

(continued)

Eyelet Cloche (continued)

YOU WILL NEED

Yarn

- Medium weight
- Shown: Lion Brand Vanna's Choice, 100% premium acrylic, 3.5 oz (100 g)/170 yds (156 m): Beige #123, 1 skein

Needles

- Sizes 8 (5 mm) and 10 (6 mm) or size to obtain gauge

Notions

- Sewing needle
- Small decorative bead (optional)

Gauge

- 12 sts = 4" (10 cm) in patt st on size 10 needles
- Take time to check gauge.

Sizes

- Finished size: 21" to 23" (53.5 to 58.5 cm)

Skill Level: Easy

Note: Stitch is loose and stretchy.

Cloche

With smaller needles, cast on 80 sts. Work in k1, p1 ribbing for 2" (5 cm). Change to larger needles and work patt as follows:

Row 1 (RS): K1, *yo, yf, sl 1 as to p, k1, psso; rep from *, end k1.

Rep Row 1 for pattern. Note: On subsequent rows, you will always be slipping the knit sts, and knit the yo sts.

Work in patt until piece measures 6½" (16.5 cm) from beg.

Shape Crown

Row 1: *K8, k2tog, rep from * across row.

Row 2: *K7, k2tog, rep from * across row.

Cont to dec 8 sts every row, always have 1 st less between decs each row, until 16 sts rem.

Cut yarn leaving a yard long end for sewing. Thread a tapestry needle with the cut end, draw thru rem sts on needle and gather up, go thru sts again and use same thread to sew back seam.

Finishing

Make 1 flower and 1 leaf (see below). Sew to side of hat.

Five-Petal Flower

With larger needles, cast on 62 sts.

Row 1 (WS): Purl.

Row 2: K2, *k1, sl this st back onto left needle, then lift the next 9 sts on left needle over this st and off the needle, yo, knit the first st again, k2, rep from * across (22 sts).

Row 3: P1, *p2tog, k1 in front, back, front and back of the yo, p1, rep from * to last st, end p1 (32 sts).

Row 4: K1, *sl 2, k1, p2sso, rep from *, end k1 (12 sts).

Row 5: *P2tog, rep from * across (6 sts), sl 2nd, 3rd, 4th, 5th, and 6th st over first st. Fasten off.

Sew a seam to form flower, place bead in center or work a French knot in center.

Leaf

With larger needles, cast on 5 sts.

Row 1 (RS): K2, yo, k1, yo, k2 (7 sts).

Row 2 and all even-numbered rows: Purl.

Row 3: K3, yo, k1, yo, k3 (9 sts).

Row 5: K4, yo, k1, yo, k4 (11 sts).

Row 7: K5, yo, k1, yo, k 5 (13 sts).

Row 9: K6, yo, k1, yo, k6 (15 sts).

Row 11: Ssk, k11, k2tog (13 sts).

Row 13: Ssk, k9, k2tog (11 sts).

Row 15: Ssk, k7, k2tog (9 sts).

Row 17: Ssk, k5, k2tog (7 sts).

Row 19: Ssk, k3, k2tog (5 sts).

Row 21: Ssk, k1, k2tog (3 sts).

Row 23: Sl 1, k2tog, psso (1 st).

Fasten off.

Ripples and Chevrons

The ripple stitch, with its many variations, is a classic pattern loved by knitters around the world. These are favored patterns for knitting blankets and shawls, but they also appear in everything from high-fashion clothing to baby items. Ripples and chevrons require a little patience on the part of beginners, but most of these patterns are easy to grasp. You can achieve amazing results by using a ripple pattern with self-striping yarn.

Chevron

Skill Level: Intermediate

Cast on a multiple of 18 plus 1.

Rows 1 and 3: P1, *(k2, p2) twice, k1, (p2, k2) twice, p1, rep from * across row.

Rows 2 and 4: K1, *(p2, k2) twice, p1, (k2, p2) twice, k1, rep from * across row.

Rows 5 and 7: P1, *p1, k2, p2, k2, p3 (k2, p2) twice, rep from * across row.

Rows 6 and 8: K1, *k1, p2, k2, p2, k3, (p 2, k2) twice, rep from * across row.

Rows 9 and 11: Same as Rows 2 and 4.

Rows 10 and 12: Same as Rows 1 and 3.

Rows 13 and 15: Same as Rows 6 and 8.

Rows 14 and 16: Same as Rows 5 and 7.

Rep Rows 1–16 for pattern.

Parasol

Skill level: Intermediate

Cast on a multiple of 18 plus 1.

Row 1 (RS): Purl.

Row 2: P2, *(k3, p1) 3 times, k3, p3, rep from *, end last rep p2.

Row 3: K1, *yo, k1, p2tog, p1, (k1, p3) twice, k1, p1, p2tog, k1, yo, k1, rep from * across row.

Row 4: P3, *k2, (p1, k3) twice, p1, k2, p5 rep from *, end last rep p3.

Row 5: K2, *yo, k1, p2, (k1, p1, p2tog) twice, k1, p2, k1, yo, k3, rep from *, end last rep k2.

Row 6: P4, *(k2, p1) 3 times, k2, p7, rep from *, end last rep p4.

Row 7: K3, *yo, k1, p2tog, (k1, p2) twice, k1, p2tog, k1, yo, k5, rep from *, end last rep k3.

Row 8: P5, *k1, (p1, k2) twice, p1, k1, p9, rep from *, end last rep p5.

Row 9: K4, *yo, k1, p1, (k1, p2tog) twice, k1, p1, k1, yo, k7, rep from *, end last rep k4.

Row 10: P6, *k1, (p1, k1) 3 times, p11, rep from *, end last rep p6.

Rep Rows 1–10 for pattern.

Feather and Fan

Skill Level: Intermediate

Cast on a multiple of 18 plus 2.

Row 1: Knit.

Row 2: K1, purl to last st, k1.

Row 3: K1, (yo, k1) 3 times, *(k2tog) 6 times, (yo, k1) 6 times, rep from * to last 4 sts, end (yo, k1) 3 times, k1.

Row 4: Knit.

Rep Rows 1–4 for pattern.

Feather and Fan II

Skill Level: Easy

Cast on a multiple of 18 plus 2.

Row 1 (RS): Knit.

Row 2: Purl.

Row 3: K1, *(k2tog) 3 times, (yo, k1) 6 times, (k2tog) 3 times, rep from * to last st, end k1.

Rows 4, 5, and 6: Knit.

Rep Rows 1–6 for pattern.

Simple Ripple

Skill Level: Easy

Cast on a multiple of 8 plus 6.

Row 1 (RS): K6, *p2, k6, rep from * across row.

Row 2: K1, *p4, k4 rep from *, end p4, k1.

Row 3: P2, *k2, p2, rep from * across row.

Row 4: P1, *k4, p4, rep from *, end k4, p1.

Row 5: K2, *p2, k6, rep from *, end p2, k2.

Row 6: P6, *k2, p6, rep from * across row.

Row 7: P1, *k4, p4, rep from *, end k4, p1.

Row 8: K2, *p2, k2, rep from * across row.

Row 9: K1, *p4, k4, rep from *, end p4, k1.

Row 10: P2, *k2, p6, rep from *, end k2, p2.

Rep Rows 1–10 for pattern.

Simple Ripple II

Skill Level: Easy

Cast on a multiple of 12 plus 4.

Rows 1 and 3: K1, *k in front and back of next st (inc made), k4, sl 1, k2 tog, psso, k4, inc in next st, rep from *, end k1.

Row 2: K1, purl to last st, k1.

Row 4: Knit.

Rep Rows 1–4 for pattern.

Fans

Skill Level: Intermediate

Note: In this pattern, unlike some other fan stitch patterns, the stitches are not increased and decreased on the same row. You will be decreasing on Rows 3, 4, and 5, then increasing on Row 6, so do not try counting your stitches each row.

Cast on a multiple of 15 plus 4.

Row 1 (WS): P4, *k11, p4, rep from * across row.

Row 2: K4, *p11, k4, rep from * across row.

Row 3: P2, *p2tog, p11, p2tog tbl, rep from *, end p2tog, p2.

Row 4: K2, *ssk, k9, k2tog, rep from *, end k2.

Row 5: P2, *p2tog, p7, p2tog tbl, rep from *, end p2.

Row 6: K4, *(yo, k1) 5 times, yo, k4, rep from * across row.

Rep Rows 1–6 for pattern.

Ripples and Ribs

Skill Level: Easy

Cast on a multiple of 14 plus 1.

Rows 1, 3, 5, 7, and 9 (WS): Purl.

Rows 2, 4, 6, 8, and 10: K1, *yo, k3, ssk, yo, sl 1, k2tog, psso, yo, k2tog, k3, yo, k1, rep from * across row.

Row 11: Knit.

Row 12: Purl.

Rep Rows 1–12 for pattern.

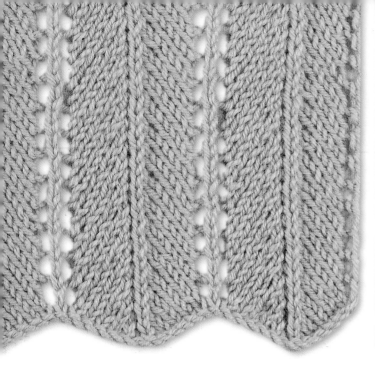

Ripples and Ribs II

Skill Level: Easy

Cast on a multiple of 13 plus 1.

Row 1: Purl.

Row 2: *K1, yo, k4, (k2tog) twice, k4, yo, rep from * across row, end k1.

Rep Rows 1 and 2 for pattern.

Ripples and Ribs III

Skill Level: Intermediate

Notes: To make the double decrease (DD) for this pattern, skip next stitch, insert point of right-hand needle as to knit in the next stitch and the skipped stitch, slip them together to right-hand needle, knit the next stitch, then pass both slipped stitches together over the knit stitch.

To purl, k one in the double yarn over, purl first, drop first wrap from needle, knit into the back of second wrap.

Cast on a multiple of 22 plus 3.

Foundation Row: Purl.

Row 1 (RS): K1, k2tog, k4, yo twice, k4, *DD, k4, yo twice, k4, rep from * to last 3 sts, end k2tog, k1.

Row 2: P6, (p1, k1) in the yo, *p9, (p1, k1) in the yo, rep from * to last 6 sts, end p6.

Rep Rows 1 and 2 for pattern.

Rocky Road

Skill Level: Easy

Cast on a multiple of 11.

Row 1 (RS): *K2tog, k2, inc 1 st in next st, k1, inc 1 st in next st, k2, k2tog tbl, rep from * to end of row.

Rows 2, 4, and 6: K1, p to last st, k1.

Rows 3 and 5: Same as Row 1.

Rows 7, 9, and 11: K1, p to last st, k1.

Rows 8 and 10: Knit.

Row 12: Knit.

Rep Rows 1–12 for pattern.

Striped Garter

Skill Level: Easy

Notes: Made with two colors A and B, follow pattern Rows 1 and 2 working 4 rows color A, 6 rows Col B.

Cast on with Col A.

Cast on a multiple of 14 plus 3.

Row 1 (RS): K1, sl 1, k1, psso, *k5, yo, k1, yo, k5, sl 2, k1, pass both sl sts over, rep from * to last 14 sts, end k5, yo, k1, yo, k5, k2tog, k1.

Row 2: K7, *k1 tbl, k1, k1 tbl, k11, rep from * to last 10 sts, end k1 tbl, k1, k1 tbl, k7.

Rep Rows 1 and 2 for pattern.

Waves

Skill Level: Experienced

Cast on a multiple of 10 plus 6.

Rows 1 and 2: Knit.

Row 3 (RS): K6, *yo twice, k1, yo 3 times, k1, yo 4 times, k1, yo 3 times, k1, yo twice, k6, rep from * across row.

Row 4: Knit across row, dropping all the yo's off the needle.

Rows 5 and 6: Knit.

Row 7: K1, rep from * of Row 3, end last rep k1.

Row 8: Same as Row 4.

Rep Rows 1–8 for pattern.

The Pines I

Skill Level: Intermediate

Note: This is one of those stitches where both sides of the work make a uniquely different fabric and can be used either way. This version begins the pattern on a right side row.

Cast on a multiple of 14 plus 5.

Row 1 (RS): K3, *yo, k2, p3, p3tog, p3, k2, yo, k1, rep from * to last 2 sts, end k2.

Row 2: K2, *p4, k7, p3, rep from * to last 3 sts, end p1, k2.

Row 3: K3, *k1, yo, k2, p2, p3tog, p2, k2, yo, k2, rep from * to last 2 sts, end k2.

Row 4: K2, *p5, k5, p4, rep from * to last 3 sts, end p1, k2.

Row 5: K3, *k2, yo, k2, p1, p3tog, p1, k2, yo, k3, rep from * to last 2 sts, end k2.

Row 6: K2, *p6, k3, p5, rep from * to last 3 sts, end p1, k2.

Row 7: K3, *k3, yo, k2, p3tog, k2, yo, k4, rep from * to last 2 sts, end k2.

Row 8: K2, *p7, k1, p6, rep from * to last 3 sts, end p1, k2.

Row 9: K3, *k4, yo, k1, sl 1, k2tog, psso, k1, yo, k5, rep from * to last 2 sts, end k2.

Row 10: K2, purl to last 2 sts, k2.

Row 11: K3, *k5, yo, sl 1, k2tog, psso, yo, k6, rep from * to last 2 sts, end k2.

Row 12: K2, purl to last 2 sts, k2.

Rep Rows 1–12 for pattern.

The Pines II

Skill Level: Intermediate

Note: This is one of those stitches where both sides of the work make a uniquely different fabric and can be used either way. This version begins the pattern on a wrong side row.

Cast on a multiple of 14 plus 5.

Row 1 (WS): K3, *yo, k2, p3, p3tog, p3, k2, yo, k1, rep from * to last 2 sts, end k2.

Rows 2–12: Same as Rows 2–12 of The Pines I.

Rep rows 1–12 for pattern.

Seed Chevron

Skill Level: Easy

Cast on a multiple of 98 plus 3.

Rows 1, 2, 3, and 4: K1, *p1, k1, rep from * across row.

Row 5: K1, *k1, yo, sl 1, k1, psso, k3, k2tog, yo, rep from *, end k2.

Row 6: K1, purl to last st, k1.

Row 7: K1, *k2, yo, sl 1, k1, psso, k1, k2tog, yo, k1, rep from *, end k2.

Row 8: K1, purl to last st, k1.

Row 9: K1, *k3, yo, sl 1, k2tog, psso, yo, k2, rep from *, end k2.

Row 10: K1, purl to last st, k1.

Rep Rows 1–10 for pattern.

Parasol Ripples Scarf

Ripples and chevrons work beautifully for creating fashion scarves. This one, knitted in a luxurious silk and bamboo blend yarn, feels like heaven against your neck. To make the curved scarf ends match, knit both sides separately from the end and sew the scarf together at the center. Crisscrossed ends are held in place with a large button. Wear the scarf with the tails tossed over one shoulder.

YOU WILL NEED

Yarn

- Lightweight
- Shown: Patons Silk Bamboo, 70% bamboo, 30% silk, 2.20 oz (85 g)/102 yds (93 m): Coral #85511, 2 balls

Needles

- Sizes 6 (4 mm) and 9 (5.5 mm) or size to obtain gauge

Notions

- One large button

Gauge

- 22 sts and 28 rows = 4" (10 cm) in patt st on size 9 needles
- Take time to check gauge.

Size

- Approximately 7" × 17" (18 × 43 cm)

Skill Level: Intermediate

Note: Scarf is made in two sections; join at back of neck.

Left Side

With size 9 needles, cast on 37 sts.

Foundation row: Knit.

Beg patt (multiple of 18 plus 1) as follows:

Row 1 (RS): Purl.

Row 2: P2, *(k3, p1) 3 times, k3, p3, rep from *, end last rep p2 instead of p3.

Row 3: K1, *yo, k1, p2tog, p1, (k1, p3) twice, k1, p1, p2tog, k1, yo, k1, rep from * to end.

Row 4: P3, *k2, (p1, k3) twice, p1, k2, p5, rep from *, end last rep p3 instead of p5.

Row 5: K2, *yo, k1, p2, (k1, p1, p2tog) twice, k1, p2, k1, yo, k3, rep from *, end k2.

Row 6: P4, *(k2, p1) 3 times, k2, p7, rep from *, end last rep p4 instead of p7.

Row 7: K3, *yo, k1, p2tog, (k1, p2) twice, k1, p2tog, k1, yo, k5, rep from *, end k3.

Row 8: P5, *k1, (p1, k2) twice, p1, k1, p9, rep from *, ending last rep p5 instead of p9.

Row 9. K4, *yo, k1, p1, (k1, p2tog) twice, k1, p1, k1, yo, k7, rep from *, end k4.

Row 10: P6, *k1, (p1, k1) 3 times, p11, rep from *, end last rep p6 instead of p11.

Rep Rows 1–10 until 5" (12.5 cm) from beg, ending with Row 10.

Change to size 6 needles. Knit 6 rows.

Change to size 9 needles. Beg with Row 1, work patt until piece is approximately 17" to 17½" (43 to 45 cm) long, ending with Row 10. Place sts on holder.

Right Side

Work same as Left Side until piece measures 5" (12.5 cm), ending with Row 10.

Change to size 6 needles. Knit 2 rows.

Buttonhole row: K16, bind off next 5 sts, k16.

Next row: K across, casting on 5 sts over the bound-off sts.

Knit 2 more rows.

Change to size 9 needles. Beg with Row 1, work patt until piece is approximately 17" to 17½" (43 to 45 cm) long, ending with Row 10. Place sts on holder.

Finishing

Join at back of neck: Using 3-needle bind off (page 21), with RSs facing, join Left and Right Sides together. Sew on button. Do not block.

YOU WILL NEED

Yarn

- Sport weight
- Shown: Lion Brand LB Collection Silk, 100% silk, 1.75 oz (50g)/163 yds (150 m): Aquarius #200, 4 skeins

Needles

- Size 9 (5.5 mm) or size to obtain gauge

Notions

- Stitch holder
- Tapestry needle

Gauge

- One complete patt repeat = 3" (7.5 cm)
- Take time to check gauge.

Size

- 18" × 68" (45.5 cm × 173 cm)

Ripples and Ribs Shawl

Wrap yourself in a luxurious silk shawl. This gorgeous yarn, available in rich colors, has beautiful drape. Knitted with a fun stitch, the result is a garment ready for the runway.

Skill Level: Easy

Note: This shawl is worked in two pieces to be joined at the neck edge using three-needle bind-off (page 21).

Shawl

Cast on 85 sts.

Work Ripples and Ribs pattern (page 159) until piece measures 34" (86 cm) from beg; do not fasten off, place sts on holder to be joined later.

Work another piece the same. Join two pieces at neck edge, using three-needle bind-off, to form shawl.

Finishing

If blocking is desired, lay shawl on a padded surface, spritz lightly with water, pat into shape, allow to dry.

Slip Stitches

These stitch patterns are formed by slipping stitches, without working them, from one needle to the other and passing the working yarn over these stitches. You can create a variety of intriguing patterns by varying the number of stitches slipped and by carrying the working yarn to the front or back of these stitches.

Butterfly

Skill Level: Intermediate

Cast on a multiple of 10 plus 9.

Rows 1, 3, 5, 7, and 9 (RS): K2, * with yarn in front (wf), sl 5, with yarn in back (wyb), k5, rep from *, end wyf, sl 5, wyb, k2.

Rows 2, 4, 6, and 8: Purl.

Row 10: P4, *in the next st (which is at the center of the slipped group) insert right-hand needle down through the 5 loose strands, bring needle up and transfer the 5 strands to left-hand needle, purl the 5 strands and the next st together as one st, p9, rep from *, end last rep p4.

Rows 11, 13, 15, 17, and 19: K7, *wyf, sl 5, wyb, k5, rep from *, end last rep with k7.

Rows 12, 14, 16, and 18: Purl.

Row 20: P9, *insert needle down through 5 loose strands, bring them up and purl them together with the next st as before, p9, rep from * across row.

Rep Rows 1–20 for pattern.

Little Butterfly

Skill Level: Intermediate

Cast on a multiple of 10 plus 7.

Rows 1, 3, and 5 (RS): K1, *k5, with yarn in front (wyf), sl 5, wyb, rep from *, end k6.

Rows 2 and 4: Purl.

Row 6: P8, *insert right-hand needle from below under the 3 loose strands on right side of work, yarn over needle and draw up a loop (gathering loop), purl the next st and sl gathering loop over purled st, p9, rep from *, end last rep p8.

Rows 7, 9, and 11: K1, *wyf, sl 5, wyb, k 5, rep from *, end wyf, sl 5, wyb k1.

Rows 8 and 10: Purl.

Row 12: P3, *lift 3 loose strands with gathering loop, purl the next st and slip loop over purl st as in Row 6, p9, rep from *, end last rep p3.

Rep Rows 1–12 for pattern.

Quilted Diamonds

Skill Level: Intermediate

Cast on a multiple of 4 plus 1.

Row 1: P1, *yarn in back (yb), sl 3, yarn in front (yf), p1, rep from * across row.

Row 2: Knit.

Row 3: Purl.

Row 4: K2, *place needle under loop formed by sl 3 in Row 1 and knit the loop and next st tog, k3, rep from * across row, end k2.

Row 5: P3, *yb, sl 3, yf, p1, rep from * across row, end last rep p3.

Row 6: Knit.

Row 7: Purl.

Row 8: K4, *place needle under loop formed by sl 3 in Row 5 and knit the loop and next st tog, k3, rep from * across row, end last rep k4.

Rep Rows 1–8 for pattern.

Columns

Skill Level: Intermediate

Cast on a multiple of 8 plus 1.

Rows 1 and 3 (WS): K2, *p5, k3, rep from *, end p5, k2.

Row 2: K2, *yarn front (yf), sl 5, yarn back (yb), k3, rep from *, end yf, sl 5, yb, k2.

Row 4: K4, *insert needle under the loose strand in Row 2 and knit this strand with the next st, k7, rep from *, end last rep k4.

Rep Rows 1–4 for pattern.

Twists

Skill Level: Experienced

Cast on a multiple of 8 plus 2.

Rows 1, 3, 5, and 7: Knit.

Rows 2, 4, 6 and 8: K1, p3, *k2, p6, rep from * to last 6 sts, end k2, p3, k1.

Row 9: K1, *p2, yarn back (yb), sl 1, k2, sl 1, yarn front (yf), k2, rep from * to last st, end k1.

Row 10: K1, *k2, yf, sl 1, yb, k2, yf, sl 1, yb, k2, rep from * to last st, end k1.

Row 11: K3, *drop next slipped st off needle toward front, sl next 2 sts to right-hand needle, drop next slipped st off needle to front, pick up first dropped st with left-hand needle, replace the 2 sts back on left-hand needle, pick up 2nd dropped st, place on left needle, k these 4 sts, k next 4 sts, rep from *, end last rep k3.

Row 12: Same as Row 2.

Rep Rows 1–12 for pattern.

Ladders

Skill Level: Intermediate

Cast on a multiple of 8 plus 7.

Rows 1 and 3 (RS): K1, *yarn back (yb), k5, yarn front (yf), sl 3 as to purl, rep from * until last 6 sts, end k6.

Row 2: K1, p5, *yb, sl 3 as to purl, yf, p5, rep from *, end k1.

Rows 4 and 8: K1, purl to last st, k1.

Rows 5 and 7: K2, *yf, sl 3 as to purl, yb, k5, rep from *, end last rep k2.

Row 6: K2, *yb, sl 3 as to purl, p5, rep from *, end last rep p1, k1.

Rep Rows 1–8 for pattern.

Ridges

Skill Level: Intermediate

Note: Always slip as if to purl.

Cast on a multiple of 4 plus 1.

Rows 1 and 3: K4, *sl 1, k3, rep from * across, end last rep k4.

Row 2: K1, p3, *sl 1, p3, rep from * to last st, k1.

Row 4: Knit.

Rows 5 and 7: K2, *sl 1, k3, rep from *, end last rep k2.

Row 6: K1, p1, *sl 1, p3, rep from * to last 3 sts, end sl 1, p1, k1.

Row 8: Knit.

Rep Rows 1–8 for pattern.

Waffle

Skill level: Intermediate

Cast on a multiple of 5 plus 4.

Row 1 (WS): *K4, yo, k1, rep from * to last 4 sts, end k4.

Row 2: *K4, yarn back (yb), sl 1 as to purl, drop yo from previous row, rep from * to last 4 sts, end k4.

Rows 3 and 5: *P4, sl 1, rep from * to last 4 sts, end p4.

Rows 4 and 6: *K4, sl 1, rep from * to last 4 sts, end k4.

Rep Rows 1–6 for pattern.

Cable Slip Stitch I

Skill Level: Intermediate

Notes: Slip all slipped stitches as to purl.

C3L: Slip next st onto cable needle and hold in front of work, k next 2 sts from left-hand needle, then k st from cable needle.

C3R: Slip next 2 sts onto cable needle and hold in back of work, k next st from left-hand needle, then k sts from cable needle.

Cast on a multiple of 4 plus 3.

Row 1 (RS): K2, *sl 1, k3, rep from *, end last rep k4.

Row 2: K1, *p3, sl 1, rep from * to last 2 sts, end p1, k1.

Row 3: K2, *C3L, k1, rep from *, end last rep k2.

Row 4: Purl.

Row 5: K6, *sl 1, k3, rep from *, end last rep k4.

Row 6: K1, *p3, sl 1, rep from * to last 6 sts, end p5, k1.

Row 7: K3, *C3R, k1, rep from *, end last rep k4.

Row 8: K1, purl to last st, k1.

Rep Rows 1–8 for pattern.

Cable Slip Stitch II

Skill Level: Intermediate

Notes: Slip all slipped stitches as to purl.

C3L: Slip next st onto cable needle and hold in front of work, k next 2 sts from left-hand needle, then k st from cable needle.

C3R: Slip next 2 sts onto cable needle and hold in back of work, k next st from left-hand needle, then k sts from cable needle.

Cast on a multiple of 3.

Row 1 (RS): K2, *sl 1, k2, rep from * to last st, end k1.

Row 2: P3, *sl 1, p2, rep from * to end.

Row 3: K2, *C3L, rep from * to last st, end k1.

Row 4: Purl.

Row 5: K2, *yo, k2tog, k1, rep from * to last st, end k1.

Row 6: Purl.

Row 7: K4, *sl 1, k2, rep from * to last 2 sts, end sl 1, k1.

Row 8: P1, *sl 1, p2, rep from * to last 2 sts, end p2.

Row 9: K2, *C3R, rep from * to last st, end k1.

Row 10: Knit.

Row 11: Purl.

Row 12: Purl.

Rep Rows 1–12 for pattern.

Linen Stitch

Skill Level: Easy

Cast on a multiple of 2 plus 1.

Row 1 (RS): K1, *yarn front (yf), sl 1, yarn back (yb), k1, rep from * to end.

Row 2: K1, purl to last st, k1.

Row 3: K2, *yf, sl 1, yb, k1, rep from *, end last rep k2.

Row 4: K1, purl to last st, k1.

Rep Rows 1–4 for pattern.

YOU WILL NEED

Yarn

- Fine weight
- Shown: Blue Heron Yarns, Silk Merino, 50% silk, 50% merino, 375 yds (353 m): Anemone, 1 skein

Needles

- Size 6 (4 mm) or size to obtain gauge

Notions

- Two stitch markers
- Tapestry needle
- Four ½" (1.3 cm) buttons

Gauge

- 20 sts = 4" (10 cm) in Little Butterfly stitch
- Take time to check gauge.

Size

- 8½" x 32" (21.5 x 81 cm)

Little Butterfly Cowl

The Little Butterfly Cowl only takes one skein of yarn. This project is a perfect opportunity to try a fantastic designer yarn and one of the interesting slip stitches.

Skill Level: Easy

Cowl

Cast on 47 sts. Work Seed/Moss St (page 49) for 5 rows.

Buttonhole row: Work seed st on first 5 sts, pm, k1, *bind off next 3 sts, k8, rep from * 2 times more, bind off 3 sts, pm, seed st on last 5 sts.

Next row: Work seed st on first 5 sts, *cast on 3 sts over 3 bound-off sts from previous row, p8, rep from * 2 times more, cast on 3 sts over the bound-off sts, p1, seed st on last 5 sts.

Next row: Keeping the 5 sts each side in seed st, knit 1 row.

Next row: Keeping the 5 sts each side in seed st, purl 1 row.

Continue 5 sts each side in seed st and center 37 sts in Little Butterfly stitch (page 169) until piece measures 30" (76 cm) from beg.

Next row: Keeping the 5 sts each side in seed st, knit 1 row.

Next row: Keeping the 5 sts each side in seed st, purl 1 row.

Work seed st for 5 rows. Bind off in patt.

Finishing

Sew 4 buttons on opposite side to align with buttonholes. Weave in ends. If blocking is required, spritz lightly with water, pat into shape.

Color Combos

Working with two or three colors of yarn in the same stitch pattern sometimes intimidates knitters, but the result is well worth the effort. You'll find that multicolor knitting is a lively alternative to solid-color fabric. Many of these color combinations use a variety of slipped stitches to create the look of intricate Fair Isle knitting, but they are surprisingly easy to knit. Slipped stitches of one color are knit into a following row of a different color. Blending the rhythm of stitches with different color combinations will offer you many exciting design options.

Puffy Stripes

Skill Level: Easy

Notes: Worked with two colors A and B; do not end colors, carry loosely up sides.

When slipping stitches be sure to carry yarn loosely to avoid puckering.

With Col A, cast on a multiple of 6 plus 5.

Row 1 (RS): Col A, knit.

Row 2: Col A, k1, *p3, k3, rep from *, end p3, k1.

Row 3: Col B, k1, *yarn back (yb), sl 3, k3, rep from *, end yb, sl 3, k1.

Row 4: Col B, k1, p1, *yarn front (yf), sl 1, p5, rep from *, end sl 1, p1, k1.

Row 5: Col B, knit.

Row 6: Col B, k4, *p3, k3, rep from *, end last rep k4.

Row 7: Col A, k4, *yb, sl 3, k3, rep from *, end last rep k4.

Row 8: Col A, k1, p4, *yf, sl 1, p5, rep from *, end sl 1, p4, k1.

Rep Rows 1–8 for pattern.

Bi-Color Sand Stitch

Skill Level: Easy

Note: Made with two colors A and B. Do not cut yarn at end of rows, carry up sides as you work.

Cast on a multiple of 2 plus 1.

Row 1 (RS): With A, knit.

Row 2: With A, knit.

Row 3: With B, k1, *sl 1 pwise, k1, rep from * across row.

Row 4: With B, k1, *yarn forward (yf), sl 1 pwise, yarn back (yb), k1, rep from * across row.

Rep Rows 1–4 for pattern.

Vertical Stripes

Skill Level: Easy

Note: Worked with two colors A and B; when carrying colors along wrong side, be sure to carry loosely to avoid puckering.

With Col A, cast on a multiple of 4.

Foundation row: Col A, purl.

Row 1 (RS): Col B, k1, *yarn back (yb), sl 2, k2, rep from *, end sl 2, k1.

Row 2: Col B, k1, *yarn front (yf), sl 2, p2, rep from *, end sl 2, k1.

Row 3: Col A, k1, *k2, yb, sl 2, rep from *, end k3.

Row 4: Col A, k1, *p2, yf, sl 2, rep from *, end p2, k1.

Rep Rows 1–4 for pattern.

Lattice

Skill Level: Experienced

Note: Worked with two colors A and B. After cast on and knit row, change to Col B. The rep of the pattern always begins with Row 1.

With Col A, cast on a multiple of 6 plus 2.

Foundation Row: Knit one row.

Row 1 (RS): Col B, yarn back (yb), k1, sl 1, *k4, sl 2, rep from *, end k4, sl 1, k1.

Row 2: Col B, yarn front (yf), p1, sl 1,*p4, sl 2, rep from *, end p4, sl 1, p1.

Row 3: Col A, same as Row 1.

Row 4: Col A, k1, yf, sl 1, *yb, k4, yf, sl 2, rep from *end, k4, yf, sl 1, k1.

Row 5: Col B, k3, *yb, sl 2, k4, rep from *, end sl 2, k3.

Row 6: Col B, p3, *yf, sl 2, p4, rep from *, end sl 2, p3.

Row 7: Col A, Same as Row 5.

Row 8: Col A, k3, *yf, sl 2, yb, k4, rep from *, end yf, sl 2, k3.

Rep Rows 1–8 for pattern.

Slip Stitch I

Skill Level: Intermediate

Note: Worked with three colors A, B, C.

With Col A, cast on a multiple of 4 plus 3.

Rows 1–4: Col A, knit.

Row 5: Col B, k3, *sl 1, k3, rep from * across row.

Row 6: Col B, p3, *sl 1, p3, rep from * across row.

Row 7: Col C, k1, *sl 1, k3, rep from *, end sl 1, k1.

Row 8: Col C, k1, *yarn front (yf), sl 1, yarn back (yb), k3, rep from *, end yf, sl 1, yb, k1.

Rows 9 and 10: Col B, same as Rows 5 and 6.

Row 11: Col A, same as Row 7.

Row 12: Col A, p1, *sl 1, p3, rep from *, end sl 1, p1.

Rep Rows 1–12 for pattern.

Slip Stitch II

Skill Level: Intermediate

Note: Worked with three colors A, B, and C; do not cut yarn at end of rows, carry inactive yarn up sides.

With Col A, cast on a multiple of 2 plus 1.

Foundation rows: Col A, knit 2 rows.

Row 1 (RS): Col B, *k1, sl 1, rep from * across row, end k1.

Row 2: Col B, k1, *yarn front (yf), sl 1, yarn back (yb), k1, rep from * to end.

Rows 3 and 4: Col B, knit across row.

Row 5: Col A, k2, *sl 1, k1, rep from * across row, end last rep k2.

Row 6: Col A, k2, *yf, sl 1, yb, k1, rep from * across row, end last rep k2.

Rows 7 and 8: Col A, knit across row.

Rows 9–12: Col C, Same as Rows 1–4.

Rep Rows 1–12 for pattern.

Slip Stitch III

Skill Level: Intermediate

Note: Worked with three colors A, B, and C.

Cast on a multiple of 4 plus 3.

Row 1 (RS): With A, knit.

Row 2: With A, purl.

Row 3: With B, k3, *with yarn in back (wyb), sl 1, k3, rep from * across row.

Row 4: With B, p3, *with yarn in front (wyf), sl 1, p3, rep from * across row.

Row 5: With C, k1, *wyb sl 1, k3, rep from * end, sl 1, k1.

Row 6: With C, k1, *wyf sl 1, wyb k3, rep from * end wyf sl 1, wyb k1.

Rows 7 and 8: With B, Same as Rows 3 and 4.

Row 9: With A, Same as Row 5.

Row 10: With A, p1, *wyf, sl 1, p3, rep from *, end sl 1, p1.

Rep Rows 1–10 for pattern.

Woven Ribbons

Skill Level: Easy

Note: Worked with three colors A, B, C; do not break yarn at each color change, carry loosely up sides.

With Col A, cast on a multiple of 4 plus 3.

Row 1: Col A, knit.

Row 2: Col A, purl.

Row 3: Col B, k1, sl 1, *k3, sl 1, rep from * to last st, end k1.

Row 4: Col B, k1, yarn front (yf), sl 1, *yarn back (yb), k3, yf, sl 1, rep from *, end yb, k1.

Row 5: Col A, knit.

Row 6: Col A, purl.

Row 7: Col C, *k3, sl 1, rep from *, end last rep k3.

Row 8: Col C, *k3, yf, sl 1, yb, rep from *, end last rep k3.

Row 9: Col C, same as Row 7.

Row 10: Col C, same as Row 8.

Rep Rows 1–10 for pattern.

Forget Me Not

Skill Level: Experienced

Notes: Worked with two colors A and B.

In order to elongate a stitch, it is necessary to wrap twice around the needle before completing the stitch.

With Col A, cast on a multiple of 4.

Row 1 (WS): Col A, wrapping yarn twice for each st, purl across row.

Row 2: Col A, *sl 4 sts, dropping extra wraps to right-hand needle, place the 4 elongated sts back on left-hand needle, then (k4tog, p4tog) twice into the same 4 sts, rep from * across row.

Row 3: Col B, p2, *wrapping yarn twice around needle, p1, rep from * to the last 2 sts, end p2.

Row 4: Col B, *k2, rep from * of Row 2 across to last 2 sts, end k2.

Rep Rows 1–4 for pattern.

Triple Loops

Skill Level: Experienced

Notes: Worked with two colors A and B; do not cut yarn but carry loosely up sides of work.

In order to elongate the slipped stitches, it is necessary to wrap yarn twice around needle before completing the stitch (place right-hand needle in next stitch, wrap yarn around twice, complete stitch as usual).

On Rows 3 and 11 extra wraps are dropped when slipping sts.

With Col A, cast on a multiple of 10 plus 3.

Row 1 (RS): Col A, knit.

Row 2: Col A, k1, k1 wrapping yarn twice around needle, *k3, k3 wrapping yarn twice around needle for each st, k3, k1 wrapping yarn twice, rep from *, end k1.

Row 3: Col B, k1, yarn back (yb), sl 1, *k3, yb, sl 3, k3, yb, sl 1, rep from *, end k1.

Rows 4 and 6: Col B, p1, yarn front (yf), sl 1, *p3, yf, sl 3, p3, yf, sl 1, rep from *, end p1.

Row 5: Col B, same as Row 3.

Row 7: Col B, k1, yb, sl 1, *k1, yb, sl 2, drop the first st of the group of 3 sl sts off needle to front of work, sl the same

2 sts back to left needle, pick up the dropped st and k it, k2, yb, sl 1, drop next sl st off needle to front of work, k2, pick up dropped st and k it, k1, yb, sl 1, rep from *, end k1.

Row 8: Col B, p1, *yf, sl 1, p9, rep from *, end sl 1, p1.

Row 9: Col A, knit.

Row 10: Col A, k1, k2 wrapping twice for each st, *k3, k1 wrapping twice, k3, k3 wrapping twice for each st, rep from *, end last rep k2 wrapping twice for each st, k1.

Row 11: Col B, k1, yb, sl 2, *k3, yb, sl 1, k3, yb, sl 3, rep from *, end last rep yb, sl 2, k1.

Rows 12 and 14: Col B, p1, yf, sl 2, *p3, yf, sl 1, p3, yf, sl 3, rep from *, end last rep yf, sl 2, p1.

Row 13: Col B, same as Row 11.

Row 15: Col B, k1, *yb, sl 1, drop next sl st off needle to front of work, k2, pick up dropped st and k it, k1, yb, sl 1, k1, yb, sl 2, drop next sl st off needle to front of work, sl the same 2 sts back to left needle, pick up dropped st and k it, k2, rep from *, end yb, sl 1, k1.

Row 16: Col B, p6, yf, sl 1, *p9, yf, sl 1, rep from *, end p6.

Rep Rows 1–16 for pattern.

Two-Color Trinity

Skill Level: Easy

Note: Worked with two colors A and B.

With Col A, cast on a multiple of 3 plus 2.

Foundation row: Col A, purl.

Row 1 (RS): Col A, k1, *k3, pass first of the 3 k sts over the 2nd and 3rd sts, rep from *, end k1.

Row 2: Col B, p1, *insert needle from behind under the thread between the st just worked and the next st, and purl this thread, p2, rep from *, end p1.

Row 3: Col B, k2, then rep from * of Row 1, ending last rep k3, pass first of the 3 k sts over the 2nd and 3rd sts.

Row 4: Col A, p2, rep from * of Row 2, end with p2.

Rep Rows 1–4 for pattern.

Two-Color Fences

Skill Level: Easy

Notes: Worked with two colors A and B.

All slip stitches are made as if to purl.

Carry colors loosely up sides.

With Col A, cast on a multiple of 6 plus 7.

Row 1: Col A, k3 *sl 1, k5, rep from *, end sl 1, k3.

Row 2: Col A, k1, purl across row, slipping all the slip sts from previous row.

Row 3: Col B, k1, *k5, sl 1, rep from * across row to last 6 sts, end k6.

Row 4: Col B, k1, *k5, yarn front (yf), sl 1, yarn back, (yb), rep from * to last 6 sts, end yb, k6.

Rep Rows 1–4 for pattern.

Garter Stitch Checks

Skill Level: Experienced

Note: Worked with two colors A and B. Do not cut yarn at end of rows; carry inactive yarn up side of work.

With Col A, cast on a multiple of 10 plus 7.

Row 1 (RS): Col A, knit.

Row 2: Col A, k1, *k5, (p1, k1) twice, p1, rep from* to last 6 sts, end k6.

Row 3: Col B, k1, *k5, (yb, sl 1, k1) twice, yb, sl 1, rep from * to last 6 sts, end k6.

Row 4: Col B, k1, *k5, (yf, sl 1, yb, k1) twice, yf, sl 1, rep from * to last 6 sts, end k6.

Row 5: Col A, knit.

Row 6: Col A k1, *k5, (p1, k1) twice, p1, rep from * to last 6 sts, end k6.

Rows 7, 8, 9, 10, 11, and 12: Rep Rows 3, 4, 5, and 6, then 3 and 4 again.

Row 13: Col A, knit.

Row 14: Col A, k1, (p1, k1) twice, p1, *k5, (p1, k1) twice, p1, rep from *, end k1.

Row 15: Col B, k1, (yb, sl 1, k1) twice, yb, sl 1, *k5, (yb, sl 1, k1) twice, yb, sl 1, rep from *, end k1.

Row 16: Col B, k1, (yf, sl 1, yb, k1) twice, yf, sl 1, *yb, k5, (yf, sl 1, yb, k1) twice, yf, sl 1, rep from *, end k1.

Row 17: Col A, knit.

Row 18: Col A, k1, (p1, k1) twice, p1, *k5, (p1, k1) twice, p1, rep from *, end k1.

Row 19: Col B, k1, (sl 1, k1) twice, sl 1, *k5, (sl 1, k1) twice, sl 1, rep from *, end k1.

Row 20: Col B, k1, (yf, sl 1, yb, k1) twice, yf, sl 1, *yb, k5, (yf, sl 1, yb, k1) twice, yf, sl 1, rep from *, end k1.

Row 21: Col A, knit.

Row 22: Same as Row 18.

Row 23: Same as Row 15.

Row 24: Same as Row 16.

Rep Rows 1–24 for pattern.

Mock Fair Isle

Skill Level: Intermediate

Note: Worked with two colors A and B.

With Col A, cast on a multiple of 5.

Row 1: Col B, purl.

Row 2: Col A, k1, *yarn back (yb), sl 1, yarn front (yf), sl 1, yb, sl 1, k1, rep from * across row.

Row 3: Col A, p1, *yb, sl 3, wrap yarn around needle, p1, rep from * across row.

Row 4: Col B, knit across row, dropping extra wraps and making long loose strands in front of work.

Row 5: Col B, purl.

Row 6: Col A , k1, *yb, sl 1, insert needle from the front, under the loose strand, and knit the loose strand and the next st as one, yb, sl 1, k1, rep from * to end of row.

Row 7: Col A, k1, *yf, sl 1, p1, yf, sl 1, k1, rep from * across row.

Row 8: Col B, knit.

Row 9: Col B, purl.

Row 10: Col A, k1, *yf, sl 1, yb, k1, rep from * across row.

Rows 11–20: Rep same as 1–10 reversing colors.

Rep Rows 1–20 for pattern.

Dots and Dashes

Skill Level: Intermediate

Note: Worked with two colors A and B.

With Col A, cast on a multiple of 16 plus 9.

Row 1 (RS): Col A, knit.

Row 2: Col A, knit across row.

Row 3: Col B (k1, sl 1) 4 times, *k9, (sl 1, k1) 3 times, sl 1, rep from *, end k1.

Row 4: Col B (yb, k1, yf, sl 1) 4 times, *p9, (yf, sl 1, yb, k1) 3 times, sl 1, rep from *, end yb, k1.

Rows 5 and 6: Col A, knit.

Row 7: Same as Row 3.

Row 8: Same as Row 4.

Row 9: Col A, knit.

Row 10: Col A, knit.

Row 11: Col B, k9, *(yb, sl 1, k1) 3 times, yb, sl 1, k9, rep from * to end.

Row 12: Col B, p9, *(yf, sl 1, yb, k1) 3 times, yf, sl 1, p9, rep from * to end.

Row 13: Col A, knit.

Row 14: Col A, knit.

Row 15: Same as Row 11.

Row 16: Same as Row 12.

Rep Rows 1–16 for pattern.

Three-Color Check

Skill Level: Intermediate

Notes: Worked with three colors A, B, C.

In order to elongate the stitch to be slipped, you will have to wrap the yarn twice around the needle before completing the stitch (place point of right-hand needle into next stitch, wrap yarn twice around needle, complete stitch as usual).

Do not end yarn after each two rows; carry inactive yarn up sides of work.

With Col A, cast on a multiple of 4 plus 3.

Row 1 (RS): Col A, knit.

Row 2: Col A, k1, *k1 wrapping yarn twice around needle, k3, rep from *, end last rep k1.

Row 3: Col B, k1, *yarn back (yb), sl 1, dropping extra wraps, k3, rep from *, end last rep k1.

Row 4: Col B, k1, *yarn front (yf), sl 1, yb, k3, rep from *, end yf, sl 1, yb, k1.

Row 5: Col C, k1, *yb, sl 2, k2, rep from *, end sl, k1.

Row 6: Col C, k1, yf, sl 1, *p2, yf, sl 2, rep from *, end yb, k1.

Rep Rows 1–6 for pattern.

Two-Color Star

Skill Level: Intermediate

Note: Worked with two colors A and B.

With Col A, cast on a multiple of 4.

Row 1: Col A, knit.

Row 2: Col A, k1, *p3tog, do not take off needle, yo by wrapping yarn around back to front again, p same 3 sts tog again, sl sts off needle, k1, rep from *, end p1, k2.

Row 3: Col B, knit.

Row 4: Col B, k1, p1, *k1, p3tog, hold on needle, yo as before, p same 3 sts tog, sl off needle, rep from *, end k2.

Rep Rows 1–4 for pattern.

Double Loops

Skill Level: Intermediate

Note: Worked with two colors A and B.

With Col A, cast on a multiple of 7 plus 1.

Row 1 (WS): Col A, k3, *p2, k5, rep from *, end p2, k3.

Rows 2 and 4: Col B, k3, *yarn back (yb), sl 2, k5, rep from *, end yb, sl 2, k3.

Rows 3 and 5: Col B, p3, *yarn front (yf), sl 2, p5, rep from *, end yf, sl 2, p3.

Row 6: Col A, *k1, yb, sl 2, drop Col A sl st from previous row off needle to front of work, sl the same 2 sts just slipped back to left needle, pick up dropped st and k it, k2, drop next Col A sl st off needle to front of work, k2, pick up dropped st and k it, rep from *, end k1.

Rep Rows 1–6 for pattern.

Powder Puffs

Skill Level: Intermediate

Note: Worked with two colors A and B. Do not end colors after each set; carry inactive yarn loosely up sides of work.

With Col A, cast on a multiple of 6 plus 1.

Rows 1 and 2: Col A, knit.

Rows 3, 5, and 7: Col B, knit.

Rows 4, 6, and 8: Col B, purl.

Row 9: Col A, k3, drop next st off left-hand needle and unravel down 6 rows to Row 2, k the st in Row 2, k1 below, *k5, k1 below, rep from *, end k3.

Row 10: Col A, knit.

Rows 11, 13, and 15: Col B, knit.

Rows 12, 14, and 16: Col B, purl.

Row 17: Col A, k6, k1 below, *k5, k1 below, rep from *, end last rep k6.

Row 18: Col A, knit.

Rep Rows 3–18 for pattern.

Two-Color Knot

Skill Level: Intermediate

Note: Worked with two colors A and B; draw colors loosely up sides as you work every 2 rows.

With Col A, cast on a multiple of 2 plus 1.

Row 1 (RS): Col A, knit.

Row 2: Col A, k2, *p2tog, do not take off needle, k same 2 tog, rep from * to last st, end k1.

Row 3: Col B, knit.

Row 4: Col B, k1, *p2tog, do not take off needle, k same 2 tog, rep from * to last 2 sts, end k2.

Rep Rows 1–4 for pattern.

Three-Color Tweed

Skill Level: Intermediate

Notes: Worked with three colors A, B, and C.

Carry colors up sides, twisting as you pick up each new color.

Pay attention to color changes, some row repeats are with a different color.

With Col A, cast on a multiple of 4 plus 3.

Row 1: Col A, k1, `*sl 1, k3, rep from *, end sl 1, k1.

Row 2: Col A, k1, *yarn front (yf), sl 1, yarn back (yb), k3, rep from *, end yf, sl 1, yb, k1.

Row 3: Col B, k3, *sl 1, k3, rep from * to end.

Row 4: Col B, k3, *yf, sl 1, yb, k3, rep from * to end.

Row 5: Col C, same as Row 1.

Row 6: Col C, same as Row 2.

Row 7: Col A, same as Row 3.

Row 8: Col A, same as Row 4.

Row 9: Col B, same as Row 1.

Row 10: Col B, same as Row 2.

Row 11: Col C, same as Row 3.

Row 12: Col C, same as Row 4.

Rep Rows 1–12 for pattern.

Anvils

Skill Level: Experienced

Notes: Worked with two colors A and B.

After cast-on and first row, each color is worked for 4 rows. Do not cut yarn after each set; carry inactive yarn loosely up sides of work.

With Col A, cast on a multiple of 8 plus 6.

Foundation row: Col A, purl.

Row 1 (RS): Col B, knit.

Row 2: Col B, k6, *yarn front (yf), sl 2, yarn back (yb), k6, rep from * across row.

Row 3: Col B, k6, *yb, sl 2, k6, rep from * across row.

Row 4: Col B, same as Row 2.

Row 5: Col A, k6, *yb, sl 2, k6, rep from * across row.

Row 6: Col A, p6, *yf, sl 2, p6, rep from * across row.

Row 7: Same as Row 5.

Row 8: Same as Row 6.

Row 9: Col B, knit.

Row 10: Col B, k2, *yf, sl 2, yb, k6, rep from *, end yf, sl 2, yb, k2.

Row 11: Col B, k2, *yb, sl 2, k6, rep from *, end yb, sl 2, k2.

Row 12: Same as Row 10.

Row 13: Col A, k2, *yb, sl 2, k6, rep from * across row, end yb, sl 2, k2.

Row 14: Col A, p2, *yf, sl 2, p6, rep from *, end yf, sl 2, p2.

Row 15: Same as Row 13.

Row 16: Same as Row 14.

Rep Rows 1–16 for pattern.

Gingham

Skill Level: Experienced

Notes: This pattern is worked in an unusual manner. You are working with two colors and, while still working back and forth, you are turning every other row instead of every row, working each color across a row before turning. Because of this, it is very important to pay attention to the instructions at the end of each row. This method of working also requires use of either two double-pointed needles for a small amount of stitches or a circular needle for a larger amount of stitches so that you can work from either end of the needle.

It is important to keep the yarn very loose as you carry it across the slipped stitches.

Cast on with Col A; however, Row 1 is immediately worked with Col B.

With Col A, cast on a multiple of 10 plus 7.

Row 1 (RS): Col B, k6, *(yf, sl 1, yb, sl 1) twice, yf, sl 1, k5, rep from *, end k1, do not turn.

Row 2: Col A, k1, *yb, sl 5, k5, rep from *, end k1, turn.

Row 3: Col B, k1, *p5, (yf, sl 1, yb, sl 1) twice, yf, sl 1, rep from *, end k1, p5, k1, do not turn.

Row 4: Col A, k1, *yf, sl 5, p5, rep from *, end yf, sl 5, k1, turn.

Row 5: Same as Row 1.

Row 6: Same as Row 2.

Row 7: Same as Row 3.

Row 8: Same as Row 4.

Row 9: Same as Row 1.

Row 10: Col A, k1, *(yf, sl 1, yb, sl 1) twice, yf, sl 1, k5, rep from *, end k1, turn.

Row 11: Col B, k1, *p5, yf, sl 5, rep from *, end k1, do not turn.

Row 12: Col A, k1, *(yf, sl 1, yb, sl 1) twice, yf, sl 1, p5, rep from *, end (yf, sl 1, yb, sl 1) twice, yf, sl 1, k1, turn.

Row 13: Col B, k6, *yb, sl 5, p5, rep from *, end k6, do not turn.

Row 14: Same as Row 10.

Row 15: Same as Row 11.

Row 16: Same as Row 12.

Row 17: Same as Row 13.

Row 18: Same as Row 10.

Row 19: Col B, k1, *p5, (yb, sl 1, yf, sl 1) twice, yb, sl 1, rep from *, end p5, k1, do not turn.

Row 20: Same as Row 4.

Row 21: Col B, k6, *(yb, sl 1, yf, sl 1) twice, yb, sl 1, k5, rep from *, end last rep k6, do not turn.

Row 22: Same as Row 2.

Row 23: Same as Row 19.

Row 24: Same as Row 20.

Row 25: Same as Row 21.

Row 26: Same as Row 22.

Row 27: Same as Row 19.

Row 28: Col A, k1, *(yb, sl 1, yf, sl 1) twice, yb, sl 1, p5, rep from *, end (yb, sl 1, yf, sl 1) twice, yb, sl 1, k1, turn.

Row 29: Same as Row 13.

Row 30: Col A, k1, *(yb, sl 1, yf, sl 1) twice, yb, sl 1, k5, rep from *, end (yb, sl 1, yf, sl 1) twice, yb, sl 1, k1, turn.

Row 31: Same as Row 11.

Row 32: Same as Row 28.

Row 33: Same as Row 29.

Row 34: Same as Row 30.

Row 35: Same as Row 31.

Row 36: Same as Row 28.

Rep Rows 1–36 for pattern.

Tic-Tac-Toe

Skill Level: Experienced

Notes: Worked with two colors A and B.

Yarn overs (yo) throughout this pattern are always made wrapping yarn twice around needle.

With Col A, cast on a multiple of 5 plus 1.

Row 1: Col A, purl.

Row 2: Col A, knit.

Row 3: Col A, p1, *yo, p3, yo, p2, rep from * to end.

Row 4: Col B, k1, sl 1 dropping extra wrap, k2, sl 1 dropping extra wrap, *[k1, yo, k1, yo, k1] into the next st (starting bobble st), sl 1 dropping extra wrap, k2, sl 1 dropping extra wrap, rep from * to last st, end k1.

Row 5: Col B, p1, sl 1, p2, sl 1, *yarn back (yb), k5, yarn front (yf), sl 1, p2, sl 1, rep from * to last st, end p1.

Row 6: Col B, k1, sl 1, k2, sl 1, *yf, p5, yb, sl 1, k2, sl 1, rep from * to last st, end k1.

Row 7: Col B, p1, sl 1, p2, sl 1, *yb, k2tog, k3tog, pass the k2tog st over the k3tog st, yf, sl 1, p2, sl 1, rep from * to last st, end p1.

Row 8 (Cross Row): Col A, k1, *drop the first long loop off needle, with yb, sl 2, drop next long loop off needle, with left-hand needle pick up the first dropped long loop, pass the 2 slipped sts from right-hand needle back to left-hand needle, then pick up the second dropped long loop, k5 (you will be knitting a long loop, 2 sts in between, second long loop, and the ending bobble stitch), rep from * to end.

Rep Rows 1–8 for pattern.

Two-Color Toddler Hat

Toddlers love bright colors, and this hat is sure to become a favorite. The two-color pattern of the hat ribbing may look intricate, but it is really easy to knit using a slip stitch pattern. Knitted in easy-care acrylic yarn, this hat easily stands up to toddler wear and tear.

(continued)

YOU WILL NEED

Yarn

- Medium weight
- Shown: Patons Canadiana, 100% acrylic, 3.5 oz (100 g)/241 yds (220 m): Super Teal #10742 (MC), 1 skein; Winter White #00101 (CC), 1 skein

Needles

- Sizes 6 (4 mm) and 8 (5 mm) or size to obtain gauge

Gauge

- 16 sts = 4" (10 cm) on size 8 needles
- Take time to check gauge.

Sizes

- Small (Medium)
- Finished Hat: 16 (18)" [40.5 (45.5) cm]

Note: Do not break yarn at end of rows but carry loosely up sides.

Hat

With size 6 needles and MC, cast on 79 (85) sts.

Row 1: Knit.

Work pattern as follows:

Row 2 (RS): With CC, k1, *sl 1, k1, rep from * across row.

Row 3: With CC, k1, *yf, sl 1, yb, k1, rep from * across row.

Row 4: With CC, p1, *yb, sl 1, yf, p1, rep from * across row.

Row 5: With CC, k1, *yf, sl 1, yb, k1, rep from * across row.

Row 6: With MC, knit.

Row 7: With MC, knit.

Rows 8 –19: Rep Rows 2–7 twice. End off CC, continue in MC.

Change to size 8 needles. Work in St st until hat measures 5½ (6)" [14 (15) cm] from beg, ending with a purl row.

Crown Shape

Row 1: Knit, dec 7 (5) sts evenly spaced across row [72 (80) sts].

Row 2 and all even-numbered rows: Purl.

Row 3: *K6, k2tog, rep from * across row [63 (70) sts].

Row 5: *K5, k2tog, rep from * across row [54 (60) sts].

Row 7: *K4, k2tog, rep from * across row [45 (50) sts].

Row 9: *K3, k2tog, rep from * across row [36 (40) sts].

Row 11: *K2, k2tog, rep from * across row [27 (30) sts].

Row 13: *K1, k2tog, rep from * across row [18 (20) sts].

Row 14: K2tog across row [9 (10) sts].

End off, leaving 36" (91.5 cm) length of yarn.

Draw this yarn through rem sts on needle, gather up, go through sts once more to reinforce, sew back seam with same yarn, then end off.

Do not steam; if blocking is required, lay on a padded surface, spritz with water, pat into shape, allow to dry.

Tic-Tac-Toe Hat and Mittens

Cozy, cute, and warm, this hat and mittens set is also fun to make using the two-color Tic-Tac-Toe stitch (page 190). Make a set for yourself or knit several sets for those on your gift list.

(continued)

Tic-Tac-Toe Hat and Mittens (continued)

Skill Level: Experienced

YOU WILL NEED

Yarn

- Medium weight
- Shown: Patons Canadiana, 100% acrylic, 3.5 oz (100 g)/205 yds (187 m): Grape Jelly #3497 (A), 1 (2, 2) skeins; Medium Amethyst #3507 (B), 1 (1, 1) skein

Needles

- Sizes 4 (3.5 mm) and 7 (4.5 mm) or size to obtain gauge
- Size 5 (3.75 mm) double-pointed needles for thumb only

Notions

- Stitch holder
- Stitch marker
- Tapestry needle

Sizes

- Small (Medium, Large)
- Finished Hat: 18 (20, 22)" [45.5 (50.5, 55.5) cm]
- Finished Mittens: 8" (20 cm) wide (all sizes) at palm; 7 (8, 9)" [17.5, (20, 22.5) cm] long from wrist to fingertips

Hat

With A and size 4 needles, cast on 84 (88, 92) sts.

Row 1: *K1, p1, rep from * across row.

Row 2: Same as Row 1.

Rep Rows 1 and 2 until piece measures 3 (3, 3)" [7.5 (7.5, 7.5) cm] from beg.

Next row (RS): K, inc 2 (3, 4) sts evenly across row—86 (91, 96) sts.

Change to size 7 needles and beg Tic-Tac-Toe patt on page 190 for 24 rows. Fasten off B; finish crown shaping with A as follows:

Shape Crown

For Small: Purl 1 row.

For Medium and Large: Purl 1 row, dec 5 (10) sts evenly across row—86 sts.

Knit 1 row, purl 1 row

For all sizes:

Row 1: K3, k2tog, *k4, k2tog, rep from * to last 3 sts, k3—72 sts.

Row 2: Purl.

Row 3: K2, k2tog, *k3, k2tog, rep from * to last 3 sts, k3—58 sts.

Row 4: Purl.

Row 5: *K2tog, rep from * across row—29 sts.

Row 6: *P2tog, rep from * across row, ending p1—15 sts.

Cut yarn, leaving 36" (91.5 cm) end for sewing. Thread a tapestry needle onto the cut end, draw yarn through rem sts on needle and gather up, go through these sts again and use same thread to sew back seam. Turn beg ribbing to inside and sew to inside.

Blocking is not recommended for this patt.

Left Mitten

With A and size 4 needles, cast on 41 (41, 41) sts.

Row 1: P1, *k1, p1, rep from * across row.

Row 2: K1, *p1, k1, rep from * across row.

Rep Rows 1 and 2 until piece measures 3 (3½, 4)" [7.5 (9, 10) cm] from beg, ending with Row 1.

Change to size 7 needles and work Tic-Tac-Toe patt on page 190 for 16 (16, 16) rows.

Shape Thumb

Row 1: P30, sl last 9 sts worked onto a holder to be worked later for thumb, p rem 11 sts.

Row 2: K, casting on 9 sts over the 9 sts on holder—41 sts.

Continue with Tic-Tac-Toe patt Row 3 and work until 14 (22, 30) more patt rows are completed. Fasten off B; finish with A.

Shape Fingertip (same for all sizes)

Row 1: P2tog, p next 19 sts, place marker on needle, p rem 20 sts—40 sts.

Row 2: K1, skp, k to 3 sts before marker, k2tog, k1, sl marker, k1, skp, k to last 3 sts, k2tog, k1.

Row 3: Purl.

Rep Rows 2 and 3, 5 times more—16 sts rem.

Place 8 sts on each needle and weave sts tog.

Cut yarn, leaving a yarn tail, then sew side seam.

Thumb

Using dpns, join yarn at thumb, pick up 9 sts along bound-off edges (first needle), k5 sts from holder onto 2nd needle, k rem 4 sts onto 3rd needle—18 sts.

Row 1: K, dec 1 st at beg and end of first needle, then k across 2nd and 3rd needles—16 sts.

Continue working in-the-round for 22 (24, 26) rounds.

Cut yarn, leaving an 8" (20 cm) end for sewing. Thread a tapestry needle onto the cut end, draw through sts on needle and gather up, go through sts again and weave in end before cutting.

Right Mitten

Work same as Left Mitten until thumb shaping.

Shape Thumb

Row 1: P20, sl last 9 sts worked onto a holder to be worked later for thumb, p rem 21 sts.

Row 2: K, casting on 9 sts over 9 sts on holder—41 sts.

Continue with Tic-Tac-Toe patt Row 3 and work until 14 (22, 30) more patt rows are completed. Fasten off B; finish with A.

Shape Fingertip (same for all sizes)

Row 1: P2tog, p next 19 sts, place marker on needle, p rem 20 sts.

Row 2: K1, skp, k to 3 sts before marker, k2tog, k1, sl marker, k1, skp, k to last 3 sts, k2tog, k1.

Row 3: Purl.

Rep Rows 2 and 3, 5 times more—16 sts rem.

Place 8 sts on each needle and weave sts tog.

Cut yarn, leaving a yarn tail, then sew side seam.

Blocking is not recommended for this patt.

Motifs

Motifs are small, individual knitted shapes that can be used to adorn a knitted garment or readymade items, such as handbags, sweatshirts, pillows, and place mats. I use many motifs in my free-form knitting. Here are directions for creating a few of my favorite motifs.

Flower

Skill Level: Intermediate

Cast on 62.

Row 1 (WS): Purl.

Row 2: K2, *k1, sl this st back onto left needle, then lift the next 9 sts on left needle over this st and off the needle, yo, knit the first st again, k2, rep from * (22 sts).

Row 3: P1, *p2tog, k front, back, front in the yo, p1, rep from * to last st, end p1 (27 sts).

Row 4: K1, *sl 2, k1, p2sso, rep from *, end k2 (11 sts).

Row 5: *P2tog, rep from *, end p1 (6 sts).

Row 6: Sl 2nd, 3rd, 4th, 5th, and 6th sts over first st. End off.

Sew a seam to form flower.

Heart

Skill Level: Easy

Cast on 31.

Rows 1–5: Knit.

Rows 6, 8, 10, 12, 14, and 16: K5, purl to last 5, k5.

Rows 7, 9, 11, 13, and 15: Knit.

Row 17: K15, p1, k15.

Row 18: K5, p9, k1, p1, k1, p9, k5.

Row 19: K13, (p1, k1) twice, p1, k13.

Row 20: K5, p7, (k1, p1) 3 times, k1, p7, k5.

Row 21: K11, (p1, k1) 4 times, p1, k11.

Row 22: K5, p5, (k1, p1) 5 times, k1, p5, k5.

Row 23: K9, (p1, k1) 6 times, p1, k9.

Row 24: K5, p3, (k1, p1) 7 times, k1, p3, k5.

Row 25: K7, (p1, k1) 8 times, p1, k7.

Row 26: K5, p2, (p1, k1) 8 times, p3, k5.

Row 27: Same as Row 25.

Row 28: Same as Row 26.

Row 29: K8, (k1, p1) 3 times, k3, (p1, k1) 3 times, k8.

Row 30: K5, p4, (p1, k1) twice, p5, (k1, p1) twice, p4, k5.

Rows 31, 33, 35, 37, 39, and 41: Knit.

Rows 32, 34, 36, 38, and 40: K5, purl to last 5 sts, k5.

Rows 42, 43, 44, and 45: Knit

Bind off.

Mitered Square

Skill Level: Easy

Note: Worked with two colors A and B.

With Col A, cast on 23.

Row 1: Col A, purl.

Row 2: Col A, knit.

Row 3: Col B, p10, p3tog, p10 (21 sts).

Row 4: Col B, purl.

Row 5: Col A, p9, p3tog, p9 (19 sts).

Row 6: Col A, knit.

Row 7: Col B, p8, p3tog, p8 (17 sts).

Row 8: Col B, knit.

Row 9: Col A, p7, p3tog, p7 (15 sts).

Row 10: Col A, knit.

Row 11: Col B, p6, p3tog, p6 (13 sts).

Row 12: Col B, purl.

Row 13: Col A, p5, p3tog, p5 (11 sts).

Row 14: Col A, knit.

Row 15: Col B, p4, p3tog, p4 (9 sts).

Row 16: Col B, knit.

Row 17: Col A, p3, p3tog, p3 (7 sts).

Row 18: Col A, knit.

Row 19: Col B, p2, p3tog, p2 (5 sts).

Row 20: Col B, purl.

Row 21: Col B, p1, p3tog, p1 (3 sts).

Row 22: Col B, k3tog. End off.

Small Fan

Skill Level: Easy

Note: Worked with two colors.

With Col A, cast on 26.

Row 1: Col A, knit.

Row 2: Col A, k1, *yo, k2tog, rep from *, end k1.

Row 3: Col A, knit.

Row 4: Col A, knit.

Row 5: Col B, *k1, sl 1, rep from *, end k2tog.

Row 6: Col B, *k1, yarn front (yf), sl 1, yarn back (yb), rep from *, end yb, k1.

Row 7: Col A, knit.

Row 8: Col A, knit.

Row 9: Col B, *k1, sl 1, rep from *, end k1.

Row 10: Col B, same as Row 6.

Row 11: Col A, knit.

Row 12 (first dec row): Col A, k1, *k2tog tbl, rep from * across (13 sts).

Row 13: Col B, *k1, sl 1, rep from * to last st, end k1.

Row 14: Col B, same as Row 6. End off Col B.

Row 15: Col A, knit.

Row 16 (2nd dec row): Col A, k1, *k2tog, rep from * across (7 sts).

Row 17: Col A, knit.

Row 18: Col A, k2tog, k3, k2tog (5 sts).

Row 19: Col A, knit.

Row 20: Col A, k2tog, k1, k2tog (3 sts).

Row 21: Col A, knit.

Row 22: Col A, k3tog. End off.

Large Fan

Skill Level: Intermediate

Notes: Worked in two colors A and B.

Do not break yarn after each color change; carry loosely up sides.

With Col A, cast on 31.

Rows 1, 2, and 3: Knit.

Row 4: K1, *yo, k2tog, rep from * across row.

Row 5: Knit; drop Col A, join Col B.

Row 6: Col B, k1, *sl 1, k3, rep from *, end sl 1, k1.

Row 7: K1, *yarn front (yf), sl 1, yarn back (yb), k3, rep from *, end yf, sl 1, yb , k1.

Row 8: P1, *yb, sl 1, yf, p3, rep from *, end yb, sl 1, yf, p1.

Row 9: Same as Row 7; drop Col B.

Row 10: Col A, knit.

Row 11 (first dec row): *K2 , k2tog, rep from *, end k3 (24 sts). Drop Col A.

Row 12: Col B, k1, *sl 1, k2, rep from *, end sl 1, k1.

Row 13: K1, *yf, sl 1, yb, k2, rep from *, end yb, k1.

Row 14: P1, *yb, sl 1, yf, p2, rep from *, end yb, sl 1, yf, p1.

Row 15: Same as Row 13; drop Col B.

Row 16: Col A, knit.

Row 17 (dec row): K2, *k2tog, k1, rep from *, end last rep k2 (17 sts). Drop Col A.

Row 18: Col B, *k1, sl 1, rep from *, end k1.

Row 19: K1, *yf, sl 1, yb, k1, rep from * across row.

Row 20: P1, *yb, sl 1, yf, p1, rep from * across row.

Row 21: Same as Row 19; drop Col B.

Row 22: Col A, knit.

Row 23 (dec row): K2, *k2tog, rep from * to last 3 sts, end k3 (11 sts). Drop Col A.

Row 24: Col B, *k1, sl 1, rep from *, end k1.

Row 25: K1, *yf, sl 1, yb, k1, rep from * across row.

Row 26: Same as Row 20.

Row 27: Same as Row 19. End off Col B, finish with Col A.

Row 28: Knit.

Row 29: K1, *k2tog, rep from * across row (6 sts).

Row 30: (K2tog) 3 times (3 sts).

Row 31: Knit.

Row 32: Sl 1, k2, psso both k sts.

Bind off rem 2 sts.

Large Fan with Trinity Border

Skill Level: Intermediate

Notes: Worked in two colors A and B.

Do not end colors each time but carry loosely up sides of work.

With Col A, cast on 32 sts.

Row 1 (RS): Purl.

Row 2: *(K1, p1, k1) in same st, p3tog, rep from * across row.

Row 3: Purl.

Row 4: *P3 tog, (k1, p1, k1) in same st, rep from * across row.

Rows 5, 6, 7, and 8: Same as Rows 1–4. Drop Col A; join Col B.

Row 9: Col B, k1, *sl 1, k3, rep from *, end sl 1, k2tog.

Row 10: K1, *yarn front (yf), sl 1, yarn back (yb), k3, rep from *, end yf, sl 1, yb, k1.

Row 11: P1, *yb, sl 1, yf, p3, rep from *, end yb, sl 1, yf, p1.

Row 12: Same as Row 10; drop Col B.

Row 13: Col A, knit.

Row 14 (first dec row): *K2, k2tog, rep from *, end k3 (24 sts). Drop Col A.

Row 15: Col B, k1, *sl 1, k2, rep from *, end sl 1, k1.

Row 16: K1, *yf, sl 1, yb, k2, rep from *, end yf, sl 1, yb, k1.

Row 17: P1, *yb, sl 1, yf, p2, rep from *, end yb, sl 1, yf, p1.

Row 18: Same as Row 16; drop Col B.

Row 19: Col A, knit.

Row 20 (dec row): K2, *k2tog, k1, rep from *, end last rep k2 (17 sts). Drop Col A.

Row 21: Col B, *k1, sl 1, rep from *, end k1.

Row 22: K1, *yf, sl 1, yb, k1, rep from * across row.

Row 23: P1, *yb, sl 1, yf, p1, rep from * across row.

Row 24: Same as Row 22; drop Col B.

Row 25: Col A, knit.

Row 26 (dec row): K2, *k2tog, rep from * to last 3 sts, end k3 (11 sts). Drop Col A.

Row 27: Col B, *k1, sl 1, rep from *, end k1.

Row 28: K1, *yf, sl 1, yb, k1, rep from * across row.

Row 29: Same as Row 20.

Row 30: Same as Row 19. End off Col B, finish with Col A.

Row 31: Col A, knit.

Row 32: K1, *k2tog, rep from * across row (6 sts).

Row 33: (K2tog) 3 times (3 sts).

Row 34: Knit.

Row 35: Sl 1, k2, psso both k sts.

Bind off rem 2 sts.

Small Leaf

Skill Level: Easy

Ssk: Slip 2 sts to right needle as if to knit, slip left needle through front of sts and k2tog through the back loop.

Psso: Pass slipped st over the knit sts.

Cast on 5 sts.

Row 1 (RS): K2, yo, k1, yo, k2 (7 sts).

Row 2 and all even-numbered rows: Purl.

Row 3: K3, yo, k1, yo, k3 (9 sts).

Row 5: K4, yo, k1, yo, k4 (11 sts).

Row 7: K5, yo, k1, yo, k5 (13 sts).

Row 9: K6, yo, k1, yo, k6 (15 sts).

Row 11: K1, ssk, k9, k2tog, k1 (13 sts).

Row 13: K1, ssk, k7, k2tog, k1 (11 sts).

Row 15: K1, ssk, k5, k2tog, k1 (9 sts).

Row 17: K1, ssk, k3, k2tog, k1 (7 sts).

Row 19: K1, ssk, k1, k2tog, k1 (5 sts).

Row 21: K1, ssk, k2tog (3 sts).

Row 23: Sl 1, k2tog, psso (1 st).

Bind off rem st.

Large Leaf

Skill Level: Easy

Ssk: Slip 2 sts to right needle as if to knit, slip left needle through front of sts and k2tog through the back loop.

M1 (make one): Knit 1 stitch in the thread between the stitch just worked and the next stitch.

Cast on 7 sts.

Row 1 (RS): Knit.

Row 2 and all even-numbered rows through Row 26: K2, purl to last 2 sts, k2.

Row 3: K3, M1, k1, M1, k3 (9 sts).

Row 5: K4, M1, k1, M1, k4 (11 sts).

Row 7: K5, M1, k1, M1, k5 (13 sts).

Row 9: K6, M1, k1, M1, k6 (15 sts).

Row 11: K7, M1, k1, M1, k7 (17 sts).

Row 13: K8, M1, k1, M1, k8 (19 sts).

Row 15: K9, M1, k1, M1, k9 (21 sts).

Row 17: K10, M1, k1, M1, k10 (23 sts).

Row 19: K11, M1, k1, M1, k11 (25 sts).

Row 21: K2, ssk, k17, k2tog, k2 (23 sts).

Row 23: K2, ssk, k15, k2tog, k2 (21 sts).

Row 25: K2, ssk, k13, k2tog, k2 (19 sts).

Row 27: K2, ssk, k11, k2tog, k2 (17 sts).

Row 28: K2, p2tog, p9, p2tog, k2 (15 sts).

Row 29: K2, ssk, k7, k2tog, k2 (13 sts).

Row 30: K2, p2tog, p5, p2tog, k2 (11 sts).

Row 31: K2, ssk, k3, k2tog, k2 (9 sts).

Row 32: K2, p2tog, p1, p2tog, k2 (7 sts).

Row 33: K2, k3tog, k2 (5 sts).

Row 34: Knit.

Row 35: K1, k3tog, k1 (3 sts).

Row 36: K3tog. End off.

Leaf Coasters

Turn large leaf motifs into whimsical coasters that will protect and dress up your table. Interfacing gives them body, and a lightweight lining is hand-sewn to the back. Make a set of green leaf coasters for spring, or knit them in fall colors. They make great gifts.

YOU WILL NEED

Yarn
- Medium weight
- Shown: Ella Rae Classic, 100% wool, 3.5 oz (100 g)/219 yds (200 m): Green, 1 skein

Needles
- Size 6 (4 mm) or size to obtain gauge

Notions
- ¼ yd (0.25 m) interfacing
- ¼ yd (0.25 m) lining fabric

Gauge
- 20 sts = 4" (10 cm) in St st on size 6 needles
- Take time to check gauge.

Sizes
- 4½" × 6" (11.5 × 15 cm)

Skill Level: Easy

Ssk: Slip 2 sts to right needle as if to knit, slip left needle through front of sts and k2tog through the back loop.

M1 (make one): Knit 1 st in the thread between the st just worked and the next st.

Large Leaf Motifs (make 4)

Follow the instructions for making the Large Leaf motif, page 203.

Finishing

Block coasters before lining. Pin into shape on a padded surface. Using a pressing cloth, steam gently; allow to dry. When dry, line as follows: Trace leaf pattern onto interfacing, cut lining about ½" (1.3 cm) wider than interfacing on all sides. Pin into place, sew to bottom of leaf.

Using pressing cloth, steam again, allow to dry.

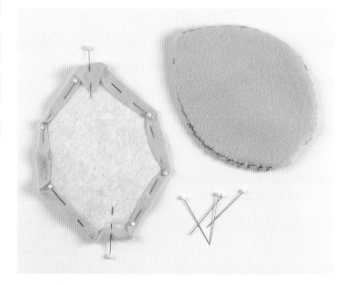

Cables

Cable patterns have intrigued knitters for generations. There are so many cable styles to try that entire books have been written on cables alone. The wide variety offers knitters countless ways to use cables, including allover patterns, panel groupings, or individual accents. They are perfect for all kinds of knitted items, including sweaters, hats, scarves, handbags, and blankets. Cables can be small and delicate or huge and chunky depending on the yarn and needles used. Once you learn the basics of knitting cables, you'll find it is great fun to experiment and create your own patterns.

Knitting cables requires some techniques not often used with other stitch patterns. A short cable needle is used to hold stitches out of the way so they can be knit out of order. The instructions are usually accompanied by charts. To make stitches cross over each other, groups of stitches are slipped from the left needle onto a cable needle and held either to the front or back of the work to be knitted later. The rule to remember is:

Hold the stitches in front of your work to make them cross to the left.

Hold the stitches in back of your work to make them cross to the right.

Cable needles have points on both ends and are available in various shapes, sizes, and materials. They may be straight with a narrower section in the middle, straight with a hump in the middle, or hook shaped. As a general rule, use a cable needle similar in size (diameter) to the needles used for the project.

Here is an example of a left-crossing cable.

1. Slip the designated number of stitches off the left needle and onto the cable needle. Drop the cable needle and let it hang loosely in the front of your knitting.

2. Working behind the cable needle, knit the next stitches (as designated by the pattern) from the left needle.

3. Knit the stitches from the cable needle.

4. Continue knitting. Note that the cable stitches cross to the left.

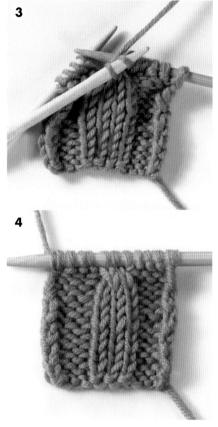

Here is an example of a right-crossing cable:

1. Slip the designated number of stitches off the left needle and onto the cable needle. Maneuver the cable needle behind your knitting needles and let it hang loosely.

2. Working in front of the cable needle, knit the next stitches (as designated by the pattern) from the left needle. Then knit the stitches from the cable needle.

3. Continue knitting. Note that the cable stitches cross to the right.

Charts

Knitting charts give you a map of the directions as seen from the right side of the work. Every square on the chart represents one stitch. The rows are numbered with odd numbers representing the right side rows listed on the right and even numbers representing the wrong side rows listed on the left. Read the chart from bottom to top, reading right to left for odd rows and left to right for even rows.

Stitch Legend

Charts are accompanied by a legend or key to explain what each symbol means.

□ Knit on RS, purl on WS

⊟ Purl on RS, knit on WS

⊡ K2tog in knit stitches

⊠ P2tog in purl stitches

⊠ SSK

⊙ Yarn over (yo)

▨ 3-St RKC (right knit cross)

Slip next stitch to cable needle and hold at back of work, knit next 2 stitches from left needle, knit stitch from cable needle.

▨ 3-St RPC (right purl cross)

Slip next stitch to cable needle and hold at back of work, knit next 2 stitches from left needle, purl stitch from cable needle.

▨ 3-St LKC (left knit cross)

Slip next 2 stitches to cable needle and hold at front of work, knit next stitch from left needle, knit 2 stitches from cable needle.

▨ 3-St LPC (left purl cross)

Slip next 2 stitches to cable needle and hold at front of work, purl next stitch from left needle, knit 2 stitches from cable needle.

▨ 4-St RKC (right knit cross)

Slip next 2 stitches to cable needle and hold at back of work, knit next 2 stitches from left needle, knit 2 stitches from cable needle.

▨ 4-St RPC (right purl cross)

Slip next 2 stitches to cable needle and hold at back of work, knit next 2 stitches from left needle, purl 2 stitches from cable needle.

▨ 4-St LKC (left knit cross)

Slip next 2 stitches to cable needle and hold at front of work, knit next 2 stitches from left needle, knit 2 stitches from cable needle.

▨ 4-St LPC (left purl cross)

Slip next 2 stitches to cable needle and hold at front of work, purl next 2 stitches from left needle, knit 2 stitches from cable needle.

▨ 5-St RC (right cross)

Slip next 3 stitches to cable needle and hold at back of work, knit next 2 stitches from left needle, slip next stitch from cable needle back to left needle and purl it, knit remaining 2 stitches from cable needle.

▨ 5-St RPC (right purl cross)

Slip next 2 stitches to cable needle and hold at back of work, knit next 3 stitches from left needle, purl 2 stitches from cable needle.

▨ 5-St LPC (left purl cross)

Slip next 3 stitches to cable needle and hold at front of work, purl next 2 stitches from left needle, knit 3 stitches from cable needle.

(continued)

6-St RKC (right knit cross)

Slip next 3 stitches to cable needle and hold at back of work, knit next 3 stitches from left needle, knit 3 stitches from cable needle.

 6-St LKC (left knit cross)

Slip next 3 stitches to cable needle and hold at front of work, knit next 3 stitches from left needle, knit 3 stitches from cable needle.

6-St RC (right cross)

Slip next 4 stitches to cable needle and hold at front of work, knit next 2 stitches from left needle, slip next 2 stitches from cable needle back to left needle, pass cable needle with remaining 2 sts to back of work, purl 2 sts from left needle, knit next 2 sts from cable needle.

 7-St LKC (left knit cross)

Slip next 4 stitches to cable needle and hold at front of work, knit next 3 stitches from left needle, knit 4 stitches from cable needle.

 8-St RKC (right knit cross)

Slip next 4 stitches to cable needle and hold at back of work, knit next 4 stitches from left needle, knit 4 stitches from cable needle.

 8-St LKC (left knit cross)

Slip next 4 stitches to cable needle and hold at front of work, knit next 4 stitches from left needle, knit 4 stitches from cable needle.

8-St RPC (right purl cross)

Slip next 4 stitches to cable needle and hold at back of work, purl next 4 stitches from left needle, knit 4 stitches from cable needle.

8-St LPC (left purl cross)

Slip next 4 stitches to cable needle and hold at front of work, knit next 4 stitches from left needle, purl 4 stitches from cable needle.

12-St RKC (right knit cross)

Slip next 6 stitches to cable needle and hold at back of work, knit next 6 stitches from left needle, knit 6 stitches from cable needle.

12-St LKC (left knit cross)

Slip next 6 stitches to cable needle and hold at front of work, knit next 6 stitches from left needle, knit 6 stitches from cable needle.

16-St RC (right cross)

Slip next 6 stitches to cable needle and hold at back of work, slip next stitches to second cable needle and hold at front of work, knit next 6 stitches from left needle, purl next 4 stitches from front cable needle, knit next 6 stitches from back cable needle.

Basic Cable

Skill Level: Intermediate

As shown on left side of swatch.	*As shown on right side of swatch.*
Cast on 12 sts (cable worked on center 8 sts).	Cast on 12 sts (cable worked on center 8 sts).
Row 1 (RS): P2, k8, p2.	**Row 1 (RS):** P2, k8, p2.
Row 2: K2, p8, k2.	**Row 2:** K2, p8, k2.
Row 3: P2, 8-St RKC, p2.	**Row 3:** P2, 8-St LKC, p2.
Row 4: Repeat Row 2.	**Row 4:** Repeat Row 2.
Rows 5–8: Repeat Rows 1–2 (twice).	**Rows 5–8:** Repeat Rows 1–2 (twice).
Repeat Rows 1–8.	Repeat Rows 1–8.

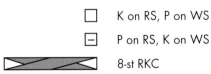

☐   K on RS, P on WS

⊟   P on RS, K on WS

   8-st RKC

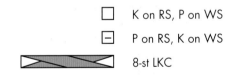

☐   K on RS, P on WS

⊟   P on RS, K on WS

   8-st LKC

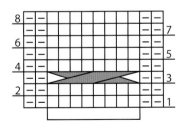

Right-slanting cable

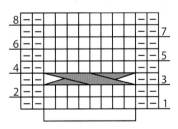

Left-slanting cable

Bamboo Cable

Skill Level: Intermediate

Cast on 8 sts (cable worked on center 4 sts).

Row 1 (RS): P2, 4-St RKC, p2.

Row 2: K2, p4, k2.

Row 3: P2, k4, p2.

Row 4: Repeat Row 2.

Row 5: Repeat Row 1.

Rows 6–11: Repeat Rows 2–3 (3 times more).

Row 12: Repeat Row 2.

Repeat Rows 1–12.

 K on RS, P on WS

P on RS, K on WS

4-st RKC

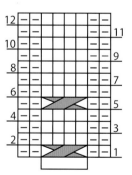

Knotted Cable

Skill Level: Intermediate

Cast on 10 sts (cable worked on center 6 sts).

Row 1: P2, k2, p2, k2, p2.

Row 2: K2, p2, k2, p2, k2.

Row 3: P2, 6-St RC, p2.

Row 4: Repeat Row 2.

Rows 5–8: Repeat Rows 1–2 (twice).

Repeat Rows 1–8.

☐   K on RS, P on WS

⊟   P on RS, K on WS

6-st RC

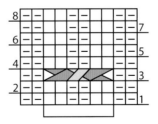

Simple Serpentine

Skill Level: Intermediate

Cast on 10 sts (cable worked on center 6 sts).

Row 1 (RS): P2, 6-St RKC, p2.

Row 2: K2, p6, k2.

Row 3: P2, k6, p2.

Rows 4–5: Repeat Rows 2–3.

Row 6: Repeat Row 2.

Row 7: P2, 6-St LKC, p2.

Rows 8–12: Repeat Rows 2–6.

Repeat Rows 1–12.

Basket Weave Cables

Skill Level: Experienced

Cast on a multiple of 6.

Row 1 (RS): Knit.

Row 2 and all even-numbered rows: K3, p to last 3 sts, k3.

Row 3: K6, *C3F, rep from * to last 6 sts, k6.

Row 5: Knit.

Row 7: K3, *C3B, rep from * to last 3 sts, k3.

Row 8: Same as Row 2.

Repeat Rows 1–8.

☐	K on RS, P on WS
⊟	P on RS, K on WS
	6-st RKC
	6-st LKC

☐	K on RS, P on WS
	6-st RKC
	6-st LKC

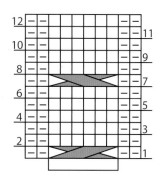

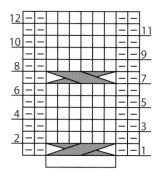

Plaited Cable

Skill Level: Intermediate

As shown on left side of swatch.

Cast on 16 sts (cable worked on center 12 sts).

Row 1 (RS): P2, k4, 8-St LKC, p2.

Row 2: K2, p12, k2.

Row 3: P2, k12, p2.

Row 4: Repeat Row 2.

Row 5: P2, 8-St RKC, k4, p2.

Rows 6–8: Repeat Rows 2–4.

Repeat Rows 1–8.

As shown on right side of swatch.

Cast on 16 sts (cable worked on center 12 sts).

Row 1 (RS): P2, k4, 8-St RKC, p2.

Row 2: K2, p12, k2.

Row 3: P2, k12, p2.

Row 4: Repeat Row 2.

Row 5: P2, 8-St LKC, k4, p2.

Rows 6–8: Repeat Rows 2–4.

Repeat Rows 1–8.

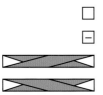

☐ K on RS, P on WS

⊟ P on RS, K on WS

8-st RKC

8-st LKC

☐ K on RS, P on WS

⊟ P on RS, K on WS

8-st RKC

8-st LKC

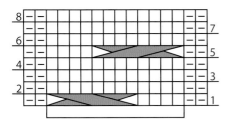

Outward Plait

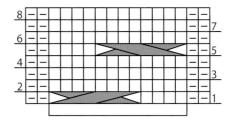

Inward Plait

Kisses and Hugs

Skill Level: Intermediate

Cast on 12 sts (cable worked on center 8 sts).

Row 1 (RS): P2, 4-St RKC, 4-St LKC, p2.

Row 2: K2, p8, k2.

Row 3: P2, k8, p2.

Row 4: Same as Row 2.

Rows 5–8: Repeat Rows 1–4.

Row 9: P2, 4-St LKC, 4-St RKC, p2.

Rows 10–12: Repeat Rows 2–4.

Rows 13–16: Repeat Rows 9–12.

Repeat Rows 1–16.

☐   K on RS, P on WS

⊟   P on RS, K on WS

   4-st RKC

   4-st LKC

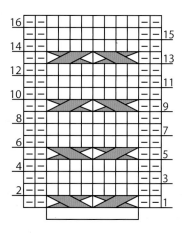

Twisted Chain

Skill Level: Intermediate

Cast on 20 sts (cable worked on center 16 sts).

Row 1 (RS): P4, (4-St LKC, p4) twice.

Row 2: K4, (p4, k4) twice.

Row 3: P4, (k4, p4) twice.

Row 4: Repeat Row 2.

Rows 5–6: Repeat Rows 1–2.

Row 7: P2, (4-St RPC, 4-St LPC) twice, p2.

Row 8: K2, p2, k4, p4, k4, p2, k2.

Row 9: P2, k2, p4, 4-St LKC, p4, k2, p2.

Row 10: Repeat Row 8.

Row 11: P2, k2, p4, k4, p4, k2, p2.

Rows 12–15: Repeat Rows 8–11.

Rows 16–18: Repeat Rows 8–10.

Row 19: P2, (4-St LPC, 4-St RPC) twice, p2.

Row 20: Repeat Row 2.

Repeat Rows 1–20.

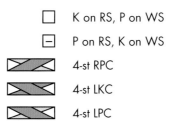

☐ K on RS, P on WS

⊟ P on RS, K on WS

▱ 4-st RPC

▱ 4-st LKC

▱ 4-st LPC

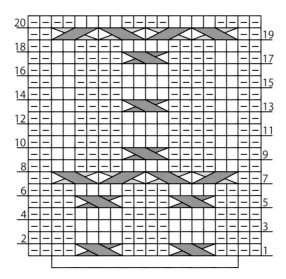

Enclosed Cable

Skill Level: Intermediate

Cast on 24 sts (cable worked on center 20 sts).

Row 1(RS): P2, k3, p4, k6, p4, k3, p2.

Row 2: K2, p3, k4, p6, k4, p3, k2.

Row 3: P2, 5-St LPC, p2, k6, p2, 5-St RPC, p2.

Row 4: K4, p3, k2, p6, k2, p3, k4.

Row 5: P4, 5-St LPC, 6-St LKC, 5-St RPC, p4.

Row 6: K6, p12, k6.

Row 7: P6, (6-St RKC) twice, p6.

Row 8: Repeat Row 6.

Row 9: P3, k3, 6-St LPC, k3, p6.

Row 10: Repeat Row 6.

Row 11: Repeat Row 7.

Row 12: Repeat Row 6.

Row 13: P4, 5-St RPC, 6-St LKC, 5-St LPC, p4.

Row 14: Repeat Row 4.

Row 15: P2, 5-St RPC, p2, k6, p2, 5-St LPC, p2.

Row 16: Repeat Row 2.

Repeat Rows 1–16.

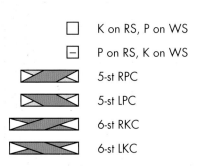

	K on RS, P on WS
	P on RS, K on WS
	5-st RPC
	5-st LPC
	6-st RKC
	6-st LKC

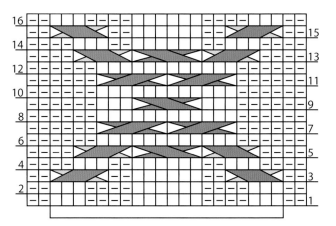

Dancing Circles

Skill Level: Intermediate

Cast on 24 sts (cable worked on center 16 sts).

Row 1 (RS): P2, 4-St RKC, (p4, 4-St RKC) twice, p2.

Row 2: K2, (p4, k4) twice, p4, k2.

Row 3: P2, k2, (4-St LPC, 4-St RPC) twice, k2, p2.

Row 4: K2, p2, (k2, p4, k2) twice, p2, k2.

Row 5: P2, k2, (p2, 4-St RKC, p2) twice, k2, p2.

Row 6: Repeat Row 4.

Row 7: P2, k2, (4-St RPC, 4-St LPC) twice, k2, p2.

Row 8: Repeat Row 2.

Rows 9–10: Repeat Rows 1–2.

Row 11: P2, k4, (p2, 4-St RPC, 4-St LPC, p2, k4) twice, p2.

Row 12: K2, (p4, k2, p2, k4, p2, k2) twice, p4, k2.

Row 13: P2, 4-St RKC, (p2, k2, p4, k2, p2, 4-St RKC) twice, p2.

Row 14: Repeat Row 12.

Row 15: P2, k4, (p2, 4-St LPC, 4-St RPC, p2, k4) twice, p2.

Row 16: Repeat Row 2.

Repeat Rows 1–16.

☐ K on RS, P on WS

⊟ P on RS, K on WS

4-st RKC

4-st RPC

4-st LPC

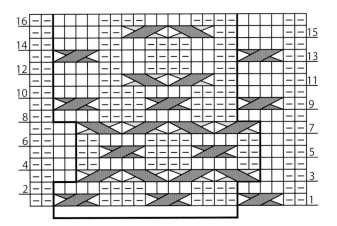

Irish Twist

Skill Level: Intermediate

Cast on 16 sts (cable worked on center 12 sts).

Row 1 (RS): P5, 3-St RKC, 3-St LPC, p5.

Row 2: K5, p3, k1, p2, k5.

Row 3: P4, 3-St RPC, k1, p1, 3-St LKC, p4.

Row 4: K4, p2, k1, p1, k1, p3, k4.

Row 5: P3, 3-St RKC, [p1, k1] twice, 3-St LPC, p3.

Row 6: K3, p3, [k1, p1] twice, k1, p2, k3.

Row 7: P2, 3-St RPC, [k1, p1] 3 times, 3-St LKC, p2.

Row 8: K2, p2, [k1, p1] 4 times, p2, k2.

Row 9: P2, 3-St LPC, [k1, p1] 3 times, 3-St RPC, p2.

Row 10: Repeat Row 6.

Row 11: P3, 3-St LPC, [p1, k1] twice, 3-St RPC, p3.

Row 12: Repeat Row 4.

Row 13: P4, 3-St LPC, [k1, p1, 3-St RPC, p4.

Row 14: Repeat Row 2.

Row 15: P5, 3-St LPC, 3-St RPC, p5.

Row 16: K6, p4, k6.

Row 17: P6, 4-St LKC, p6.

Row 18: Repeat Row 16.

Row 19: P5, 3-St RKC, 3-St LKC, p5.

Row 20: K5, p6, k5.

Row 21: P4, k6, p5.

Row 22: Repeat Row 20.

Row 23: P5, 6-St LKC, p5.

Row 24: Repeat Row 20.

Repeat Rows 1–24.

☐	K on RS, P on WS
⊟	P on RS, K on WS
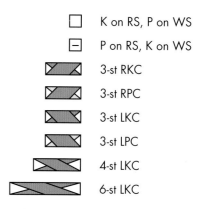	3-st RKC
	3-st RPC
	3-st LKC
	3-st LPC
	4-st LKC
	6-st LKC

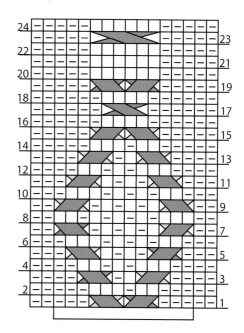

Row 22: K5, p2, k3, p2, k5.

Row 23: P4, 3-St RPC, p3, 3-St LPC, p4.

Row 24: K4, p2, k5, p2, k4.

Row 25: P4, k2, p2, MB, p2, k2, p4.

Row 26: Repeat Row 24.

Row 27: P4, 3-St LPC, p3, 3-St RPC, p4.

Row 28: K5, p2, k3, p2, k5.

Row 29: P5, 3-St LPC, p1, 3-St RPC, p5.

Row 30: K6, p2, k1, p2, k6.

Repeat Rows 1–30.

Aran Diamond

Skill Level: Experienced

Cast on 17 sts (cable worked on center 13 sts).

Row 1 (RS): P6, 5-St RC, p6.

Row 2: K6, p2, k1, p2, k6.

Row 3: P5, 3-St RPC, k1, 3-St LPC, p5.

Row 4: K5, p2, k1, p1, k1, p2, k5.

Row 5: P4, 3-St RPC, k1, p1, k1, 3-St LPC, p4.

Row 6: K4, p2, [k1, p1] twice, k1, p2, k4.

Row 7: P3, 3-St RPC, [k1, p1] twice, k1, 3-St LPC, p3.

Row 8: K3, p2, [k1, p1] 3 times, k1, p2, k3.

Row 9: P2, 3-St RPC, [k1, p1] 3 times, k1, 3-St LPC, p2.

Row 10: K2, p2, [k1, p1] 4 times, k1, p2, k2.

Row 11: P2, 3-St LPC, [p1, k1] 3 times, p1, 3-St RPC, p2.

Row 12: K3, p2, [k1, p1] 3 times, k1, p2, k3.

Row 13: P3, 3-St LPC, [p1, k1] twice, p1, 3-St RPC, p3.

Row 14: K4, p2, [k1, p1] twice, k1, p2, k4.

Row 15: P4, 3-St LPC, p1, k1, p1, 3-St RPC, p4.

Row 16: K5, p2, k1, p1, k1, p2, k5.

Row 17: P5, 3-St LPC, p1, 3-St RPC, p6.

Row 18: Repeat Row 2.

Row 19: P6, 5-St RC, p6.

Row 20: Repeat Row 2.

Row 21: P5, 3-St RPC, p1, 3-St LPC, p5.

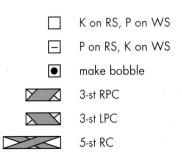

☐	K on RS, P on WS
⊟	P on RS, K on WS
⬤	make bobble
	3-st RPC
	3-st LPC
	5-st RC

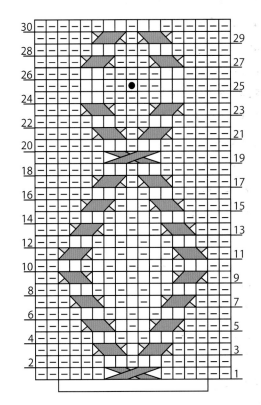

Pineapples and Vines

Skill Level: Intermediate

Cast on 11 sts (cable worked on center 7 sts).

Row 1 (RS): P2, 7-St LKC, p2.

Row 2: K2, p7, k2.

Row 3: P2, k7, p2.

Rows 4–5: Repeat Rows 2–3.

Row 6: Repeat Row 2.

Rows 7–12: Repeat Rows 1–6.

Row 13: Repeat Row 1.

Row 14: K3, [p1, k1] 3 times, k2.

Row 15: P2, k1, [p1, k1] 3 times, p2.

Rows 16–23: Repeat Rows 14–15 4 times.

Row 24: Repeat Row 14.

Repeat Rows 1–24.

☐	K on RS, P on WS
⊟	P on RS, K on WS
⧓	7-st LKC

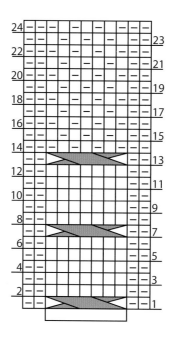

Butterfly Cable

Skill Level: Intermediate

Note: Sample shown is worked in wider columns with cable repeats that alternate from side to side.

Cast on 24 sts (cable worked on right 20 sts).

Row 1 (RS): P4, [k6, p4] twice.

Row 2: K4, [p6, k4] twice.

Rows 3–10: Repeat Rows 1–2, 4 times.

Row 11: P4, 16-St RC, p4.

Row 12: Repeat Row 2.

Repeat Rows 1–12.

☐ K on RS, P on WS

⊟ P on RS, K on WS

 16-st RC

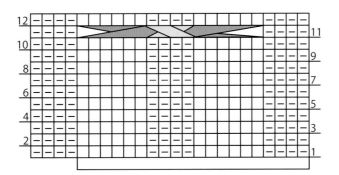

Small Claw Cables

Skill Level: Intermediate

Cast on 41.

Row 1 (RS): K1, *k5, p2, k8, p2, rep from * once, end k6.

Row 2: K1, *p1, k3, p1, k2, p8, k2, rep from * once, end p1, k3, p1, k1.

Row 3: Same as Row 1.

Row 4: Same as Row 2.

Row 5 (twist row): K1, *k5, p2, 4-st RKC, 4-st LKC, p2, rep from * once, end k6.

Rep Rows 2–5.

☐	K on RS, P on WS
⊟	P on RS, K on WS
⧅⧄	4-st RKC
⧄⧅	4-st LKC

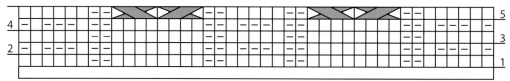

41 stitches

Double Cables

Skill Level: Experienced

Cast on 39 sts (cable worked on center 27 sts).

Row 1 (RS): K2, p4, k5, p1, k6, p3, k6, p1, k5, p4, k2.

Row 2: K6, p5, k1, p6, k3, p6, k1, p5, k6.

Row 3: K2, p4, k5, p1, 6-st LKC, p3, 6-st RKC, p1, k5, p4, k2.

Row 4: Same as Row 2.

Row 5: Same as Row 1.

Row 6: Same as Row 2.

Row 7: Same as Row 3.

Row 8: Same as Row 2.

Row 9: Same as Row 1.

Row 10: Same as Row 2.

Row 11: K2, p4, 12-st LKC, p3, 12-st RKC, p4, k2.

Row 12: K6, p6, k1, p5, k3, p5, k1, p6, k6.

Row 13: K2, p4, k6, p1, k5, p3, k5, p1, k6, p4, k2.

Row 14: Same as Row 12.

Row 15: K2, p4, 6-st RKC, p1, k5, p3, k5, p1, 6-st LKC, p4, k2.

Row 16: Same as Row 12.

Row 17: Same as Row 13.

Row 18: Same as Row 12.

Row 19: Same as Row 15.

Row 20: Same as Row 12.

Row 21: Same as Row 13.

Row 22: Same as Row 12.

Row 23: Same as Row 15.

Row 24: Same as Row 12.

Row 25: Same as Row 13.

Row 26: Same as Row 12.

Row 27: Same as Row 15.

Row 28: Same as Row 12.

Row 29: Same as Row 13.

Row 30: Same as Row 12.

Row 31: K2, p4, 12-st RKC, p3, 12-st LKC, p4, k2.

Row 32: Same as Row 2.

Row 33: Same as Row 1.

Row 34: Same as Row 2.

Row 35: Same as Row 3.

Row 36: Same as Row 2.

Row 37: Same as Row 1.

Row 38: Same as Row 2.

Row 39: Same as Row 3.

Row 40: Same as Row 2.

Rep Rows 1–40.

(continued)

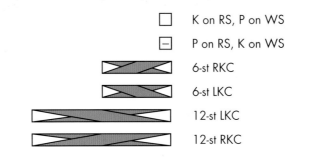

K on RS, P on WS

P on RS, K on WS

6-st RKC

6-st LKC

12-st LKC

12-st RKC

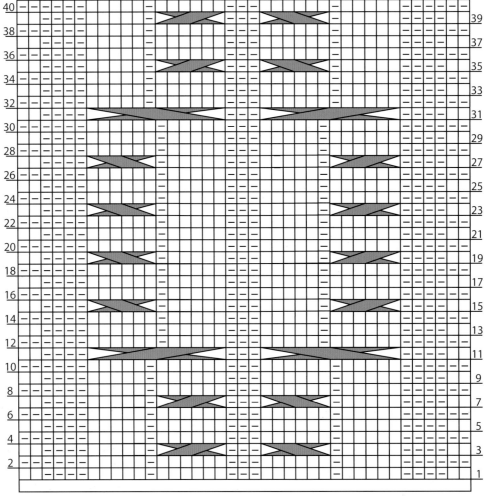

39 stitches

Double Cables Hat

Practice your cable techniques by knitting this winter hat. A wide ribbed band doubles back for a snug, warm fit. Jumbo double cables repeat around the hat, which is knitted in rows and seamed together in the back. You'll only need a skein of yarn per cap, so buy a few skeins of your favorite colors and make cabled hats for the whole family.

Skill Level: Experienced

Hat

With smaller needles, cast on 97 sts.

Ribbed Border

Row 1: K1, *p1, k1, rep from * across row.

Row 2: P1, *k1, p1, rep from * across row.

Rep Rows 1 and 2 for 4" (10 cm), dec 1 st at end of last row (96) sts.

Beg Cable Pattern

Change to larger needles.

Row 1 (RS): *P2, k5, p1, k6, p4, k6, p1, k5, p2, rep from * across row.

Row 2: *K2, p5, k1, p6, k4, p6, k1, p5, k2, rep from * across row.

(continued)

YOU WILL NEED

Yarn

- Medium weight
- Shown: Lion Brand Vanna's Choice, 100% premium acrylic, 3.5 oz (100 g)/170 yds (156 m): Antique Rose #860-143, 1 skein

Needles

- Sizes 6 (4 mm) and 9 (5.5 mm) or size to obtain gauge

Notions

- Tapestry needle

Gauge

- 16 sts = 4" (10 cm) in St st on size 9 needles
- Take time to check gauge.

Sizes

- 22" (56 cm)

Double Cables Hat (continued)

Row 3: *P2, k5, p1, sl next 3 sts to cable needle and hold in back of work, k next 3 sts, k3 from cable needle, p4, sl next 3 sts to cable needle and hold in front of work, k next 3 sts, k3 from cable needle, p1, k5, p2, rep from * across row.

Row 4: Same as Row 2.

Row 5: Same as Row 1.

Row 6: Same as Row 2.

Row 7: Same as Row 3.

Row 8: Same as Row 2.

Row 9: Same as Row 1.

Row 10: Same as Row 2.

Row 11: *P2 , sl next 6 sts to cable needle and hold in front of work, k next 6 sts, k6 from cable needle, p4, slip next 6 sts to cable needle and hold in back of work, k next 6 sts, k6 from cable needle, p2, rep from * across row.

Row 12: *K2 , p6, k1, p5, k4, p5, k1, p6, k2; rep from * across row.

Row 13: *P2, k6, p1, k5, p4, k5, p1, k6, p2, rep from * across row.

Row 14: Same as Row 12.

Row 15: *P2, sl next 3 sts onto cable needle and hold to front of work, k next 3 sts, k3 from cable needle, p1, k5, p4, k5, p1, sl next 3 sts to cable needle and hold to back of work, k next 3 sts, K3 from cable needle, p2, rep from * across row.

Row 16: Same as Row 12.

Row 17: Same as Row 13.

Row 18: Same as Row 12.

Row 19: Same as Row 15.

Row 20: Same as Row 12.

Row 21: Same as Row 13.

Row 22: Same as Row 12.

Row 23: Same as Row 15.

Row 24: Same as Row 12.

Row 25: Same as Row 13.

Row 26: Same as Row 12.

Row 27: Same as Row 15.

Row 28: Same as Row 12.

Row 29: Same as Row 13.

Row 30: Same as Row 12.

Row 31: *P2, sl next 6 sts to cable needle hold to back of work, k next 6 sts, k6 from cable needle, p4, sl next 6 sts to cable needle and hold to front of work, k next 6 sts, k6 from cable needle, p2, rep from * across.

Row 32: Same as Row 2.

Row 33: Same as Row 1.

Row 34: Same as Row 2.

Row 35: Same as Row 3.

Row 36: Same as Row 2.

Row 37: Same as Row 1.

Row 38: Same as Row 2.

Row 39: Same as Row 3.

Row 40: Same as Row 2.

Row 41: K2tog across row (48 sts).

Row 42: P2tog across row (24 sts).

Cut yarn leaving a 36" (91.5 cm) end for gathering and sewing.

Finishing

Thread 36" (91.5 cm) length of yarn onto a tapestry needle. Draw this yarn through 24 sts rem on needle and gather tightly; draw through sts again and fasten, but do not cut yarn. Use same yarn for sewing back seam.

Blocking: Wet hat under cold water. Either stretch over a hat form or lay on a towel and pin into shape. Allow to dry.

Pom-pom (optional): When hat is blocked and dry add a pompom on top.

Before starting, cut a piece of yarn about 18" (45.5 cm) long and put aside for tying. Wind yarn 125 times around a 4" (10 cm) piece of cardboard. Gently slip off cardboard and tie securely in center. Cut the looped ends, shake out, and trim. Fasten to hat with the yarn used for tying.

Men's Cabled V-Neck Vest

For the look and touch of pure luxury, knit him this fine-gauge cabled vest. It can be worn casually with slacks or jeans, but it's also great layered under a sport coat or suit jacket. Small, neat claw cables are set off by reverse stockinette stitch and separated by garter-stitch bands. A generous ribbing band at the bottom is knitted on smaller needles for a snugger fit. This is an easy cable to knit, even if cables are new to you, and you'll love the feeling of this soy silk yarn slipping through your fingers.

(continued)

YOU WILL NEED

Yarn

- Lightweight yarn
- Shown: Pure by South West Trading Company, 100% soy silk, 1.76 oz. (50 g)/164 yds (150 m): Cabernet #027, 7 (8, 8, 9) balls

Needles

- Sizes 3 (3.25 mm) and 6 (4 mm) or sizes needed to obtain gauge
- Size 3 (3.25 mm) circular needle, 24" (61 cm) long

Notions

- Four stitch holders
- Two stitch markers
- Tapestry needle

Gauge

- 26 sts = 4" (10 cm) on size 6 needles in cable patt

Sizes

- Small (Medium, Large, X-Large)
- Finished chest measurement: 44 (46, 48, 50)" [111.5 (116.5, 122, 127) cm]

Back

With size 3 straight needles, CO 142 (148, 154, 160) sts. K1, p1 in rib for 2½" (6.5 cm), inc 1 st at end of last row—143 (149, 155, 161) sts.

Change to size 6 needles and work cable pat as follows:

Row 1 (RS): K5 (8, 11, 14), *k10, p2, k8, p2, rep from * twice, k1 (center st), **p2, k8, p2, k10, rep from ** twice, end with k5 (8, 11, 14).

Row 2: K5 (8, 11, 14), *p1, k8, p1, k2, p8, k2, rep from * twice, p1 (center st), **k2, p8, k2, p1, k8, p1, rep from ** twice, end k5 (8, 11, 14).

Row 3: Rep Row 1.

Row 4: Rep Row 2.

Row 5 (cable twist row): K5 (8, 11, 14), *k10, p2, sl next 2 sts to cable needle and hold to back of work, k next 2 sts, k2 from cable needle, sl next 2 sts to cable needle, hold to front of work, k next 2 sts, k2 from cable needle (cable twist made), p2, rep from * twice, k1 (center st), **p2, cable twist on next 8 sts, p2, k10, rep from ** twice, end k5 (8, 11, 14).

Rep Rows 2–5 until back is 13½ (14, 14½, 15)" [34.5 (35.5, 37, 38) cm] from beg, ending with a WS row.

Shape Armholes

At beg of next 2 rows, BO 6 (7, 8, 9) sts—131 (135, 139, 143) sts. Making sure to keep pat as established, dec 1 st each arm side every other row 7 times—117 (121, 125,129) sts.

Making sure to keep pat as established, work even until armhole is 10½ (11, 11½, 12)" [26.5 (28, 29, 30.5) cm].

Shape Shoulders

Work across 39 (40, 41, 42) sts and place on holder to be joined later to front right shoulder, BO center 39 (41, 43, 45) sts, work across rem 39 (40, 41, 42) sts and place on holder to be joined later to front left front shoulder.

Front

Work same as back until armhole shaping is completed, ending with a WS row.

Divide for V-Neck

Left front

Work across 58 (60, 62, 64) sts, place rem 59 (61, 63, 65) sts on holder to be worked later for Right Front, turn. Work 1 row even. Cont in pat, dec 1 st at neck edge on next row, then every other row twice more, then every 4th row 16 (17, 18, 19) times—39 (40, 41, 42) sts. Work even until armhole is same length as Back to shoulder. Place rem sts on holder to be joined later to back left shoulder.

Right Front

Place center st on a pin to be worked later for V-shaping, join yarn at center, and work rem 58 (60, 62, 64) sts, turn. Work 1 row even. Dec 1 st at neck edge on next row, then every other row twice more, then every 4th row 16 (17, 18, 19) times—39 (40, 41, 42) sts. Work even until armhole is same length as Back to shoulder. Do not BO; leave sts on holder to be joined later to Back right shoulder.

Finishing

With RS together, sl sts from Right Front and Back shoulders onto size 6 needles. Join using the three-needle BO method (page 21). Join Left Front and Back shoulders in the same manner. Sew underarm seams.

V-Neck Border

Using size 3 circular needle, with RS facing you, starting at right side of Back, pick up 40 (42, 44, 46) sts along back neck (Note: When back of neck was BO there were only 39 [41, 43, 45] sts, but an even number is needed to make V-shaping), pick up 56 (58, 60, 62) sts along left side of V, place marker, k center st from pin, place marker, pick up 56 (58, 60, 62) sts along right side of V, mark this as end of row.

Row 1: *K1, p1, rep from * until 2 sts before the first marker, sl 1, k1, psso, sl marker, k center st, sl marker, k2tog, **p1, k1, rep from ** to end.

Row 2: Follow rib to center st, k center st, follow rib to end of row.

Row 3: Rep Row 1.

Row 4: Rep Row 2.

BO in rib, following Row 1 decs at center as you BO.

Armbands

Using size 3 circular needle, with RS facing, starting at underarm seam, pick up 76 (78, 80, 82) sts to shoulder seam, then pick up 76 (78, 80, 82) sts from shoulder to armhole seam—152 (156, 160, 164) sts.

Rows 1–4: *K1, p1, rep from * across row.

BO in rib.

Blocking is not recommended for this garment to preserve the texture of the stitch pattern.

(continued)

Men's Cabled V-Neck Vest (continued)

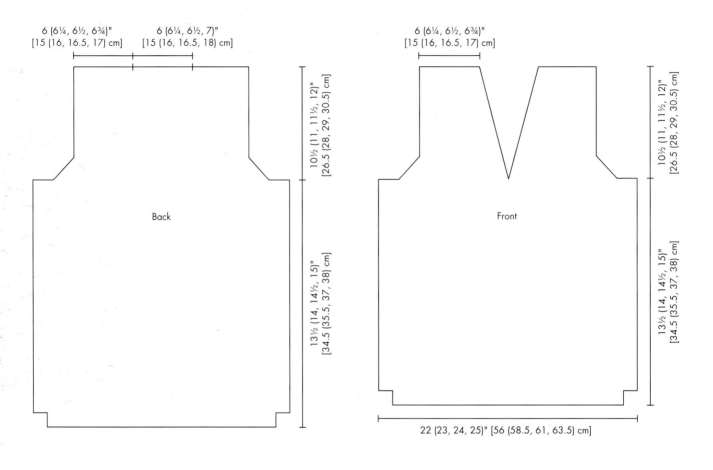

6 (6¼, 6½, 6¾)"
[15 (16, 16.5, 17) cm]

6 (6¼, 6½, 7)"
[15 (16, 16.5, 18) cm]

10½ (11, 11½, 12)"
[26.5 (28, 29, 30.5) cm]

Back

13½ (14, 14½, 15)"
[34.5 (35.5, 37, 38) cm]

6 (6¼, 6½, 6¾)"
[15 (16, 16.5, 17) cm]

10½ (11, 11½, 12)"
[26.5 (28, 29, 30.5) cm]

Front

13½ (14, 14½, 15)"
[34.5 (35.5, 37, 38) cm]

22 (23, 24, 25)" [56 (58.5, 61, 63.5) cm]

SPECIALTY KNITTING METHODS

Some knitting styles require additional techniques beyond the standard techniques used for all the previously covered stitch patterns. Some distinctive knitting styles originated in different countries and were handed down through generations of knitters. For other styles, such as intarsia (colored graphic designs), knitters have developed ways to perfect the method. Some styles, such as free-form knitting, may have developed more recently than others.

One-Piece Knitting

Most knitters have problems sewing their garment together. Even those who do it properly generally do not enjoy this step. The biggest problem knitters seem to have is setting in sleeves. One-piece knitting eliminates this task entirely.

When doing one-piece knitting, knitters start from the neck down, section off parts of the sweater (front, back, and sleeves), work to the armhole, and then place some sections on holders while others are being worked. Usually, there is just the underarm sleeve seam to sew, but the sleeves can be worked circularly to totally eliminate seams.

The T-shaped method requires working the sleeve first, adding stitches to the back and front, working across the body, and making a neck opening midway. Then, you'll complete the other body-section half, bind off, and finish the second sleeve. When finished, only the underarm seems need to be sewn. Both of these methods can be used to knit cardigans or pullovers, with pullovers being the easiest to achieve. A one-piece garment can also be knit from side to side. The garter stitch sweater shown on page 54 is an example of a garment that is knit in one piece, side to side.

Another big plus to these knitting methods is that you can easily alter one-piece knits to fit a growing child. Usually, children grow taller faster than their body size changes. It is easy to alter the size of one-piece knits (especially those made from the top down) by ripping out the bound-off row, placing stitches back on the needle, and adding a few inches to sleeves and body length. With the side-over styles, it is also easy to pick up stitches and add a few rows of trim in a complementary or contrasting color to lengthen the body and sleeves.

Once the basic technique is learned, you will become your own designer. Add your own special touches and use different stitches when working a basic pattern to create custom knitted pieces. After making your first one-piece garment, you'll be so pleased with the professional-looking results that you'll be anxious to start another.

Top-Down Toddler Cardigan

This toddler cardigan, which matches the hat shown on page 191, is knit in one piece from the top down. The color combination patterns of the yoke, wrists, and lower band are knit with slip stitches.

YOU WILL NEED

Yarn

- Medium weight
- Shown: Patons Canadiana, 100% acrylic, 3.5 oz (100 g)/241 yds (220 m): Super Teal #10742 (MC), 2 (2, 3) skeins; Winter White #00101 (CC), 1 skein

Needles

- Sizes 6 (4 mm) and 8 (5 mm) or size to obtain gauge

Notions

- Three stitch holders
- Six ½" (1.3 cm) buttons
- Tapestry needle

Gauge

- 16 sts = 4" (10 cm) in patt st on size 8 needles
- Take time to check gauge.

Sizes

- Child's 2 (4, 6)
- Finished chest: 26 (28, 30)" [66 (71, 76) cm]

Skill Level: Easy

Note: This sweater is worked from the top down.

Do not end yarn after each color change; carry loosely up sides.

When only one set of numbers is given it applies to all sizes.

Sweater Yoke

With size 6 needles and MC, cast on 61 sts.

Rows 1–4: Work in garter st (k every row).

(continued)

Top-Down Toddler Cardigan (continued)

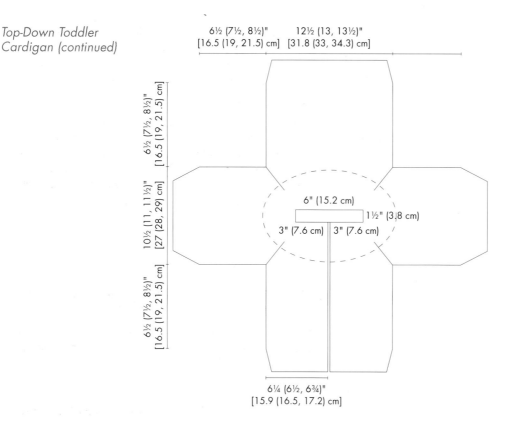

6½ (7½, 8½)" [16.5 (19, 21.5) cm]   12½ (13, 13½)" [31.8 (33, 34.3) cm]

6½ (7½, 8½)" [16.5 (19, 21.5) cm]

10½ (11, 11½)" [27 (28, 29) cm]

6½ (7½, 8½)" [16.5 (19, 21.5) cm]

6" (15.2 cm)

1½" (3.8 cm)

3" (7.6 cm)   3" (7.6 cm)

6¼ (6½, 6¾)" [15.9 (16.5, 17.2) cm]

Row 5 (RS): With CC, k1, *sl 1, k1, rep from * across row.

Row 6: K1, * yarn front (yf), sl 1, yarn back (yb) k1, rep from * across row.

Row 7: P1, *yb, sl 1, yf, p1, rep from * across row.

Row 8: K1, *yf, sl 1, yb, k1, rep from * across row.

Row 9: With MC, knit across row.

Row 10: Change to size 8 needles; knit across row.

Rows 11–15: Rep Rows 5–9.

Row 16 (first inc row): With MC, k2, inc 1 st in next st, *k3, inc 1 st in next st, rep from * 13 times more, end k2 (76 sts).

Row 17: With CC, k1, *sl 1, k2, sl 1, k1, rep from * across row.

Row 18: K1, *yf, sl 1, yb, k2, yf, sl 1, yb, k1, rep from * across row.

Row 19: P1, *yb, sl 1, yf, p2, yb, sl 1, yf, p1, rep from * across row.

Row 20: K1, *yf, sl 1, yb, k2, yf, sl 1, yb, k1, rep from * across row.

Row 21: With MC, knit across row.

Row 22 (second inc row): K5, inc 1 st in next st, *k4, inc 1 st in next st, rep from * 12 times more, k last 5 sts (90 sts).

Row 23: With CC, k1, *sl 1, k2, rep from * across row, end sl 1, k1.

Row 24: K1, *yf, sl 1, yb, k2, rep from * across row, end sl 1, k1.

Row 25: P1, *yb, sl 1, yf, p2, rep from * across row, end sl 1, p1.

Row 26: K1, *yf, sl 1, yb, k2, rep from * across row, end sl 1, k1.

Row 27: With MC, knit across row.

Row 28 (third inc row): K6, inc 1 st in next st, *k5, inc 1 st in next st, rep from * 12 times more, k last 5 sts (104 sts).

Row 29: With CC, k1, *sl 1, k2, sl 1, k3, rep from * across row, end sl 1, k1.

Row 30: K1, *yf, sl 1, yb, k2, yf, sl 1, yb, k3, rep from * across row, end sl 1, k1.

Row 31: P1, *yb, sl 1, yf, p2, yb, sl 1, yf, p3, rep from * to last 5 sts, end yb, sl 1, yf, p2, yb, sl 1, yf, p1.

Row 32: K1, *yf, sl 1, yb, k3, yf, sl 1, yb, k2, rep from * across row, end sl 1, k1.

Row 33: With MC, knit all across row.

Row 34 (fourth inc row): K10, inc 1 st in next st, *k6, inc 1 st in next st, rep from * 12 times more, end k9 (117 sts).

Row 35: CC, k1, sl 1, k2, *sl 1, k3, rep from * to last 5 sts, sl 1, k2, sl 1, k1.

Row 36: K1, yf, sl 1, yb, k2, yf sl 1, *yb, k3, yf, sl 1, rep from * to last 4 sts, yb, k2, yf, sl 1, yb, k1.

Row 37: P1, yb, sl 1, yf, p2, *yb, sl 1, yf, p3, rep from * to last 5 sts, yb, sl 1, yf, p2, yb, sl 1, yf, p1.

Row 38: K1, yf, sl 1, yb, k2, *yf, sl 1, yb, k3, rep from * to last 5 sts, yf, sl 1, yb, k2, yf, sl 1, yb, k1. End off CC.

Row 39: With MC, knit across row.

Row 40 (fifth inc row): *K3, inc 1 st in next st, rep from * 26 times more, end k4 (144 sts).

Row 41: Knit across row. This completes yoke.

Body

Next row (WS): P20, place marker (pm) on needles (right front), p32, pm on needle (first sleeve), p40, pm on needle (back), p32, pm on needle (2nd sleeve) p20 (left front).

Next row (RS): Knit across row, inc 1 st before and after each marker (8 incs).

Cont to work in St st, inc 1 st before and after each marker until there are 25 (26, 27) sts on each front section, 42 (44, 46) sts on each sleeve section, 50 (52, 54) sts on back section, ending with last knit inc row [184 (192, 200) sts].

Divide for body and sleeves as follows:

Next row (WS): P25 (26, 27) front sts to first marker, remove marker, and place sts just worked on a holder; p42 (44, 46) first sleeve sts, leave theses sts on needle and marker in place; p50 (52, 54) back sts, place back sts on holder and remove markers; p42 (44, 46) second sleeve sts, leave sleeve sts on needle, place rem front 25 (26, 27) front sts not worked onto a holder, leave marker on the holder showing this front has not been worked yet. You now have 2 fronts and back sts on holders, and both sleeve sts on needle.

Working both sleeves at once, using separate balls of yarn, work as follows:

Cast on 2 sts at beg of sleeve, k across row, cast on 2 sts at end of row [46 (48, 50) sts].

Join new ball of yarn, work second sleeve same. There are 46 (48, 50) sts on each sleeve.

Work each sleeve with separate balls of yarn until 6½ (7½, 8½)" [16.5 (19, 21.5) cm] from underarm. Change to size 6 needles. Work Rows 5–9 of Yoke sl st patt for 3 patt reps. With MC, work garter st for 4 rows. Bind off.

Join MC yarn at underarm of front with marker, work across the front 25 (26, 27) sts, turn, work same front again, cast on 4 sts for underarm, work across back, cast on 4 sts for underarm, work rem front; you now have 2 fronts and back all on needle [108 (112, 116) sts]. Work in St st for 6½ (7½, 8½)" [16.5 (19, 21.5) cm]. Change to size 6 needles and work bottom border the same as sleeves. Bind off.

Finishing

Sew underarm seams.

Front Borders: Note: When you are repeating Rows 5–15 of patt, you will not be on 5th row of border.

Left Front Button Band: With RS facing, starting at neck edge, using size 6 needles and MC, pick up and k61 (67, 73) sts.

Row 1: Knit.

Row 2 (RS): With CC, k1, *sl 1, k1, rep from * across row.

Row 3: With CC, k1, *yf, sl 1, yb, k1, rep from * across row.

Row 4: With CC, p1, *yb, sl 1, yf, p1, rep from * across row.

Row 5: With CC, k1, *yf, sl 1, yb, k1, rep from * across row.

Row 6: With MC, knit across row.

Row 7: With MC, knit across row.

Rows 8–13: Rep Rows 2–7.

Bind off loosely.

Right Front Button Band: Before beginning Right Front, mark 6 buttonholes evenly spaced on Left Front. Starting at bottom, with RS facing, work as for Left Front Band, making buttonholes opposite each marker on the 6th and 7th patt row as follows:

On the 6th patt row: *K to marker, bind off 2 sts, rep from * until 6 buttonholes are completed, finish row.

On the 7th patt row: K and cast on 2 sts over each set of bound-off sts.

Complete Rows 8–13 as for Left Front Button Band.

Bind off loosely.

Sew buttons opposite buttonholes.

If blocking is required, do not press, lay on a padded surface, spritz lightly with water, pat into shape, allow to dry.

Top-Down Mock Cable Pullover

This figure-flattering sweater is knit from the top down in one piece. A drawstring weaves through eyelet holes along the neckline. Wide mock cable ribbing accents the wrists and waist.

YOU WILL NEED

Yarn

- Medium weight
- Plymouth Baby Alpaca DK, 100% baby alpaca, 1.75 oz (50 g)/125 yds (114 m): Beige #207, 8 (8, 9, 10) skeins

Needles

- Size 6 (4 mm) and 8 (5 mm) circular and double-pointed needles or size to obtain gauge
- For size Small only size 5 (3.5 mm) circular and double-pointed needles

Notions

- Stitch markers
- Tapestry needle
- Crochet hook size G/6 (4 mm)

Gauge

- 20 sts = 4" (10 cm) worked in patt on size 8 needles
- Take time to check gauge.

Sizes

- Small (Medium, Large, X-Large)
- Finished chest: 32 (34, 36, 39)" [81.5 (86.5, 91.5, 99) cm]

Skill Level: Intermediate

Note: Sweater is made in one piece starting at neck edge.

Body

Beg at neck edge, with size 5 (6, 6, 6) circular needle, cast on 176 (176, 176, 176) sts.

Being careful not to twist sts, knit 1 rnd, placing marker at beg of rnd. Slip marker at end of every rnd. Work patt for neck border as follows:

Rnd 1: *P2, k1, yo, k1, rep from * around.

Rnd 2: *P2, k3, rep from * around.

Rnd 3: *P2, yarn back (yb), sl 1, k2, psso both k sts, rep from * around.

Rnd 4: *P2, k2, rep from * around.

Rnds 5–12: Rep Rnds 1–4 twice more (12 patt rnds in all).

Change to size 8 circular needle. Cont working body in the rnd in St st (knit every rnd) as follows:

Rnd 1: K34 (first sleeve), place marker (pm); k54 (back), pm; k34 (second sleeve), pm; k54 (front), pm.

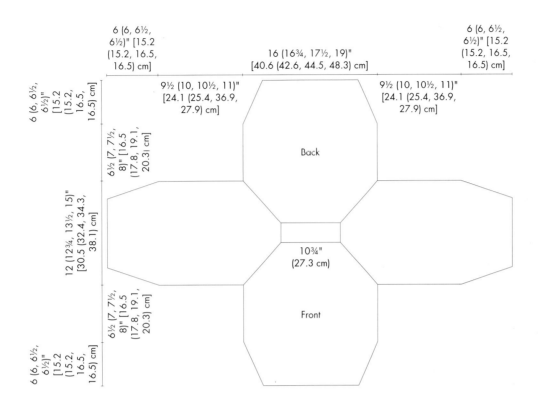

6 (6, 6½, 6½)" [15.2 (15.2, 16.5, 16.5) cm]

16 (16¾, 17½, 19)" [40.6 (42.6, 44.5, 48.3) cm]

6 (6, 6½, 6½)" [15.2 (15.2, 16.5, 16.5) cm]

6 (6, 6½, 6½)" [15.2 (15.2, 16.5, 16.5) cm]

9½ (10, 10½, 11)" [24.1 (25.4, 36.9, 27.9) cm]

9½ (10, 10½, 11)" [24.1 (25.4, 36.9, 27.9) cm]

6½ (7, 7½, 8)" [16.5 (17.8, 19.1, 20.3) cm]

Back

12 (12¾, 13½, 15)" [30.5 (32.4, 34.3, 38.1) cm]

10¾" (27.3 cm)

6½ (7, 7½, 8)" [16.5 (17.8, 19.1, 20.3) cm]

Front

6 (6, 6½, 6½)" [15.2 (15.2, 16.5, 16.5) cm]

Rnd 2: K1, inc 1 st in next st (k in front and back of same st), *k to within 2 sts before next marker, inc 1 st in next st, k1, sl marker, k1, inc 1 st in next st, rep from * twice more, then work until 2 sts before beg marker, inc 1 st in next st, k1 (8 incs made) [184 (184, 184, 184) sts].

Rnd 3: Knit, slipping all markers.

Rep the last 2 rnds until there are 80 (84, 88, 96) sts on back section, 80 (84, 88, 96) sts on front section, 60 (64, 68, 76) sts on each sleeve [280 (296, 312, 344) sts].

Divide for sleeves and body: K60 (64, 68, 76) sts of first sleeve and place on a holder, k80 (84, 88, 96) sts of back leaving marker on for now, k60 (64, 68, 76) sts of second sleeve and place on a holder, k60 (84, 88, 96) sts of front. Note: You now have 160 (168, 176, 192) sts of back and front on needles; sleeve sts rem on holders to be worked later.

Cont as follows:

Next rnd: Knit around, inc 1 st each side of back and front [164 (172, 180, 196) sts].

Cont working around in St st until 6½ (7, 7½, 8)" [16.5 (18, 19, 20.5) cm] from underarm.

Change to size 5 (6, 6, 6) needle. Rep cable patt Rnds 1–4 as on neckline for 6 (6, 6½, 6½)" [15 (15, 16.5, 16.5) cm] more, ending with patt Rnd 3. Bind off on patt Rnd 4 in p2, k2 rib.

Sleeves (make 2)

Sl 60 (64, 68, 76) sts from first sleeve holder to size 8 dp needles and work as follows:

Rnd 1: K, inc 1 st each side of underarm [62 (66, 70, 78) sts].

Work even in St st (k every rnd) until sleeve is 9½ (10, 10½, 11)" [24 (25.5, 26.5, 28) cm] from underarm, dec 2 sts on last rnd for all sizes [60 (64, 68, 76) sts].

Cuff

Change to size 5 (6, 6, 6) dp needles. Rep cable patt Rnds 1–4 for 6 (6, 6½, 6½)" [15 (15, 16.5, 16.5) cm] same as body bottom, ending on patt Rnd 3. Bind off on Rnd 4 in patt in p2, k2 rib.

Finishing

Drawstring: Using double yarn strand and size G/6 crochet hook, make a chain 56" (142 cm) long. Alternatively, make three-stitch I-cord (page 36). Weave chain in and out of top cable patt holes at neck, tie in front.

Blocking: If garment needs blocking, lay on a padded surface, spritz lightly with water, pat into shape. Do not press.

Little Princess Dress

This darling little girl's dress is a perfect project to try your hand at knitting from the top down on circular needles. This design uses three different lace stitches paired with stockinette stitch and it shows the knitter how stitches change when stitches are worked in the round, always from the right side of work, instead of back and forth.

YOU WILL NEED

Yarn

- Light worsted weight
- Shown: Lion Brand LB Collection, Superwash Merino, 100% merino, 3.5 oz (100 g)/306 yds (200 m): Sky #486-107, 2 (2, 3) skeins

Needles

- Size 6 (4 mm) circular needle or size to obtain gauge

Notions

- Three ⅝" (1.3 cm) buttons
- Three stitch holders
- Stitch marker
- Tapestry needle

Gauge

- Stockinette stitch: 20 sts = 4" (10 cm)
- First Patt: 3 patt repeats = 4" (10 cm)
- Second Patt: 5 groups = 4" (10 cm)
- Third Patt: 2½ patts = 4" (10 cm)
- Take time to check gauge.

Sizes

- Child's 2 (4, 6)
- Finished chest: 22 (24, 26)" [56 (61, 66) cm]
- Finished length: 19 (19½, 20)" [48 (49.5, 51) cm]

Skill Level: Intermediate

Notes: Garment is worked from top down, starting at neck and working back and forth to form neck opening, then joined and finished working in the round.

Garment stretches slightly when blocked.

When working a yarn over before a purl stitch, wrap yarn around needle from front to back to front.

Body

Starting at neck edge, with size 6 needles, cast on 74 (74, 74) sts. Do not join. Work back and forth in stockinette stitch (k 1 row, p 1 row) for 4 rows.

Beading row (RS): K1, *yo, k2tog, rep from * across row.

Beg with a purl row, work 3 more rows St st. Note: This completes picot hem at neckline.

Yoke

Note: All sizes same until end of Yoke rows.

Row 1: K12, yo, k1, yo, k11, yo, k1, yo, k24, yo, k1, yo, k11, yo, k1, yo, k12 (8 incs made)—82 sts.

Row 2: Purl across row.

Row 3: K13, yo, k1, yo, k13, yo, k1, yo, k26, yo, k1, yo, k13, yo, k1, yo, k13 (8 incs made)—90 sts.

Row 4: Purl across row.

Cont in this manner, always having 1 more st on each back section, 2 more sts on each sleeve, and 2 more sts on front section, between yo's until there are 28 (29, 30) sts on each back section, 43 (45, 47) sts on each sleeve, and 56 (58, 60) sts on front section, ending with a purl row. Fasten off.

Place back and front sections on holder, join yarn at underarm of one sleeve and work as follows:

Beading row: K1, *yo, k2tog, rep from * across row.

Beg with a purl row, work 3 rows in St st. Bind off.

Work other sleeve to correspond.

Bottom of Dress

Starting at back edge, with RS facing, join yarn and k across 28 (29, 30) back sts, cast on 6 (6, 6) sts sts for underarm, k across 56 (58, 60) front section sts, cast on 6 (6, 6) sts for underarm, k across rem 28 (29, 30) back sts—124 (128, 132) sts. Join to form a ring, placing a marker at beg of rnds; remainder of dress is worked in the rnd.

Rnds 1–3 (RS): Purl.

(continued)

Little Princess Dress (continued)

Size 2 only:

Rnd 4: Purl, dec 1 st at end of row—123 sts.

Size 4 only:

Rnd 4: (P15, inc 1 st in next st) 7 times, p last 16 sts—135 sts.

Size 6 only:

Rnd 4: P and inc 1 st in the first st, (p14, inc 1 st in next st) 8 times, p rem 11 sts—141 sts.

All sizes:

Rnd 5: K123 (135, 141) sts.

Beg First Patt (multiple of 6 + 3)

Rnd 1: P3, *k3, yo, p3, rep from * to end of rnd.

Rnd 2: P3, *k4, p3, rep from * to end of rnd.

Rnd 3: P3, *k1, k2tog, yo, k1, p3, rep from * to end of rnd.

Rnd 4: P3, *k2, k2tog, p3, rep from * to end of rnd.

Rnd 5: P3, *k1, yo, k2tog, p3, rep from * to end of rnd.

Rnd 6: P3, *k3, p3, rep from * to end of rnd.

Rep Rnds 1–6, 2 (2, 3) times more.

Knit 1 rnd, purl 3 rnds.

Next rnd: P, inc 18 sts evenly spaced around—141 (153, 159) sts.

Knit 1 rnd.

Beg Second Patt (multiple of 6 + 3)

Rnds 1, 3, 5, and 7: P1, knit to last st, p1.

Rnd 2: K2, *yo, ssk, k1, k2tog, yo, k1, rep from * to last st, k1.

Rnd 4: K2, *yo, k1, sl 1, k2tog, psso, k1, yo, k1, rep from * to last st, k1.

Rnd 6: K2, *k2tog, yo, k1, yo, ssk, k1, rep from * to last st, k1.

Rnd 8: K1, k2tog, *(k1, yo) twice, k1, sl 1, k2tog, psso, rep from * to last 6 sts, end (k1, yo) twice, k1, ssk, k1.

Rep Rnds 1–8, 3 (3, 4) times more.

Next rnd: Knit.

Next 3 rnds: Purl.

Size 2 only:

Next rnd: P1, inc 1 st in next st, (p 2, inc 1 st in next st) 46 times, inc 1 st in last st—189 sts.

Size 4 only:

Next rnd: P1, inc 1 st in next st, (p2, inc 1 st in next st) 50 times, inc 1 st in last st—205 sts.

Size 6 only:

Next rnd: P2, inc 1 st in next st, (p2, inc 1 st in next st) 51 times, p2, inc 1 st in last st—212 sts.

All Sizes:

Next rnd: Knit, inc 4 (6, 8) sts evenly spaced around—193 (211, 220) sts.

Beg Third Patt (multiple of 9 + 4)

Rnds 1 and 3: Knit.

Rnd 2: K3, *yo, k2, ssk, k2tog, k2, yo, k1, rep from * to last st, k1.

Rnd 4: K2, *yo, k2, ssk, k2tog, k2, yo, k1, rep from * to last 2 sts, k2.

Rep Rnds 1–4, 7 (7, 8) times more.

Knit 5 more rnds.

Next Rnd: K1, *yo, k2tog, rep from * around, end k0 (0, 1).

Knit 3 more rnds.

Bind off loosely.

Finishing

Fold hem at bottom of sleeves and at bottom of skirt to inside to form picot edges, pin and sew in place.

Back Neck Placket

Left side: With RS facing, starting at bottom of placket, pick up and k24 sts.

Row 1 (buttonhole row): P2, bind off next 2 sts, p3, bind off next 2 sts, p3, bind off next 2 sts, p rem 10 sts.

Row 2: K, cast on 2 sts over each set of 2 bo sts.

Bind off pwise.

Right side: With RS facing, starting at neck edge, pick up and k24 sts.

Row 1: Purl.

Row 2: Knit.

Bind off pwise.

Sew buttons opposite buttonholes. Weave in ends.

Blocking

Lay garment flat on a padded surface, pin into shape using rust-proof pins, spritz lightly with water and allow to dry.

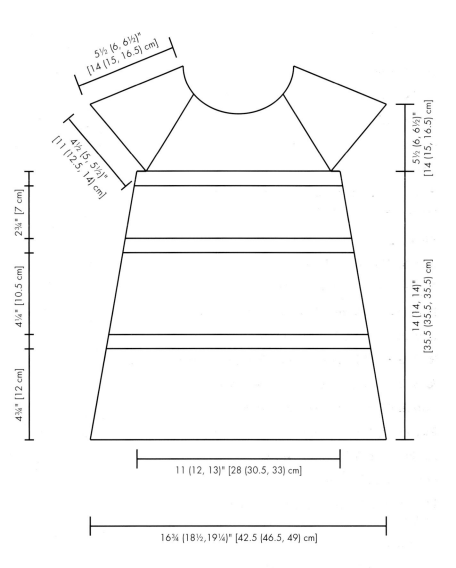

5½ (6, 6½)" [14 (15, 16.5) cm]

4½ (5, 5½)" [11 (12.5, 14) cm]

5½ (6, 6½)" [14 (15, 16.5) cm]

2¾" [7 cm]

4¼" [10.5 cm]

4¾" [12 cm]

14 (14, 14)" [35.5 (35.5, 35.5) cm]

11 (12, 13)" [28 (30.5, 33) cm]

16¾ (18½, 19¼)" [42.5 (46.5, 49) cm]

Trio Sweater Coat

The luxurious cashmere yarn makes this sweater-coat a truly special garment. The design partners the top-down method of knitting with three lace patterns. While the lace patterns can be a little challenging, when the knitting is done, there is very little finishing required.

The entire garment is worked back and forth and not joined; circular needles are used to accommodate the amount of stitches on the needle.

Skill Level: Experienced

Notes: Lion Brand LB Collection, Superwash Merino, 100% merino, 3.5 oz (100 g)/306 yds (200 m) may be substituted for the cashmere.

Coat

Starting at the top neck edge, using size 6 needles, cast on 86 (86, 94, 94) sts.

Neckband

Change to size 5 needles and work as follows:

Row 1: K4, pm, k across to last 4 sts, pm, k4.

Rows 2 and 4: K3, purl across to last 3, k3.

Row 3: K across row.

Row 5: K4, *yo, k2tog, rep from * to last 4 sts, k4.

Rows 6 and 8: Rep Row 2.

Row 7: Rep Row 3.

Yoke

Change to size 6 needles, work yoke as follows;

Notes: When working in this manner, you are working the top of the fronts, sleeves, and back all in one piece, divided by a seam stitch. The yarn over before and after the seam stitch forms the increases.

Row 1 (RS): K17 (17, 18, 18) (front), yo, k1, yo (= seam st and incs), k10 (10, 12, 12) (sleeve), yo, k1, yo (= seam st and incs), k28 (28, 30, 30) (back), yo, k1, yo (= seam st and incs), k10 (10, 12, 12) (sleeve), yo, k1, yo (= seam st and incs), k17 (17, 18, 18) (front)—94 (94,102, 102) sts.

Row 2: K3, purl to last 3 sts, k3.

Row 3: K18 (18, 19, 19), yo, k1, yo, k12 (12, 14, 14), yo, k1, yo, k30 (30, 32, 32), yo, k1, yo, k12 (12, 14, 14), yo, k1, yo, k18 (18, 19, 19)—102 (102, 110, 110) sts.

Row 4: K3, purl to last 3 sts, k3.

Cont in this manner, always having 1 more st on each front, 2 more sts on each sleeve, 2 more sts on back (8 incs every other row), and 3 sts at each front edge will be garter st (knit every row) for front border.

Cont until there are 50 (51, 52, 53) sts on each front, 76 (78, 80, 82) sts on each sleeve, 94 (96, 98, 100) sts on back, ending with a WS row. *Note: There will be 350 (358, 366, 374) sts on needle counting the 4 seam sts.*

YOU WILL NEED

Yarn

- Lightweight
- Shown: Lion Brand LB Collection Cashmere Yarn, 100% cashmere, 0.88 oz (25 g)/82 yds (75 m): Terracotta #134, 16 (17, 18, 19) skeins

Needles

- Size 6 (4 mm) size 7 (4.5 mm) 36" (91 cm) circular needles or size to obtain gauge
- Size 5 (3.75 mm)

Notions

- Two stitch holders
- Two stitch markers
- Tapestry needle
- Six buttons (optional)

Gauge

- 22 sts and 28 rows = 4" (10 cm) in stockinette stitch on size 6 needles
- Take time to check gauge.

Sizes

- S (M, L, XL)
- Finished bust: 37 (38, 39, 40)" [94 (96.5, 99, 101.5) cm]
- Finished length: Approx 32½ (33¼, 33¾, 34½)" [82.5 (84, 85.5, 87.5) cm]
- Finished chest: 32 (34, 36, 39)" [81.5 (86.5, 91.5, 99) cm]

Divide for Body and Sleeves

Note: The st next to the 3 garter st border sts will always be kept in stockinette stitch and patt will be worked in center sts.

Next Row (RS): Work across first front and 1 corner st [51 (52, 53, 54) sts], cast on 4 (4, 6, 6) sts, place 76 (78, 80, 82) sleeve sts on holder; work 1 corner st, 94 (96, 98, 100) sts of back and next corner st [96 (98 100, 102) sts], cast on 4 (4, 6, 6), place 76 (78, 80 82) sleeve sts on holder; work remaining front section—51 (52, 53, 54) sts.

(continued)

Trio Sweater Coat (continued)

Being sure to keep front border as established, cont in St st on 206 (210, 218, 222) sts for 1 (1½, 2, 2½)" [2.5 (4, 5, 6) cm] more.

At this point, place a marker 4 sts in from each side. *Note: The first and last 3 sts will still be kept in garter st and 1 st inside garter st will be kept in St st throughout.*

Lace patts will be worked inside the border sts.

Being sure to keep front border as established, work 4 rows of Rev St st (purl on RS, knit on WS) and on the 4th row; for Small size only dec 1 st—205 sts; for Medium size only inc 1 st—211 sts; for Large size only dec 1 st—217 sts; for XL size, inc 1 st—223 sts.

Begin Lace Patts

Note: Because of the different multiples of the patts, it is necessary to increase and decrease on the last row of the reverse stockinette stitch panel, always making increases and decreases evenly spaced in center of work.

Lace Patt #1 Spiral Eyelets (page 152)

Row 1 (RS): K4, p3, *k3, yo, p3, rep from * to last 4 sts, k4.

Row 2 (WS): K3, p1, k3, *p4, k3, rep from * to last 4 sts, p1, k3.

Row 3 (RS): K4, p3, *k1, k2tog, yo, k1, p3, rep from * to last 4 sts, k4.

Row 4 (WS): K3, p1, k3, *p2, p2tog, k3, rep from * to last 4 sts, p1, k3.

Row 5 (RS): K4, p3, *k1, yo, k2tog, p3, rep from * to last 4 sts, k4.

Row 6 (WS): K3, p1, k3, *p3, k3, rep from * to last 4 sts, p1, k3.

Rep Rows 1–6 of Lace Patt #1, 5 times more—approx 5½" (13.5 cm).

Making sure to keep border as established, work 4 rows Rev St st, and on the 4th row, inc 4 sts for all sizes—209 (215, 221, 227) sts.

Lace Patt #2 Small Fern (page 112)

Beg on RS with Small Fern lace patt Row 2, work Rows 2–8 once, then rep lace patt Rows 1–8 five times more—approx 6½" (16.5 cm).

Making sure to keep border as established, work 4 rows Rev St st and on the 4th row, for Small size only, inc 1 st—210 sts; for Medium size only, inc 4 sts—219 sts; for Large size only, dec 2 sts—219 sts, for XL size only, inc 1 st—228 sts.

Change to size 7 needles.

Lace Patt #3 Vertical III (page 110)

Rep Rows 1–4 of Lace Patt #3 until approx. 7¾" (20 cm), ending with WS and removing all markers.

Work 4 rows St st.

Picot row (RS): K2 (1, 1, 2), yo, *k2tog, yo, rep from * to last 2 sts, k2

Work 4 rows St st. Bind off loosely.

Sleeves

Starting at underarm, with RS facing and size 6 needles, cast on 2 (2, 3, 3) sts, k76 (78, 80, 82) sleeve sts from holder, cast on 2 (2, 3, 3) sts—80 (82, 86, 88) sts.

Keeping first and last st in knit throughout for selvedge st, work 1 (1½, 2, 2½)" [2.5 (4, 5, 6) cm] in St st, ending with a WS row.

Work 4 rows Rev St st and on 4th row, for Small size only, dec 1 st—79 sts; for Medium size only, inc 3 sts—85 sts; for Large size only, inc 5 sts—91sts; for XL size only, inc 3 sts—91 sts.

Work Lace Patt #1, making sure to keep 1 st each side in knit for selvedge st.

Rep Lace Patt #1 Rows 1–6 five more times—approx 5¼" (13.5 cm).

Work in Rev St st for 4 rows and on the 4th row, for Small size only, inc 4 sts—83 sts; for Medium size only, inc 4 sts—89 sts; for Large size only, dec 2 sts—89 sts; for XL size only, dec 2 sts—89 sts.

Keeping selvage sts on both ends, rep Lace Patt #2 Rows 1–8 five times more. Rep Row 1 one more time.

With RS facing and keeping selvage sts on both ends, work 4 rows St st.

Picot row (RS): K2, yo, *k2tog, yo, rep from * to last 3 sts, k2tog, k1.

Work 4 rows of St st. Bind off loosely.

Work second sleeve the same.

Finishing

Sew sleeve underarm seams.

Fold neckline, bottom of sleeves, and bottom of coat to inside at picot row; sew in place.

Sew on 6 buttons (optional).

Cut yarn, leaving a 2-yard (1.8 m) long end. Thread a tapestry needle onto the cut end, draw yarn through right front edge at base of neckline hem; using double strand of yarn, and size F crochet hook, chain 40; fasten off. Work left side the same.

Weave in ends.

Blocking: Place garment on a padded surface, spritz with water, pat into shape, pin using rust-proof pins, allow to dry.

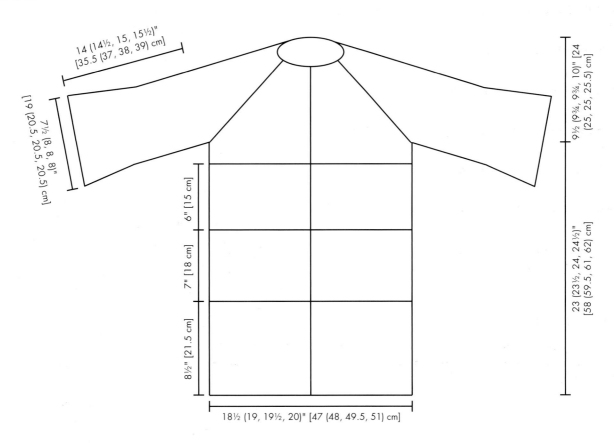

14 (14½, 15, 15½)" [35.5 (37, 38, 39) cm]

9½ (9¾, 9¾, 10)" [24 (25, 25, 25.5) cm]

7½ (8, 8, 8)" [19 (20.5, 20.5, 20.5) cm]

6" [15 cm]

7" [18 cm]

8½" [21.5 cm]

23 (23½, 24, 24½)" [58 (59.5, 61, 62) cm]

18½ (19, 19½, 20)" [47 (48, 49.5, 51) cm]

Entrelac Knitting

Entrelac knitting results in a textured diamond pattern that often looks as though narrow knitted bands were woven together in a basket-weave pattern. The fabric is actually knitted in one piece and features tiers of tipped squares; each tier is knitted to the tier below and tips in the opposite direction. Within each tier, every square is knitted of multiple rows. Entrelac requires only knitting and purling and is most often worked in stockinette stitch. The tricky part comes when connecting stitches to the previous row.

You can knit each tier with a different color to achieve the woven look. Or, you can select a self-striping yarn with long color repeats. The color change will be more subtle but fools the eye into thinking each tier was knitted with a different color.

Entrelac Handbag

Spice up your wardrobe with an entrelac handbag. This project was knitted with two different colors of yarn. There is very little shaping involved, so you can concentrate on learning the rhythm of the entrelac knitting method.

YOU WILL NEED

Yarn

- Medium weight
- Shown: Patons Décor, 75% acrylic, 25% wool, 3.5 oz (100 g)/208 yds (190 m): Taupe #87631 (MC), Aran #87602 (CC), 1 skein each

Needles

- Sizes 4 (3.5 mm) and 8 (5 mm) or size to obtain gauge

Notions

- 1 pair round bamboo handles
- ½ yd (0.5 m) lining
- Sewing needle and matching thread
- ½ yd (0.5 m) interfacing
- Tapestry needle

Gauge

- 1 rectangle = 2" (5 cm) on size 8 needles
- Take time to check gauge.

Size

- 12" × 12" (30.5 × 30.5 cm)

Skill Level: Experienced

Handbag (Make 2 sides.)

With MC and size 4 needles, cast on 51 sts.

Note: You are starting at top border of bag.

Row 1: K1, *p1, k1, rep from * across row.

Row 2: P1, *k1, p1, rep from * across row.

Rep Rows 1 and 2 for 2" (5 cm).

Next (dec) row: Knit, dec 11 sts evenly spaced across row (40 sts).

(continued)

Change to size 8 needles and work as follows:

Base Triangles (WS): Still using MC, *p2, turn and k2, turn and p3, turn and k3, turn and p4, turn and k4, turn and p5* (first triangle completed), rep from * to * to end of row. Fasten off MC.

First Tier of Rectangles: Join CC, k2, turn and p2, turn, inc 1 st in the first st (k and p into same st), sl 1, k1, psso, turn and p3, turn, inc 1 st in first st, k1, sl 1, k1, psso, turn and p4, turn, inc 1 st in first st, k2, sl 1, k1, psso (side edge triangle complete), then cont as follows: *pick up and k5 sts evenly along edge of next triangle, (turn and p5, turn and k4, sl 1, k1, psso) 5 times*, rep from * to * to edge of last triangle, pick up and k5 sts evenly along edge of last triangle, turn and p2tog, p3, turn and k4, turn and p2tog, p2, turn and k3, turn and p2tog, p1, turn and k2, turn and p2tog (1 st rem on right-hand needle and side edge triangle is complete). Fasten off CC.

Second Tier of Rectangles: Join MC. With WS facing, using MC and cont from the st on right-hand needle, *pick up from front of work and p4 sts evenly along edge of triangle just worked, (turn and k5, turn and p4, purl tog the last in MC and the next st in CC) 5 times*, rep from * to * (5 sts will be picked up on all rem triangles, after first) to end. Fasten off MC.

Third Tier of Rectangles: Same as First Tier of Rectangles but pick up sts along side of rectangles instead of triangles.

Rep Second and Third Tiers of Rectangle for patt until about 11" (28 cm) from beg, end with 3rd row. Fasten off CC.

Final Tier of Triangles: Join MC. With WS facing, using MC, *cont from st on right-hand needle, pick up from front of work and p4 sts along edge of triangle just worked, turn and k5, turn and p2tog, p2, p2tog, turn and k4, turn and p2tog, p1, p2tog, turn and k3, turn and (p2tog) twice, turn and k2, turn and p1, p2tog, turn and k2, turn and p3tog*, rep from * to *, picking up sts along side of rectangle instead of triangle. Fasten off rem st.

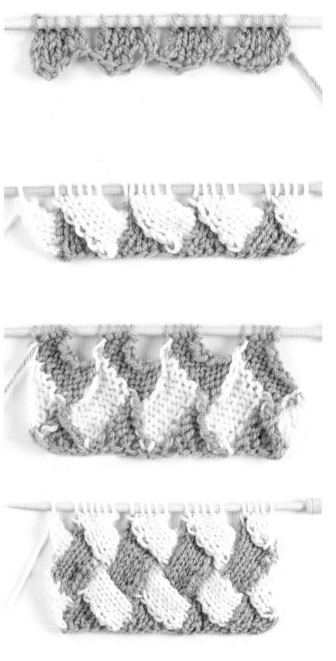

Finishing

Do not block.

Place bag pieces WS together. Sew sides and bottom seam. Cut interfacing ¼" (6 mm) narrower than bag and twice the length from base of ribbing. Fold in half and slip into bag. Cut lining ½" (1.3 cm) wider than bag and 1" (2.5 cm) longer than twice the length from base of ribbing. Fold in half, and sew side seams. Slip lining into bag, turn under top, and stitch in place, encasing interfacing.

Center handles on top border, fold border over handle, sew in place.

Colorful Entrelac Bag

This cheery handbag was knitted with four different colors of yarn. Front and back panels of entrelac knitting are joined to a gusset. I-cord straps that end with leaf motifs are tied together at the shoulder.

YOU WILL NEED

Yarn

- Bulky weight

- Shown: Cascade 128 Superwash, 100% merino wool, 3.5 oz (100 g)/128 yds (117 m): MC, #1964, 2 skeins; A, #1096, 1 skein; B, #1952, 1 skein; C, #822, 1 skein

Needles

- Size 10 (6 mm) straight needles or size to obtain gauge

- Two size 8 (5 mm) double-point needles for I-cord shoulder strap

Notions

- Tapestry needle

- ½ yd (0.5 m) fleece for inner lining

- ½ yd (0.5 m) silky lining

- One 12" (30.5 cm) zipper

Gauge

- 1 rectangle = 1¾" (4.5 cm) on size 10 (6 mm) needle

- Take time to check gauge.

Size

- 13" × 14" (33 × 35.5 cm)

(continued)

Colorful Entrelac Bag (continued)

Skill Level: Experienced

Sides (make 2)

With MC and size 10 needles, cast on 40 sts.

Base Triangles (WS): With MC, *p2, turn; k2, turn; p3, turn; k3, turn; p4, turn; k4, turn; p5* (first triangle completed), rep from * to * to end of row. Fasten off MC.

First Tier of Rectangles: Join A, k2, turn; p2, turn; inc 1 st in first st (k and p into same st), skp (dec), turn; p3, turn; inc 1 st in first st, k1, skp, turn; p4, turn; inc 1 st in first st, k2, skp (side edge triangle complete). Cont as follows: *Pick up and k5 sts evenly along edge of next triangle, (turn; p5, turn; k4, skp) 5 times*, rep from * to * to edge of last triangle, pick up and k5 sts evenly edge of last triangle, turn and p2tog, p3, turn and k4, turn and p2tog, p2, turn and k3, turn and p2tog, p1, turn and k2, turn and p2tog (1 st rem on right-hand needle and side edge triangle is complete). Fasten off A.

Second Tier of Rectangles: Join B. With WS facing, cont from the st on right-hand needle, *pick up from front of work and p4 sts evenly along edge of triangle just worked, (turn and k5, turn and p4, purl tog the last in B and the next in A) 5 times*, rep from * to * (5 sts will be picked up on all rem triangles, after first) to end. Fasten off B.

Third Tier of Rectangles: Join C. As with first row of Rectangles, but pick up sts along side of rectangles instead of triangles; fasten off C.

Rep Second and Third Tiers of Rectangle, alternating MC, A, B, and C, until 11 tiers in all, ending with C. Fasten off C.

Join MC. Work 2 more Tiers in MC; do not fasten off MC.

Final Tier of Triangles: With MC and WS facing, *cont from st on right-hand needle, pick up from front of work and p4 sts along edge of triangle just worked, turn and k5, turn and p2tog, p2, p2tog, turn and k4, turn and p2tog, p1, p2tog, turn and k3, turn and (p2tog) twice, turn and k2, turn and p1, p2tog, turn and k2, turn and p3tog*, rep from * to *, picking up sts along side of rectangle instead of triangle.

With MC, knit 4 rows. Bind off.

Gusset and Shoulder Strap (make 2)

Note: Gusset is made in 2 pieces and seamed at bottom. Gusset is intentionally made slightly smaller than outside of bag and stretched slightly to fit.

With MC and size 10 needles, cast on 10 sts. Work garter st (k every row) for 42 rows.

Next row: Dec 1 st each side—8 sts.

Cont in garter st for 42 rows.

Next row: Dec 1 st each side—6 sts.

Cont in garter st for 42 rows.

Next row: Dec 1 st each side—4 sts.

Using size 8 dpns, work I-cord as shown on page 36 for 21" (53 cm).

Make leaf tab and cont with MC and size 10 needles as follows:

Rows 1 and 3: Purl.

Row 2: Knit.

Row 4: K1, (inc 1 st in next st) twice, k1—6 sts.

Rep the last 4 rows, working inc 1 st in from each end—12 sts.

Next row: Purl.

Next row: K1, skp, k to last 3 sts, k2tog, k1.

Next row: Purl.

Rep last 2 rows until 4 sts rem.

K2tog twice—2 sts.

P2tog. Fasten off.

Finishing

Sew 2 gusset pieces tog at widest part (this is center bottom of bag).

Before sewing bag tog, cut inner lining to fit back and front and sew in place. Insert zipper for closure as shown on page 44. Sew silky lining in place.

Mark center bottom of bag, mark halfway on each side of bag. Pin gusset in place, centering gusset seam at center bottom, stretch gusset to bottom corner of bag to first dec point. Stretch gusset so that second dec reaches center side marker. Stretch gusset to top of bag. When gusset is pinned in, sew in place.

When bag is completed, lining can be added to gussets if desired.

Tie knots in shoulder strap to fit desired lengths.

Blocking is not recommended for this pattern stitch.

Free-form Knitting

What does the term "free-form" mean? It usually refers to a type of fabric created by using many different yarns in a multistitch, multidirectional manner. Free-form can also be achieved by using only one yarn and one color worked in many different stitches. Free-form knitted fabric can be used to create wearable garments, bags, hats, pillows, and other accessories.

I made my first free-form knitted piece about seven years ago. I had been doing free-form crochet, with a little knitting added, for quite some time, but had never done an entirely knitted piece. I was teaching a free-form crochet workshop when one of the attendees, who was president of Big Apple Knitting Guild, asked me if I could develop a free-form knitting workshop for her group. I started working on a small bag, and enjoyed it so much I kept on experimenting with free-form knitting. Before the year was over, I developed the workshop and introduced a video on free-form knitting.

For me, the challenge was using free-form techniques to create something different and exciting. The little bag design kick-started my passion for the artistry of free-form knitting.

The wonderful thing about free-form knitting is that there are no rules, usually no instructions, no right or wrong way. There are as many different approaches to the method as there are artists creating free-form knitted pieces.

You will note that I said usually no instructions. Many free-formers believe that trying to write instructions for free-form knitting defeats the purpose. It is, after all, supposed to be "free." After quite a few years of teaching workshops in conventional and free-form styles, I find that beginners appreciate a little instruction to get them started. But, you'll find that after completing a single free-form project (sometimes even before completion) that your own creativity takes over and you are no longer following instructions.

Generally, the instructions I share to inspire free-form beginners include two methods and a single rule. The rule: Use the most intricate stitches, like two-tone lattice, with the plainest yarns, and use the simplest stitches, such as garter stitch, with highly textured eyelash yarns. The methods: Use a lining, a template, or a mesh base to shape your work. Have a definite project in mind when you begin, but remember that as you work, the piece may become something far removed from your original idea.

Once you have decided what you would like to make, choose a color combination. Not confident about combining colors? Choose a multicolored yarn and pull solid-hued yarns to match the colors in the multicolored yarn. Begin experimenting with small pieces of knit, using several yarns and stitches in the same piece. Adding some of the lovely designer yarns makes a piece really special. Dye lot is not a problem when working free-form.

Choose a shaping method that best suits your project. For lighter weight garments, use a template, such as a garment that fits you well or a paper pattern. For a heavier weight jacket, use the lining method.

For the lining method, you will need a suitable fabric on which to sew your pieces. I have used polar fleece, muslin, and a sweatshirt as lining. You can use a commercial pattern or make your own by tracing an existing garment. The lining can become a permanent part of your garment or be used as a template and removed when the project is done. After you have knitted a few pieces, pin them onto your lining. When you have an arrangement you love, sew the pieces to the lining and to each other. Do not start sewing until you are satisfied with your arrangement. If the lining will be a permanent part of your garment, sew the knitted pieces on with small secure stitches. If using the lining as a template, baste knitted pieces to the lining with big stitches. After sewing all the pieces together, clip the basting stitches and remove the lining.

Use shaped plastic mesh as bag interlining. These plastic shapes make a great free-form base and a great looking bag. The plastic shapes are available in a few different styles. The form used for the project on page 254 is one that I use in my workshops. These are available online at www.lacis.com or at many craft shops.

The template method is worked similarly to the lining method, but the pieces are only sewn to each other and not to the lining. To begin, measure an existing garment that fits you well to use as your model. If pinning pieces to this garment won't harm the fabric, use the actual garment as your template. If this is not possible, trace the garment onto a piece of poster board. As you make your knitted pieces, lay them onto the drawing. Be very sure of your knitted-fabric placement before sewing. I continually lay my in-progress work on the template to check size and placement.

One of the easiest template methods is embellishing a mesh base, such as the project on page 258. After making an entire garment in an open-work eyelet stitch, embellish the piece with as many or as few motifs as you like.

Free-form does require a lot of finishing and leaves lots of ends to "bury." I recommend tucking in yarn ends after attaching each piece, leaving only one long end for sewing pieces together. I do not block free-form pieces because I want to preserve their highly textured look.

Free-form Knitted Bag

This free-form knitted handbag is made by knitting various motifs and securing them to a plastic canvas base. The plastic canvas gives the bag a sturdy shape while providing a base to which the motifs are sewn. An inner lining finishes it off and hides all the construction. Look for these handbag forms at your local yarn shop or online.

YOU WILL NEED

Yarn

- Various weights and fibers

- Shown: Lion Brand Yarns, 1 skein each of: Moonlight Mohair, 57% acrylic, 28% mohair, 9% cotton, 6% metallic, 1.75 oz (50 g)/82 yds (75 m): Glacier Bay

- Superwash Merino, 100% superwash merino, 3.5 oz (100 g)/306 yds (280 m): Denim Jeans Blue

- Lion Cotton, 100% cotton, 5 oz (146 g)/236 yds (212 m): Wedgewood

- Lion Cotton, 100% cotton ombre, 4 oz (113 g)/189 yds (170 m): Denim Swirl

Needles

- Sizes #6 (4 mm) and #8 (5 mm)

- Sewing needle and matching thread

- Tapestry needle

- Crochet hook

Notions

- One plastic bag form

- One 1" (2.5 cm) button

- ½ yd (0.5 m) washable felt for lining

Gauge

- Not important, different for all sections

Note: When sewing knitted motifs to your plastic backing, stretch motifs slightly to fit a section and meet the next motif.

Before beginning bag assembly make motifs as follows:

Large Leaf

Follow directions on page 203.

Using size 6 needles, make 1 in Superwash Merino. Using size 8 needles, make 1 in Wedgewood Cotton.

Flower

Follow directions on page 196.

Using size 6 needles and Superwash Merino, make 2. Using size 6 needles and Wedgewood Cotton, make 1. Using size 8 needles and Denim Swirl Cotton, make 2 (one used with purl side as RS; one used with knit side as RS).

Mitered Square

Follow directions on page 198.

Using size 8 needles, make 2 using Wedgewood Cotton as Col A, Moonlight Mohair as Col B.

Lattice Motif

Make 1 using size 8 needles, Wedgewood Cotton as Col A, Moonlight Mohair as Col B.

With Col A, cast on 20 sts and knit 1 row (note that after cast on and knit row, change to Col B. The repeat of the pattern always begins with Row 1).

Row 1 (RS): With Col B, with yarn in back (wyb), k1, sl 1, *k4, sl 2, repeat from *, end k4, sl 1, k1.

Row 2: With B, with yarn in front (wyf), p1, sl 1, *p4, sl 2, rep from *, end p4, sl 1, p1.

Row 3: With A, repeat Row 1.

Row 4: With A, k1, wyf, sl 1, *wyb, k4, wyf, sl 2, rep from *, end k4, wyf, sl 1, k1.

Row 5: With B, k3, *wyb, sl 2, k4, rep from *, end sl 2, k3.

Row 6: With B, p3, *wyf, sl 2, p4, rep from *, end sl 2, p3.

Row 7: With A, repeat Row 5.

Row 8: With A, k3, *wyf, sl 2, wyb, k4, rep from *, end wyf, sl 2, k3.

Repeat Rows 1–8 for 32 rows; bind off.

Ruffle Flower

Make 1 using size 8 needles and Moonlight Mohair.

Cast on 28 sts.

Row 1: K, inc 1 in each st (56 sts).

Row 2: Knit.

Bind off and curl into a spiral.

Slip Stitch Motif

Using size 8 needles, make 1 using Cotton Wedgewood as Col A, Denim Swirl as Col B.

With Col A, cast on 17 sts and knit 1 row.

Row 1: Col B, k3, *sl 1, k3, repeat from * across.

Row 2: Col B, k3, *wyf, sl 1, wyb, k3, rep from * across.

Row 3: Col B, p3, *wyb, sl 1, wyf, p3, rep from * across.

Row 4: Col B, same as Row 2.

Rows 5 and 6: Col A, knit across row.

Rep Rows 1–6 once more; bind off.

Large Fan

Follow directions on page 200.

Make 1 using size 8 needles, Wedgewood Cotton as Col A, Denim Swirl as Col B.

(continued)

Free-form Knitted Bag (continued)

Garter Stitch Fill-in for Sides (make 2)

Using #8 needles, Moonlight Mohair and cotton yarn,
working in garter stitch (knit every row), work 2 rows mohair,
2 rows cotton for 10 rows; bind off.

Small Fan

Follow directions on page 199.

Make 1 using size 8 needles, Moonlight Mohair as Col A and
Wedgewood Cotton as Col B. Make 1 using size 6 needles,
Wedgewood Cotton as Col A and Moonlight Mohair as
Col B.

Strap

Make a twisted cord using 5 strands of Wedgewood Cotton.
Before beginning, have a 10" (25 cm) strand of yarn ready
to use for a tie. Cut 5 strands of yarn, each 4 yards (3.6 mm)
long. Fold the strands over an anchor (something that the
twisted strands can easily be lifted off), and twist them together
over and over until they are tightly twisted. Without letting
go of the ends, bring the end that you are holding to the
anchored end and lift off. Being sure to hold both ends, allow
to twist, straighten out, and tie loose end securely.

Assembly

Using the photo as a guide, place your motifs on the plastic
mesh. Using your tapestry needle and matching yarn, sew
them directly to the mesh. When entirely covered and before
assembling, cut felt to shape and sew to inside. Tuck ends
of strap inside lining at sides before sewing. Fold bag into
shape. Using matching yarn, sew sides together.

Button Loop

Mark center front of flap with a pin. Using a crochet hook
and any one of the yarns, attach yarn piece to right side of
the center and chain 8 stitches. Attach other end of yarn piece
to left of center and weave in ends to secure button loop. Sew
on button.

Another free-form handbag.
This bag was not made on a rigid form. Rather, I cut color-coordinating interlining of polyester fleece to the shape I wanted, and stitched the motifs directly to the interlining and each other. Then, I added a lining to cover the stitches and give it a smooth finish.

Free-form Vest

Applying knitted motifs to a mesh-knit base garment is another way to get creative with free-form knitting. Begin by knitting this simple mesh vest. Then add a few motifs at the shoulders. If you want to embellish further, keep adding motifs. You can also hand-stitch beads or crystals to the motifs for a little sparkle.

YOU WILL NEED

Yarn

• Medium weight

• Shown: Lion Brand Wool Ease, 80% acrylic, 20% wool, 3 oz (85 g)/180 yds (177 m): Vibrant Purple #620-147, 3 (3, 4, 4) skeins

Needles

• Sizes 8 (5 mm) and 10 (6 mm) or size to obtain gauge

Notions

• Five ¾" (2 cm) buttons

• Tapestry needle

• Beads (optional)

Gauge

• 12 sts = 4" (10 cm) in patt on size 10 needles

• Take time to check gauge.

Sizes

• Small (Medium, Large, X-Large)

• Finished chest: 34 (36, 38, 40)" [86.5 (91.5, 96.5, 101.5) cm]

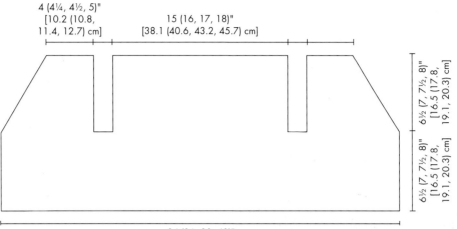

4 (4¼, 4½, 5)"
[10.2 (10.8, 11.4, 12.7) cm]

15 (16, 17, 18)"
[38.1 (40.6, 43.2, 45.7) cm]

6½ (7, 7½, 8)"
[16.5 (17.8, 19.1, 20.3) cm]

6½ (7, 7½, 8)"
[16.5 (17.8, 19.1, 20.3) cm]

34 (36, 38, 40)"
[86.4 (91.4, 96.5, 101.6) cm]

Skill Level: Intermediate

Notes: The vest is made in one piece to armhole.

This pattern will stretch if blocked.

Body

With size 10 needles, cast on 102 (108, 114, 120) sts.

Knit 4 rows.

Beg patt as follows:

Row 1: K1, *yo, p2tog, rep from * to last st, yarn back (yb), k1.

Row 2: K1, *yo, p next st and yo tog, rep from * to last st, yb, k1.

Rep Row 2 until 6½ (7, 7½, 8)" [16.5 (18, 19, 20.5) cm] from beg, end with a WS row.

Divide for back and fronts as follows:

Being sure to keep patt as est, work 24 (25, 26, 27) sts and place on holder for front, bind off next 4 (5, 5, 6) sts for underarm, work next 46 (48, 52, 54) sts and place on holder for back, bind off next 4 (5, 5, 6) sts for underarm, work last 24 (25, 26, 27) sts for left front and cont on left front sts as follows:

Left Front

Dec 1 st front edge (k1, k2tog with no yo) every other row until 12 (13, 14, 15) sts rem. Cont even until armhole is 6½ (7, 7½, 8)" [16.5 (18, 19, 20.5) cm]. Bind off.

Right Front

Place 24 (25, 26, 27) right front sts from holder onto needle. Beg at armhole edge dec 1 st at front edge every other row (keeping armhole edge even) until 12 (13, 14, 15) sts rem. Work even until armhole is 6½ (7, 7½, 8)" [16.5 (18, 19, 20.5) cm]. Bind off.

Back

Place 46 (48, 52, 54) back sts from holder onto needle. Work patt as established until armhole is 6½ (7, 7½, 8)" [16.5 (18, 19, 20.5) cm]. Bind off.

Knitted Five-Petal Flower (make 2)

Ssk: Sl 2 sts to right needle as if to knit, sl left needle through front of sts and k2tog through the back loop.

Psso: Pass slipped st over the knit sts.

With size 8 needles, cast on 62 sts.

Row 1 (WS): Purl

Row 2: K2, *k1, sl this st back onto left needle, then lift the next 9 sts on left needle over this st and off the needle, yo, k first st again, k2, rep from * (22 sts).

Row 3: P1, *p2tog, k1 in front, back, front and back of the yo space, p1, rep from * to last st, p1 (32 sts).

(continued)

Free-form Vest (continued)

Row 4: K1, *sl 2, k1 p2sso, rep from *, end k1 (12 sts).

Row 5: *P2tog, rep from * (6 sts); sl 2nd, 3rd, 4th, 5th and 6th st over first st. Fasten off.

Sew a seam to form flower, place bead in center or work a French knot in center.

Simple Knitted Leaf (make 4)

With size 8 needles, cast on 5 sts.

Row 1 (RS): K2, yo, k1, yo, k2 (7 sts).

Row 2 and all even-numbered rows: Purl.

Row 3: K3, yo, k1, yo, k3 (9 sts).

Row 5: K4, yo, k1, yo, k4 (11 sts).

Row 7: K5, yo, k1, yo, k5 (13 sts).

Row 9: K6, yo, k1, yo, k6 (15 sts).

Row 11: Ssk, k11, k2tog (13 sts).

Row 13: Ssk, k9, k2tog (11 sts).

Row 15: Ssk, k7, k2tog (9 sts).

Row 17: Ssk, k5, k2tog (7 sts).

Row 19: Ssk k3, k2tog (5 sts).

Row 21: Ssk, k1, k2tog (3 sts).

Row 23: Sl 1, k2tog, psso (1 st).

Fasten off.

Finishing

Sew back and front at shoulders.

Blocking

Lay garment on padded surface. Spritz with water until moist, not soaked. Using hands stretch to lay flat. Pin in place if necessary (use rust-proof pins). When dry embellish with leaves and flowers and beads if desired.

Knitting with Beads

There are different ways to work beads into your knitted projects. Of course beads could be hand-stitched onto the knitted fabric after completion, to accent specific areas. Often, beads are strung onto the yarn before you start knitting, and then they are brought forward on the yarn and worked into stitches as they are needed. Judy Pascale shows you how to work beads into the fabric without first stringing them onto the yarn.

In this method, Judy uses a very small crochet hook to slide one bead at a time onto a stitch before it is knitted, thus locking the bead into the fabric with two strands of yarn running though it.

Beaded Slip Stitch Bag
by Judy Pascale

A slip stitch pattern is used to knit this small shoulder bag. Beads are slid onto the slipped stitches before they are knitted. Try knitting a swatch of the pattern first to become familiar with the method.

YOU WILL NEED

Yarn

• Lightweight

• Shown: Koigu, 100% Premium Merino Wool, 1.75 oz (50 g) 175 yds (160 m): Red, 1 skein

Needles

• Size 2 (2.75 mm) or size to obtain gauge

Notions

• Cable needle

• Steel crochet hook size 9 (1.4 mm)

• Stitch markers

• 418 beads (2–3 tubes #6 beads)

Gauge

• 39 sts = 4" (10 cm) in patt st on size 2 needles

• Take time to check gauge.

Size

• 5" × 6" (12.5 × 15 cm)

Skill Level: Intermediate

Notes: When winding the yarn, make a small ball for the strap and wind the remainder.

Slip all slipped stitches as if to purl.

Beads are placed on all elongated slipped stitches before the stitch is knit.

Continental knitters be sure yarn is in front of work before slipping the sts.

Special Abbreviations

C3L: Slip next st onto cable needle and hold in front of work, k next 2 sts from left-hand needle **(1)**, then BK st from cable needle.

C3R: Slip next 2 sts onto cable needle and hold in back of work, BK next st from left-hand needle, then k sts from cable needle.

BK: Insert crochet hook through the center of a bead. Insert beaded crochet hook into the stitch purlwise and remove stitch from needle **(2)**. With the stitch secure in the hook, slip the bead over the hook and onto the stitch **(3)**. *Note: If you apply a little tension on the stitch secured in the hook, the bead should go right over and onto the stitch.* Replace the beaded stitch onto the left needle. The beaded stitch is now ready to be knitted **(4)**.

Beaded Slip Stitch Pattern

(multiple of 4 plus 1)

Row 1 (RS): K1, *sl 1, k3, rep from * to end.

Row 2: *P3, sl 1, rep from * to last st, p1.

Row 3 (bead row): K1, *C3L, k1, rep from * to end.

Row 4: Purl.

Row 5: K5, *sl 1, k3, rep from * to end.

Row 6: *P3, sl 1, rep from * to last 5 sts, p5.

Row 7 (bead row): K3, *C3R, k1, rep from * to last 2 sts, k2.

Row 8: Purl.

Rep Rows 1–8 for pattern.

Purse

Beg with Purse overlap, using size 2 needles cast on 4 sts (long-tail cast-on; see page 14).

(continued)

Beaded Slip Stitch Bag (continued)

Knit 3 rows (foundation).

Row 1: K2, dbl yo, k2.

Row 2: K2, drop 1 yo, k other yo, k2 (buttonhole formed).

Row 3 (RS): K2, yo, k1, yo, k2.

Row 4 (WS): Knit.

Row 5: K2, yo, k until 2 sts rem, yo, k2.

Row 6: Knit.

Rep Rows 5 and 6 until you have 43 sts on needle, ending with a WS row.

Setting Up for Beaded Slip St Patt

Row 1: K2, pm, k across, inc 6 sts evenly, pm, k2 (49 sts).

Row 2: K2, p45, k2 (49 sts).

Beaded Slip St Patt

K2, work Beaded Sl St Patt, k2.

**Note:* Follow instructions for strap at same time while working purse.*

Work 2 reps of 8-row Beaded Sl St Pattern. Work Rows 1–7 of 3rd rep, ending with RS row. DO NOT work Row 8.

**Begin strap. Use size 2 needles. (Optional: For tighter tension strap, use size 1 needles.)*

With smaller ball of yarn placed on outside of purse, come through purse with crochet hook from inside to outside right under Row 4 of first set of 8-row pattern. Hook yarn with crochet hook and pull long strand of yarn from small ball through the purse to WS.

Insert crochet hook from outside to inside in next st. From under the strand, pull yarn through to front of purse, creating a st to be placed on the needle immediately. Rep in next st, creating a new st. Cont until you have the size strap you desire. The small ball of yarn is at the right of the new sts.

Using dpn size 2 (or size 1) allows you to start knitting these new sts. Knit in garter st for 12 ridges (24 knitted rows) or until the garter strap measures the same as the Beaded Sl St Patt already established on the needle.

Join strap to beaded purse.

K2, sl marker, purl across purse until you reach the sts on the dpn, purl together 1 st from the strap with the next st from the purse, cont to purl together 1 st from each needle until all strap sts are worked together with sts from the purse. Then purl until the marker, sl marker, k2. Row 8 is now completed and the strap is attached to the beaded pattern.

Cont with the Beaded Sl St Patt until you have ten 8-row reps. DO NOT work Row 8 of last rep. Sl these sts to a holder.

Front Top

Cast on 44 sts; turn and knit across.

Rows 1 and 2: Knit.

Row 3: K2, pm, k next 40 sts inc'ing 5 sts evenly spaced across these sts, pm, k2.

Row 4: K2, p45, k2 (49 sts).

Work 8-row Beaded Sl St Patt 9 times, ending with a RS row. DO NOT work Row 8 on last rep.

With RS together, work 3-needle bind off (page 21) purlwise. Sew side seams. Weave in ends. Lightly mist while shaping and allow to air-dry. Add a button on the front closure.

Mock Rib Strap

M1 in purl: Pick up horizontal bar from back to front. Purl lifted bar.

Cast on 3 sts.

Row 1: K1, p1, k1.

Row 2: K1, M1 in purl, k1, M1 in purl, k1.

Row 3: K2, p1, k2.

Row 4: K1, (p1, k1) twice.

Rep Rows 3 and 4.

Buttonhole row: K1, k2tog, yo, k2.

Next row: K1, (p1, k1) twice.

Rep Rows 3 and 4 until strap measures 50" (127 cm) or almost at desired length. End on Row 4.

Buttonhole row: K1, k2tog, yo, k2.

Next row: K1, (p1, k1) twice.

Work Rows 3 and 4 twice.

Next row: K2tog, p1, k2tog.

Bind off in rib.

Intarsia Knitting

Multicolored designs knitted with different yarns are achieved by one of two knitting methods: intarsia or Fair Isle knitting. Traditionally, intarsia designs are graphic, color-block images. For ease in controlling the yarns, lengths of each yarn are wound onto knitting bobbins. Where the colors change, one yarn is dropped and the other begins, so there is only one layer of yarn throughout the design. Fair Isle patterns are generally bands or stripes of intricate multicolor patterns. As the colors change, the nonworking color is carried along behind the stitches, either travelling behind them (called stranding) or woven invisibly into the stitches. This doubles the yarn in the design, so the design has a padded appearance.

Sasha Kagan has developed a method of intarsia that incorporates elements of the two methods. Individual motifs are worked into the knitted fabric by weaving the background yarn along behind each motif in the area specified on the graph chart. When a color appears on the graph, change to the appropriate bobbin of yarn. Weave the background yarn in behind the motif colors, catching it in every other stitch. You will have a double thickness of yarn where the motif appears, giving a slightly 3D effect. If you have worked the weaving correctly, the yarns will cross evenly and remain at the same depth. If the design puckers, you have pulled the yarns too tightly. It is better for the yarns to be woven too loosely than too tightly. The beginning and end tails of the motif colors are darned back into the color they came from.

Queen of Hearts Beret
by Sasha Kagan

Sasha Kagan used her intarsia method for this beret that she designed. If intarsia knitting is new to you, you may want to try the technique first on a swatch of the heart pattern. If you weave the nonworking yarn behind every other stitch and darn your ends in carefully, the back of your design will look nearly as neat as the front.

YOU WILL NEED

Yarn

• Lightweight

• Shown: Rowan Cashsoft DK .75oz (50 g)/142 yds (130 m), 57% merino, 33% acrylic, 10% cashmere: 1 ball Balad Blue #508 (A), 1 ball

• Rowan Pure Wool DK,100% wool 1.75 oz (50 g)/137 yds (125 m.): 1 ball each, Hyacinth #26, Dalia #42 (B), Glacier #05

• Rowan Tapestry 1.75 oz (50 g)/131 yds (120 m), 70% wool, 30% soya bean protein fiber: Lakeland #180, 1 ball

Needles

• Sizes 3 and 6 (3.25 mm) and (4 mm) or size to obtain guage

Gauge

• 22 sts and 28 rows = 4" (10 cm) over intarsia pattern using size 6 needles

Size

• 21½" (55 cm) circumference, to fit average head

Hat

Using size 3 needles and A, cast on 107 sts.

Work 11 rows k1, p1 twisted rib.

Next row: Rib 1, M1 (rib 2, M1) to last 2 sts, rib 2 (160 sts).

Change to size 6 needles and follow chart (using the woven intarsia method) from Row 1 to Row 20 and again from Row 1 to Row 10. Continue in St st with A until piece measures 6¼" (16 cm), ending with a RS row.

Shape Crown

Row 1 (WS): With A (P2tog, p6) to end.

Rows 2–4: Work even in St st.

Row 5: (P2tog, p5) to end.

Rows 6–8: Work even in St st.

Row 9: (P2tog, p4) to end.

Ballad Blue #508 (A)
Lakeland #180
Dalia #42 (B)
Hyacinth #26 (B)
Glacier #05

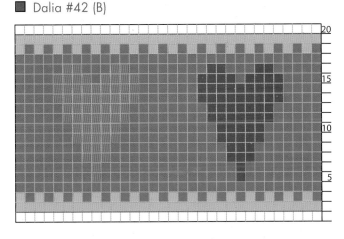

Right Side

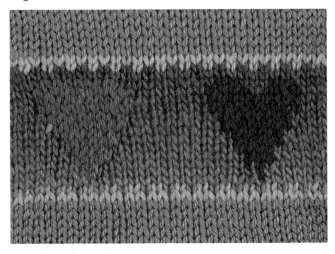

Wrong Side

Rows 10–12: Work even in St st.

Row 13: (P2tog, p3) to end.

Rows 14–16: Work even in St st.

Row 17: (P2tog, p2) to end.

Rows 18–20: Work even in St st.

Row 21: (P2tog, p1) to end.

Rows 22–24: Work even in St st.

Row 25: (P2tog) to end.

Row 26: (P2tog) to end.

Break yarn.

Thread yarn through rem sts. Draw up and secure.

Make Stalk

Using A and size 3 needles, cast on 12 sts, turn, cast off all sts.

Fold stalk in half and secure in the center of the beret. Sew up seam and tidy in loose ends.

Steam gently.

About the Author

Margaret Hubert has written a dozen books for Creative Publishing international over the last several years, including *The Complete Photo Guide to Crochet, The Complete Photo Guide to Knitting, Knit or Crochet—Have It Your Way, Knits for Men, The Granny Square Book, Lacework for Adventurous Crocheters, Runway Crochet,* and *Granny Square Flowers.* Through her books, classes, and convention seminars, Margaret has been instrumental in fostering and developing new generations of knitters and crocheters. In a fitting tribute to her lifelong work as a needle art designer, the Crochet Guide of America honored Margaret in 2012 by naming her to their Hall of Fame.

Contributors

Sasha Kagan

Internationally known textile artist Sasha Kagan has built a multifaceted knitwear design business from her home in Wales. She studied fine art and printmaking at Exeter College of Art and gained her MA in printmaking at the Royal College of Art. This led her to a fascination with William Morris and the Arts and Crafts movement. On moving to Wales, Sasha used hand knitting and crochet to create her trademark nature-inspired designs. Sasha has published six books and contributed articles to books and magazines. Her most recent books, *Crochet Inspiration* and *Knitwear,* continue her exploration of handcrafted textiles. Her mission is to inspire handcrafters to be creative and enjoy the process of making textiles by hand.

Judy Pascale

Judy Pascale, a Connecticut native and lifelong knitter, launched her career as a professional knitting instructor and designer in the early 1990s. She has sold her knitwear both privately and at juried shows. Presently, she teaches knitting and design classes that emphasize customizing to achieve desired fit. She has taught classes and workshops at XRX Stitches Conventions, for The National NeedleArts Association (TNNA), and at yarn shops and guilds. Judy is an active member of the Nutmeg Knitters, the Soundview Knitting Guild, and the Big Apple Knitting Guild. Judy joins other talented and enthusiastic members of the knitting community in creating a renaissance for the ageless art of knitting.

Some of the cable stitch patterns and charts on pages 207 to 224 were excerpted from *Ready Set Knit Cables* by Carri Hammett, published by Creative Publishing international.

Contributing Vendors

Blue Heron Yarn
www.blueheronyarns.com

Cascade Yarns,
www.cascadeyarn.com

Coats and Clark
www.coatsandclark.com

Hampden Hills Alpacas
www.hampdenhillsalpacas.net

Lion Brand Yarn
www.lionbrand.com

Lucci Yarns
www.Lucciyarn.com

Patons Yarn
www.patonsyarns.com

Plymouth Yarns
www.plymouthyarn.com

Index

DON'T MISS THE OTHER BOOKS IN THE SERIES!

The Complete Photo Guide to Crochet,
2nd Edition
Margaret Hubert
ISBN: 978-1-58923-798-8

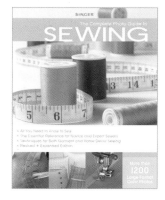

The Complete Photo Guide to Sewing,
Revised and Expanded
Editors of CPi
ISBN: 978-1-58923-434-5

MORE BOOKS ON KNITTING

First Time Knitting
Carri Hammett
ISBN: 978-1-58923-805-3

Fun and Fantastical Hats to Knit
Mary Huff
ISBN: 978-1-58923-794-0

Knitting Clothes Kids Love
Kate Oates and Nancy Langdon
ISBN: 978-1-58923-675-2

Colorwork for Adventurous Knitters
Lori Ihnen
ISBN: 978-1-58923-706-3